The Newman Guide to Choosing a Catholic College

The Newman Guide to Choosing a Catholic College

What to Look For and Where to Find It

Edited by Joseph A. Esposito

Cardinal Newman Society

Manassas, Virginia

The Newman guide to choosing a Catholic college: what to look for and where to find it / edited by Joseph A. Esposito—1st ed.—Washington, D.C. : Cardinal Newman Society, 2007.

    p. ; cm.
    ISBN: 978-0-9786502-1-6 (paper)

1. Catholic universities and colleges—United States—Directories. 2. College choice—United States—Handbooks, manuals, etc. I. Esposito, Joseph A. II. Cardinal Newman Society. I. Title. II. Choosing a Catholic College.

LC501.N49 2007   2007937139
378.071/273—dc22   0711

Cover photo by Ron Kerman, courtesy of Ave Maria University, Ave Maria, Florida (www.avemaria.edu)
Cover design by Sam Torode
Interior layout by Beer Editorial and Design

Published by: Cardinal Newman Society
                9167 Key Commons Court
                Manassas, VA 20110–5300
                www.cardinalnewmansociety.org
                (703) 367-0333

Printed in the United States of America

Dedicated to the ideals of the
Venerable John Henry Cardinal Newman (1801–1890)

God our Father,
your servant John Henry Newman
upheld the faith by his teaching and example.

May his loyalty to Christ and the Church,
his love of the Immaculate Mother of God,
and his compassion for the perplexed
give guidance to the Christian people today.

We beg you to grant the favors we ask
through his intercession
so that his holiness may be recognized by all
and the Church may proclaim him a saint.
We ask this through Christ our Lord.
Amen.

Table of Contents

The Colleges

Joyfully Catholic

Born from the Crisis

Fighting the Tide

Epilogue

Appendices

Acknowledgments

This *Guide* was the result of a broad collaborative effort undertaken over a two-year period. Perhaps the most visible example of this is reflected in the essays. We appreciate the contributions of Archbishop Elden Curtiss, Father Benedict Groeschel, C.F.R., Father C. John McCloskey III, Peter Kreeft and Eileen Cubanski.

But there were many who worked behind the scenes to produce this publication. Foremost among them was Evangeline Jones, deputy director of research at the Cardinal Newman Society, who performed a wide range of editorial and research duties.

Patrick Reilly, the founder and president of the Cardinal Newman Society, saw the need for this *Guide* and provided the support, knowledge and guidance to see this project through to completion. Tom Mead, executive vice president of the Cardinal Newman Society, consistently provided insights that helped strengthen the work and provided essential technical and management support.

There also was a cadre of researchers who did interviews, checked countless websites and did endless fact checking. Four stand out for their substantial contributions to this *Guide*: Mary Heisler, Jennifer Kelly, Marc Perrington and Christopher Zehnder.

We are also grateful for the assistance of the following (in alphabetical order): Zachary Akers, Sophie Coy, Jonathan Dittert, Scott Faley, Thomas Harmon, Breana Harrington, Daniel Henson, Patrick MacDougall, Kelly Mulhern, Doreen Nagurney, Ryan Ostendorf, Mark Schwerdt, Jeremy Sheiko, Noelle Temple, Nancy Vercio and Adam Wilson.

We are indebted to the many individuals who offered insights into the colleges through interviews. These include staff and faculty, students and alumni. College representatives were very gracious in providing photographs, checking facts and in other ways helping us better understand the finer points of their institutions.

Many members of the Cardinal Newman Society also volunteered helpful information. Further, this *Guide* would not have been possible without the very substantial generosity of donors to the Cardinal Newman Society. Although they are too numerous to identify by name, certain of them stand out for their early support and enthusiasm for the *Guide* when it was but a prayer: Andrew and Lori Citsay and Mari Lou Hernandez have our very special gratitude.

Kara Beer was responsible for a quick, accurate and highly professional layout and managed final production of the publication. Sam Torode and Shawna Kunz did the artwork. Jeremy Beer, Christopher Michalski and their colleagues at ISI Books, the imprint of the Intercollegiate Studies Institute, provided substantial assistance with marketing, sales and distribution.

Finally, we acknowledge the enthusiasm and support of Diane Frances Barberini. Diane, a much-loved teacher and filmmaker, was diagnosed with a terminal illness as she was beginning to work on this project. She died on July 28, 2007. She touched many lives, and she will be remembered.

Joseph A. Esposito
Editor
September 1, 2007

Introduction

Joseph A. Esposito

Since the Cardinal Newman Society was established in 1993, interested Catholics have contacted the organization to discuss concerns about the Catholic identity of specific colleges. Often they bring to our attention professors, speakers, curriculum, events or other issues that are at variance with Catholic teachings. Such input has and continues to be very helpful to us, and we have been able to address and often help reverse practices that are clearly inappropriate.

At least as often, we also receive many inquiries asking how we assess the fidelity of certain colleges. Generally, these are from parents who want to know whether their son or daughter would be spiritually nourished at these institutions.

Sometimes the queries are very broad, such as whether we can recommend, say, the top ten U.S. Catholic colleges. There also are many instances when we are asked to recommend a solid Catholic college that has a good pre-med program, which colleges have strong women's athletic teams, or which offer the most notable study-abroad semesters.

More than two years ago, the inquiries about how we might match students with their needs and interests became so numerous that we were convinced of the need for a guide to Catholic colleges. You hold the final result in your hands.

A Tool for Catholic Families

At first we believed that a comprehensive guide to all Catholic colleges in the United States would be the best approach. We hired researchers who combed through websites and published materials and conducted interviews. We sent a detailed questionnaire to all 224 Catholic colleges but received few responses from the many colleges that were well aware of our concerns about their problematic approach to Catholic education. We accumulated a large amount of information—some of it heartening, some fairly predictable and, alas, much that was disturbing.

The more we looked at the data, the more we came to believe that publishing a guide to Catholic colleges in which a majority were neutral or conflicted in their Catholic identity would be of little help to parents looking for information on where to send their college-bound son or daughter. Our goal is to help with the challenge of the college search.

In this first edition of *The Newman Guide*, we have identified 21 Catholic colleges—including one in Ontario, Canada, which we felt compelled to include—where students can reasonably expect a faithful Catholic education and a campus culture that upholds the values taught in their homes and parishes. No such guide has ever been published, and the Cardinal Newman Society is uniquely qualified to provide the information and analysis entirely absent from typical college rankings and guides.

What we provide, then, is invaluable information to supplement the traditional guides and promotional materials that are also an essential part of the college search process. Each profile in *The Newman Guide* highlights the college's mission, governance, spiritual life, curriculum, residential life and extracurricular programs. We provide information that we consider to be most useful in making a college selection—assuming that Catholic identity is an important criterion.

We have tried to provide primarily objective information in order to offer a comprehensive aid to parents and students. While our focus is on Catholic identity, we also discuss issues that are of use to any student, such as notable academic programs, sports opportunities and even characteristics of the surrounding town.

How We Selected Colleges

No college is perfect, and no college is right for everyone. There are wide variations, even among some of the most orthodox Catholic institutions. Some emphasize a Great Books curriculum, while others are more career-oriented. Some have a tiny enrollment, while others are good-sized universities. Some are located in remote rural areas, and others in large cities.

And all, despite their Catholic identity, are impacted to a greater or lesser extent by the surrounding culture; there is no substitute for proper formation before entering college and a student's ability to choose the best courses, professors, friends and activities.

The criteria for selection reflect an art, not a science. We do not give points to individual colleges, nor have we attempted to weight certain characteristics. The colleges included are characterized by the following:

❖ They give a priority to their Catholic identity and actively practice it in most, if not all, aspects of campus life;

❖ They are generally assiduous in ensuring that critics of Catholic Church teaching are not given a platform for their work;

❖ They are committed to providing a quality education for their students; and

❖ Any deficiencies are more than outweighed by success in other areas.

The result is a listing of 20 Catholic colleges in the United States and one in Canada. We are impressed by all of these included here. Could others have been added? Perhaps. In a few instances, we encountered school officials who were reluctant to cooperate and prevented us from doing the in-depth study to determine whether they belonged in this group.

We hope to add additional colleges in the next edition, including those that are working to enhance their Catholic identity. We look forward to helping facilitate dialogue between the colleges in this *Guide* and those that seek to emulate them.

The colleges included in the following pages are grouped into three categories and an epilogue. The first, "Joyfully Catholic," are those that we find to be the most thoroughly orthodox institutions, those whose Catholic identity informs most of what they do as an institution and how they present their programs to prospective students and donors. They are not necessarily "more Catholic" than the other institutions, but their commitment to fidelity above all else ensures that secularizing influences are not likely to have much impact here.

The second group is an intriguing one, those "Born from the Crisis" in Catholic higher education. These are new colleges, some of which are just getting underway, most seeking to occupy a particular niche. Although they are evolving and some still working on accreditation, they offer great potential and are clearly worth considering. All of these suggest a commitment to Catholic identity that rivals that of the "Joyfully Catholic" colleges.

One-third of the colleges are in a category that we have designated "Fighting the Tide." They are well-established institutions that have weathered the vicissitudes of the times and continue to provide a good Catholic education—some of them reversing past trends in a sincere effort to comply with *Ex corde Ecclesiae*, the document on Catholic higher education issued by Pope John Paul II in 1990. In most cases, they are working to bolster their Catholic identity.

Finally, we discuss the University of Notre Dame in an epilogue. In our opinion, it would be difficult to produce such a guide without addressing what is perhaps the most widely recognized Catholic university in the United States. Notre Dame is an excellent academic institution that offers a vibrant spiritual life to students and includes many of the best Catholic minds in several disciplines.

But we believe it has suffered from various missteps from its top officials that give us deep concern. Notre Dame's leaders need to resolve a decades-long struggle to reconcile ambitions toward become a leading national research university—with all of the pressures from external stakeholders and secular academe that accompany that role—and Notre Dame's Catholic mission.

So we offer a candid and detailed assessment of Notre Dame's notable strengths and disappointing weaknesses as a Catholic institution.

Helping You Get Started

To help place the college selection process in the proper context, we have included essays from several prominent Catholics who are knowledgeable about Catholic higher education. We start with a forward from renowned Father Benedict Groeschel, C.F.R., and a letter to students from Archbishop Elden Curtiss of the Archdiocese of Omaha.

The founder and president of the Cardinal Newman Society, Patrick Reilly, contributed an essay on the status of Catholic higher education. We also are fortunate to have an essay on the essentials of a Catholic college education by the well-known evangelist Father C. John McCloskey III, an Opus Dei priest.

The prolific writer and philosopher Dr. Peter Kreeft of Boston College has written a thoughtful article about why philosophy and theology are important to all students. Eileen Cubanski, founder and executive director of the National Association of Private Catholic and Independent Schools, wrote the last essay, which discusses the value of a Catholic education.

We conclude our first section with answers to some key questions of interest to college-searching students and their families.

We hope that after you have read these essays framing the issue of how to select a Catholic college, you will consider the opportunities presented by each of the institutions described in the following pages. Don't forget to look at the material at the end, which also provides comparative insights into this group.

The Newman Guide, in our opinion, is a starting point. After you identify colleges which most interest you and your family, we suggest that you study their websites, visit their campuses and ask all the specific questions that will help you make an informed college selection decision.

Choosing a college is a major decision and encompasses many different issues. Our goal in producing this guide has been to create a resource that will help point you toward to solidly Catholic institutions. In this effort, we have taken inspiration from the great work of the Venerable John Henry Cardinal Newman and Pope John Paul II. We hope that you will find it in that spirit.

Foreword

Father Benedict Groeschel, C.F.R.

If nothing else, my 40 years of teaching in Catholic higher education have convinced me that much of it is going in the wrong direction. The command of Our Lord Jesus Christ "Go and teach all nations" was the foundation of the educational endeavors of the Catholic Church. This was true when I was a student, and thousands of faithful priests and religious brothers and sisters worked very hard for generations to produce a magnificent network of fine institutions of Catholic higher education.

I have seen all of this sadly and tragically erode. Some of the religious communities best known in the past now run colleges that are the furthest removed from Catholic identity. As a result, I often encourage parents to send their children to secular colleges and universities that have an active and involved campus ministry loyal to the Catholic faith rather than use what I call a phony Catholic school. The word "phony" is not a slang word; it comes from the Greek word for sound, and it means that something sounds like what it is not.

There is, however, cause for hope, and it is manifested in those oases of Catholicism profiled in this publication. Colleges listed in *The Newman Guide* are genuinely Catholic, with an indication of those that are most loyal to the Catholic tradition. The colleges and universities mentioned vary considerably, but they have in common a serious attempt to teach the Catholic faith in an orthodox manner and to preserve a campus atmosphere that encourages good Christian life.

You will not find the moral decadence that pervades our culture at these institutions. On the contrary, if you were to visit them, you would be surprised at the large number of students who voluntarily attend daily Mass and receive the sacraments devoutly. Some smaller colleges have a strong emphasis on literature and Catholic culture. They go far beyond the usual meaning of the term "liberal arts." They communicate great cultural values in an exceptional manner. Others are more typical broadly based colleges and universities, but again, when it comes to religious and cultural values, they are clearly dedicated to what is meant by a Catholic education.

I am impressed when I see colleges that reflect their Catholic identity in every aspect of their campus life. It is truly heartening to see this devotion to the Lord, which is in so many ways countercultural.

Some of the colleges profiled here are quite small—institutions whose purpose is unabashedly to help form young Catholic men and women. They emphasize the riches of the remarkable Catholic intellectual tradition. And they provide the spiritual nourishment for which many students hunger and most need.

A few of the colleges are brand new. They are hoping to add their voice as a second generation of orthodox Catholic colleges born after the tumult in Catholic higher education in the 1960s. These new colleges offer a further example of hope.

I also am excited about the older institutions that through strong leadership and often with student activism are successfully navigating the shoals of modernism. We are indebted to those colleges that are battling outside pressures—including financial challenges and the allure of "academic freedom"—to adhere to their historical identity.

When Cardinal Newman Society president Patrick Reilly asked me to assist in putting out this guide, I was both delighted and concerned. When you make a presentation like this, there is always the danger of leaving out a college that should be included. There is also the necessity of selecting those that are on the border. For example, there are a number of Catholic universities and colleges not included in this guide where a sizable portion of the administration and faculty is trying to preserve or restore the school's Catholic identity.

However, in many cases they have not so far been particularly successful. If you find that some are annoyed that their college is not mentioned in this guide, encourage them to examine the guide and see how their institution could come closer to the realization of an authentic Catholic school. Along with providing Catholic parents and students with good guidance on where to go for college, I hope that the guide will encourage institutions that also ran but didn't "make the cut," as they say in athletics. Let them do a little soul-searching and with it some housecleaning.

It is a sad fact that our country is currently squandering its most essential valuable resource, namely, its youth. They are exposed to advanced technical training masquerading as education. In the process they are also exposed to all kinds of values that are contrary to life and their good as human beings, especially their spiritual good. In response to this, one would expect Catholic education to present a broad and clear humanistic approach to culture with emphasis on the Catholic tradition in Western civilization.

We have every right also to expect Catholic institutions to inspire and lead students to the pursuit of an intelligent and good life despite the present situation. Sad to say, many institutions with a Catholic name do just the opposite. The reason for their lethargy and failure to fulfill their purposes is not an attack on faith, but stems rather from greed. Somehow or other the belief is still strong that the more buildings they build and the more students they have, the better the education will be. This is absolute nonsense, which becomes obvious if we only give it some thought. Saint Paul's observation (1 Timothy 6:10) that greed is the root of all evil is certainly pertinent to understanding the large-scale apostasy of much of Catholic higher education.

There is a Christian way to teach anything, Chesterton said. He mentioned that even if you teach the alphabet and you do it in such a way that those who learn it do not despise those who do not know it, you have taught it in a Christian way. How important it is for every student to want to bring his or her life in agreement with the Gospel and the saving message of Our Lord Jesus Christ. There is no other purpose ultimately to life.

What we do in the following of Christ is what we will bring with us through the doors of death at the end of life. Nothing else will come with us. A faithful educational institution is going to prepare people not only for the immediate future of job and career but also for the ultimate future, which is our entrance into the kingdom of God. A college that does not have this as its top priority does not deserve to call itself Catholic. In this guide you will find a list of colleges that understand their responsibility and wholeheartedly embrace it.

I am delighted to be a supporter of the Cardinal Newman Society and hope that this guide will be the beginning of a series of directories that will indicate that Catholic higher education is getting back on course.

ARCHDIOCESE OF OMAHA

Office of the Archbishop

100 North 62nd Street
Omaha, Nebraska 68132

A Letter to Catholic High School Students
About Choosing a College or University

Dear Students:

You are preparing to embark on an amazing journey: a college education. The fact that you are considering a Catholic college or university indicates that you are already making wise choices, the key to a successful and fulfilling college experience.

Many Catholic students choose to attend non-Catholic colleges because of important financial, geographical, academic and other considerations. But it can be said truly that only a faithful Catholic college or university lives up to the full promise of higher education: the search for and transmission of all truth.

Pope John Paul II wrote in *Ex corde Ecclesiae*, the Apostolic Constitution for Catholic Universities: "Without in any way neglecting the acquisition of useful knowledge, a Catholic University is distinguished by its free search for the whole truth about nature, man and God. The present age is in urgent need of this kind of disinterested service, namely of *proclaiming the meaning of truth,* that fundamental value without which freedom, justice and human dignity are extinguished. By means of a kind of universal humanism, a Catholic University is completely dedicated to the research of all aspects of truth in their essential connection with the supreme Truth, who is God."

At a Catholic college or university, then, the revealed truths of faith and the observed truths of science and beauty are equally appreciated. The theology major seeks understanding in the liberal arts and sciences; the pre-medical student seeks wisdom in the teachings of the Church; and the business major tempers his ambitions with ethical behavior rooted in a Christian concern for serving the common good. Moreover, the intellectual, literary, artistic and cultural treasures of the Catholic heritage are available to all those who seek them.

The teachings of Jesus Christ have no boundaries; they apply to every facet of life. So it should be expected and appreciated that at a Catholic college or university, the institution's Catholic identity impacts activities outside the classroom. Expectations for moral Christian behavior extend to the residence halls, the student clubs, the athletic fields and the social gathering places.

If you are considering a Catholic college, chances are you welcome a campus life that respects the dignity of its members and shuns the excesses that have become commonplace on many American campuses. Some have argued that the Catholic Church's moral teachings improperly limit the freedom that should characterize a college education. To the contrary, a college or university that rejects the distractions of unhealthy and disrespectful behavior and the tyranny of radical relativism offers students an environment where all topics can be explored freely with genuine concern for the truth and the common good.

Most young men and women yearn for freedom. That is natural and healthy, a sign that you are excited to take responsibility for yourself and make independent decisions about your behavior and course of life. Unfortunately, it is all too common for college students to rebel against their faith and upbringing, making choices that enslave them to immoral habits and cause serious physical, psychological and spiritual harm to themselves and others around them. If you want freedom, you will find it in Christ!

Sadly, even at a Catholic college or university, you will be confronted sometimes by critics of religion and, especially, Christian morality. The contention is that ancient taboos and unenlightened moral prohibitions are thwarting human progress—especially with regard to sexuality. They will say that human sexuality is a biological phenomenon that should be free of all religious (and therefore all moral) restraints. People must be able to experience their sexuality in any way that they choose, otherwise their freedom is curtailed, the critics say.

But on the typical American college campus, one finds many examples of alcohol abuse and other drug addictions and sexual activity outside the proper context of marriage. These are having a serious negative impact on students. If a total lack of restraint is supposed to lead to more human freedom, then why is it leading to addiction and slavery for so many people?

It is because of God's spirit in us that we hunger for truth and beauty and love. Only God Who is all truth and total beauty and the fullness of love can totally satisfy us. This is why Catholic colleges and universities are such blessings to the Church, because they offer young men and women important opportunities to grow closer to God without artificial separations between faith and reason, freedom and love, vocation and career.

Regardless of which college you choose, set an example for others and lead them to Jesus, who is waiting for them with open arms. Avoid sin and seek out worthwhile activities. Get involved with your Catholic campus ministry and find ways to serve the less fortunate people in your community. Practice sharing the good news of Jesus and his Church with others, witness to the great promise of chastity and proclaim the dignity of all human life.

Take your studies seriously, but remember that your spiritual development is always the greatest priority. Pray often, spend time quietly before the Blessed Sacrament and ask Jesus to lead you. Worry less about choosing a major than listening to God's calling in your life. Seek out guidance from priests, faculty and counselors to ponder how you can be leaven to the world.

Pope Benedict XVI tells young people like yourself that when God calls, you must "be prepared to respond with a generous 'yes' without compromise." Ultimately there is great joy in this, but our Holy Father reminds you that embracing God's calling in total love and obedience always "comes at a price, that price which Christ paid first and which every one of His disciples must also pay, although at a far cheaper price than the one paid by the Teacher."

That price which you must be prepared to pay "is the price of sacrifice and self-denial, of faithfulness and perseverance, without which there is not and cannot be true love, which is entirely free and a source of joy."

Your parents and your Church have prepared you for this sacrifice of love, to put your talents at the service of God and your brothers and sisters. I know most of you have had an excellent education and upbringing. This has prepared you to bring the love of Christ to your peers.

I pray that God will guide you in your choice of colleges and bless your college experience. As disciples of Jesus, you are well prepared to help transform the world and renew all things in Christ!

I am sincerely yours in the Lord,

Most Reverend Elden Francis Curtiss
Archbishop of Omaha

The State of Catholic Higher Education

Patrick J. Reilly

The Newman Guide gives the Cardinal Newman Society the opportunity to highlight Catholic colleges which consistently and enthusiastically embrace the mission of Catholic higher education.

But what about the Catholic colleges that are not included?

The reasons why we have chosen not to profile other Catholic colleges vary with each institution, most ranging from a lukewarm Catholic identity to serious scandal. Generally, however, families seeking a Catholic education outside the colleges identified here will discover a sad state of affairs.

Most Catholic colleges have secularized considerably over the past 40 years, such that anyone who attended these colleges in the 1960s or earlier would scarcely recognize them today. It is no surprise that more than half the colleges in *The Newman Guide* were established after 1970, most in reaction to the rapid decline of faithful Catholic education in this country.

The good news is that a nationwide renewal of Catholic higher education is underway. Not only are new, faithful Catholic colleges springing up—bishops, religious orders and lay leaders are planning to establish several more in the next decade—but nearly every Catholic college in the United States has increased attention to its core mission. We hope to be able to recommend even more colleges in the near future.

How does knowledge of these trends help families who are currently seeking a Catholic college? A basic understanding of the state of Catholic higher education today is valuable not only as a precaution, but also as confirmation of the great treasures we have in the 21 colleges profiled herein.

Identity Crisis

Notwithstanding the great strides the Church is making with regard to Catholic higher education, currently most U.S. Catholic colleges that are not in this *Guide* fall into two categories. First, most of them have retained some degree of Catholic identity, but their leaders seem preoccupied with other concerns—such as conforming to a "feel good" sort of spirituality, ensuring diversity in the student body and faculty, providing career training or simply keeping the doors open. Second, there are many other historically Catholic colleges that have been seriously compromised by disdain for the Church and active dissent from Catholic teaching. This latter group is smaller but includes most of the large Catholic universities.

In either category of institution, the curricula and official policies of the colleges are not well-designed to effectively uphold Catholic identity. Even a small number of problematic faculty, staff or students have significant opportunities to push the envelope and loosen a college's historical ties to the Church. We see this time and time again, with college leaders scratching their heads about what went wrong.

A student at the typical Catholic college will find:

❖ a significant number of faculty who may appreciate theology, philosophy and the arts as useful for presenting ideas and critiquing others' ideas, but who reject any claim to truth outside the natural sciences;

❖ a curriculum featuring a broad course selection with some required courses but no integrated core and little exposure to the Catholic intellectual tradition, unless the student majors in philosophy or theology and actively seeks appropriate courses;

❖ a religious studies or theology department including faculty who dissent from Catholic teaching and offering courses with no clear indication of whether they are genuine Catholic theology courses;

❖ a faculty with a significant portion (sometimes a large majority) of non-Catholics and non-practicing Catholics, often including openly homosexual and dissenting professors;

❖ guest lecturers, often with a decidedly liberal-progressive point of view, including pro-abortion politicians and others whose public actions and statements oppose Catholic moral teaching;

❖ a campus ministry that is generally weak and understaffed, minimizes catechesis and spiritual formation, and often plays loosely with Catholic teaching and the liturgy of the Mass—which is attended by a minority of Catholic students;

❖ student clubs which often include some that oppose Catholic teaching, usually on abortion or homosexuality, and few (if any) that provide opportunities for spiritual growth;

❖ coed residence halls with some restrictions that are generally ineffective in discouraging sexual activity and alcohol abuse; and

❖ campus health and counseling services that are under no obligation to support Catholic moral teaching.

Some of this may astonish you. It is, in fact, a list of the more common concerns. We have identified much more unusual and appalling problems, both at large universities and at small, seemingly traditional Catholic colleges. These include homosexual film festivals, transvestite drag shows, conferences featuring pagan rituals and New Age workshops, lectures by notorious pornographers and pro-abortion activists, etc. Once the door is opened, there is no telling what might come in.

How Did It Happen?

For several centuries, fidelity to the Church was largely taken for granted at Catholic colleges and universities—but the secularization of Catholic colleges in the U.S. transpired quickly in the span of a few decades.

It is no exaggeration that higher education grew out of the Catholic Church. The great medieval universities in Europe were established, funded and staffed by Catholics. For centuries, Catholic colleges around the world have been among the most highly respected.

The Church's involvement in higher education has also had its critics. In 1852 this led the Venerable John Henry Cardinal Newman, the celebrated convert from Anglicanism, to publish perhaps the best-known defense of Catholic higher education.

In *The Idea of a University*, Cardinal Newman argued that a college should have education for its own sake as its only objective, thereby fostering "growth in certain habits, moral or intellectual." With its promise of "teaching universal knowledge," a college cannot rightly exclude any branch of knowledge—most importantly theology, which teaches truths that make sense of all other truths. The Catholic Church cannot rightly be excluded from an active role in higher education, because the bishops have the authority and responsibility to ensure the integrity of theological teaching and the dialogue of faith and reason.

Contrary to Newman's vision, American higher education has largely followed the model of the German research university. This means that even many small colleges are concerned with faculty research and publication as well as teaching; emphasize faculty freedom and departmental independence over interdisciplinary studies and an integrated core curriculum; and underemphasize theology, philosophy and the arts.

To their credit, most of the Catholic colleges held on to their Catholic identity even as the leading Protestant universities, including Yale, Harvard, Princeton, Dartmouth, and many others, abandoned their initial Christian foundations. The Catholic colleges stayed Catholic primarily because the college sponsors, officials, faculty and students were almost entirely Catholic. The curriculum and campus culture largely reflected the interests and culture of the Catholic Church.

It was the turmoil of the 1960s and the aftermath of Vatican II that threw into disarray the Catholic culture in the U.S., of which college campuses were a microcosm. The G.I. Bill, other financial aid programs and new taxpayer funding for public universities enticed growing numbers of Catholic students to forego Catholic education. Meanwhile, the aid programs brought increasing numbers of non-Catholic students to Catholic colleges, which also began to hire non-Catholic faculty. Soon Catholic colleges were faced with an identity crisis.

Competition for students and a desire for greater acceptance by secular colleges led 26 American college officials, scholars and bishops in 1967 to produce the "Land O'Lakes Statement." It publicly declared Catholic colleges' independence from "authority of whatever kind, lay or clerical, external to the academic community itself."

The aftermath was shameful. Bowing to the anti-authoritarian movement of the 1960s and the interests of increasing numbers of non-Catholic students and faculty, most Catholic colleges watered down their emphasis on Catholic identity and their expectations for moral behavior. Fearful that courts would restrict government funding to faith-based colleges—a fear that never materialized on the federal level—college officials removed crucifixes from the classroom walls and reorganized under boards of trustees outside Church control. Conforming to secular academia, they whittled away at their core curricula and focused on preparing students for successful careers.

The resulting problems at Catholic colleges can largely be summed up into two categories. First, Catholic colleges embraced a distorted definition of "academic freedom" such that it is difficult to imagine what offensive speech or perverse activity might not be protected by it, so long as the ever-changing priorities of political correctness are not violated.

Second, most Catholic colleges have abandoned responsibility for students' moral, social and spiritual development. The operating principle for most American colleges was once *in loco parentis*; today colleges provide campus facilities, support services and some programming for students, but most without clear objectives for personal growth or moral standards to define a Catholic campus culture.

Reform and Renewal

It seems this very damaging period may have reached a turning point. The courage and vision of Pope John Paul II helped slow the momentum of secularization and, we hope, reversed the trend.

The 1983 revision of the Code of Canon Law created a new section for Catholic colleges, including the requirement that any Catholic theology professor must have a *mandatum* (or "mandate") from the local bishop, affirming that they will teach within the full communion of the Catholic Church. Students now have reasonable assurance of the orthodoxy of theology professors at colleges that require the *mandatum* or which at least strive to hire theology professors who are obvious candidates for the *mandatum*.

In 1990, Pope John Paul II issued *Ex corde Ecclesiae*, the apostolic constitution on Catholic higher education, by which he defined what constitutes Catholic identity at Catholic colleges. More than a statement of principle, the constitution's General Norms are binding on Catholic colleges as an application of Canon Law. *Ex corde Ecclesiae* gives each local bishop the legal authority and responsibility to declare a college "Catholic"—or in the case of a persistently wayward college, to remove the Catholic label. It requires that every "official action or commitment of the [college] is to be in accord with its Catholic identity." Catholic professors are "to be faithful to, and all other teachers are to respect, Catholic doctrine and morals in their research and teaching."

The results have been encouraging. Even though compliance with *Ex corde Ecclesiae* varies widely, most Catholic colleges are taking steps in a positive direction. The Association of Catholic Colleges and Universities, which once argued that *Ex corde Ecclesiae* is unworkable in the U.S., now pledges to implement it. Many U.S. bishops are pushing quietly for reform, and in more than a few instances have publicly decried scandal on Catholic campuses. Lay Catholics have also urged reform—more than 20,000 of them as members of the Cardinal Newman Society, and others through local efforts and alumni organizations.

The unity of faith and reason continues to be a key theme for Pope Benedict XVI, who—like his predecessor—is a scholar with great appreciation for Catholic higher education. As philosopher Ralph McInerny has said, "It sometimes seems that the only voice insisting on the power of human reason is that of the Holy Father." His great intellect and insight are having their impact especially in theology courses, and college leaders are intently watching the former Vatican prefect who successfully defused the liberation theology movement and disciplined wayward theologians.

The renewal of Catholic higher education is slowly becoming reality, despite the doubts of some of the Church's brightest observers. But it will take many years to reach completion.

Distinctively Catholic

In the meantime, one of the most exciting developments in the Church today is the establishment of new, faithful Catholic colleges. We are in the midst of a new wave of colleges, with plans underway for several more in the coming years. An earlier wave in the 1970s gave rise to Christendom College, Thomas Aquinas College, and others that have since built strong reputations. Each of the new colleges is unique and offers something special to Catholic families: one concentrates on the increasingly important New Media, three serve the rapidly growing Catholic population in the South, one emphasizes the outdoors and stewardship of nature, etc. Finding one's niche at a good Catholic college is becoming much easier.

Also very exciting are the colleges that have maintained or restored their Catholic identity despite prevailing trends in the opposite direction. More are joining this group, but the ones profiled in this *Guide* deserve praise for their heroism, often amid much scorn from faculty and officials at other Catholic colleges.

Many of the schools in the *Guide* provide an outstanding education in the Catholic intellectual tradition by means either of studying the Great Books of Western culture or through a core curriculum that coherently integrates the traditional liberal arts disciplines. These point to a renaissance of traditional Catholic education, an encouraging development.

What makes these colleges different from largely secularized Catholic colleges? A few examples:

❖ Instead of graduating students with no substantial exposure to the Catholic intellectual tradition, the colleges in the *Guide* generally have a strong core curriculum or several requirements to study faithful Catholic theology and philosophy.

❖ Whereas most Catholic colleges gamble on the maturity of students to refrain from sexual activity, the *Guide* colleges set clear expectations for moral behavior with same-sex residence halls or visitation policies that are strictly enforced. For example, the Franciscan University of Steubenville pioneered an innovative "household" program that encourages students to support their peers in healthy Christian lifestyles.

❖ About ten percent of Catholic colleges annually host the morally offensive play *The Vagina Monologues* as part of a national

fundraiser to support the worthy cause of preventing violence against women. The colleges in the *Guide*, however, strive to build a Catholic campus culture. Very Rev. David O'Connell, C.M., president of the Catholic University of America, said the *Monologues* has "become a symbol each year of the desire of some folks to push Catholic campuses over the edge of good and decent judgment." The University of St. Thomas in Houston instead presented a play, *Traffic in Women*, written by English professor Janet Lowery to bring attention to the centuries-old problem of trafficking women for prostitution, pornography or domestic labor.

Catholic families, then—and others who are attracted to the benefits of a Catholic education—have good opportunities for a college education that is steeped in the Catholic intellectual tradition while offering a moral campus environment. Already today there are 21 excellent colleges profiled in *The Newman Guide* which feature a variety of charisms, academic offerings, numbers of students, locations, extracurricular programs and more. For future students, the numbers of faithful Catholic colleges are increasing.

The renewal of historically Catholic colleges, which built their reputations upon the dedication of faithful Catholic leaders and faculty, is essential. Whether or not you are a student or graduate of one of these colleges, your prayers and support for renewal will have an important impact.

But today, with this *Guide* to 21 excellent colleges, we also celebrate the rising tide of Catholic higher education which Cardinal Newman so fervently hoped for: "[T]his is our hour, whatever be its duration, the hour for great hopes, great schemes, great efforts, great beginnings . . . to recommence the age of Universities."

Finding God on a Catholic Campus

Father C. John McCloskey III

The late futurist Herman Kahn once said there are only two times in life when one's ideas, attitudes and convictions are radically altered: before you are six and when you go to college.

In my own pastoral work with college students, especially where it pertains to religious belief and behavior, I have found Kahn's observation to be true. Given what is at stake, the choice of a college for one's child should be an overriding concern of any Catholic parent. The university is usually the last place to form the pre-adult Catholic. The important transition between the teen years and young adulthood should be one from dependence to responsible independence in all areas of one's life, most especially the moral and the spiritual.

Character formation, built upon the natural law and perfected with grace, will determine the question of happiness or unhappiness both in this life and the next. There also is the financial question. The large sum—sometimes exceeding $150,000—shelled out for college expenses could easily be invested elsewhere for the real benefit of the Church, society or one's family. Prudence calls for serious deliberation.

Through the years many parents have asked my advice on selecting a Catholic college for their child. Their concern about making a wise choice is well-justified. The United States once had the largest and best network of Catholic colleges in the world. Millions of Catholic men and women for much of our history received a coherent, faithful education and formation, preparing them to form families, serve God, Church, society and country and to value their roles as father or mother, husband or wife above wealth, pleasure or personal realization. These Catholic colleges were staffed by tens of thousands of dedicated men and women, clerical, religious and lay, to whom great glory and credit are due.

Over the last 40 years, in large part due to an eagerness to assimilate, most Catholic colleges and universities have thrown away their heritage, traditions and truth claims, resulting in a loss of an understanding of their mission. Pope Benedict XVI, in a June 2007 address in Rome, described our present "educational emergency" as "inevitable"

in a culture which too often makes relativism its creed. In such a society the light of truth is missing; indeed, it is considered dangerous... to speak of truth, and the end result is doubt about the goodness of life and the validity of the relationships and commitments that constitute it. Hence, education tends to be reduced to the transmission of specific abilities or capacities for doing, while people endeavor to satisfy the new generation's desire for happiness by showering them with consumer goods and transitory gratification. Thus, both parents and teachers are easily tempted to abdicate their educational duties and no longer even understand what their role, or rather the mission entrusted to them, is.

That mission, as Pope John Paul II told American bishops in 1998, is "the integral formation of students, so that they may be true to their condition as Christ's disciples and as such work effectively for the evangelization of culture and for the common good of society." The key word is "integral": the formation of the whole human person. Formation, of course, covers lots of ground. It is clear, however, that university education cannot simply be a matter of transmitting knowledge, but of transforming the whole personality through a lived assent to the truths of Revelation.

The primary way for the Catholic university to help undergraduates is by means of a liberal arts education in the Western tradition. Through this education, students can learn to think, reason and communicate as adults in such a way that they can fulfill their vocations as parents of Catholic families who will make Christ and his Church present in the wider secular world of work, social activity and friendship.

Today, however, with notable exceptions, "college" has largely become at best a place for excellent pre-professional training and at worst an extended and expensive four-year vacation from reality. The great majority of college students today cannot articulate why they are studying, other than vague references to career or "service to humanity." Their uncertainty and confusion reflect the lack of clear vision on the part of educational institutions themselves, which mirrors the prevailing culture marked by secularism, utilitarianism and relativism.

What remains is an atmosphere where power, physical attractiveness, sexual conquests, leisure time, economic security and the amassing of wealth are the underlying, if unarticulated, goals of life. A relatively few young men and women are capable, after some reflection, of understanding that they are living in a polluted atmosphere, and that holiness, commitment, marriage and family, truth, character and virtue should be the ends of an integral education.

Under these circumstances, how does one find a Catholic college that offers a coherent, faithful education and formation?

Check with the Church

A good first place to look for basic criteria is the Church herself. Pope John Paul II laid out what the Church expects of institutions that label themselves Catholic in *Ex corde Ecclesiae*. You will find this document reprinted in the pages of this *Guide*; read it, and then apply it to the colleges you research. In *Ex corde Ecclesiae*, the Church applies her perennial wisdom to the contemporary scene and provides a sure guide for distinguishing private whimsy from authentic teaching regarding the university. After all, it was the Church that gave birth to the university.

At the heart of a truly Catholic university will be a sound theology department, since the Catholic Church recognizes theology as the "Queen" of sciences. Apart from considerations of academic competence, parents and prospective students need to determine the all-important question of the theology department's loyalty to the teaching authority of the Church. The majority of Catholic colleges have a two- or three-course requirement in theology for its undergraduates, who presumably will consider the teaching of their professors as authoritative. Sometimes it is difficult to ascertain what type of theology is taught at any given school.

Ask the authorities if the criteria of the "Instruction on the Ecclesial Vocation of the Theologian" of the Congregation for the Doctrine of the Faith have been applied to its theology faculty, and if they have taken the oath required of them. A list of the on-campus speakers during the last academic year who dealt with themes concerning Catholic doctrine and morals would also be revealing.

Another investigative technique is to probe the knowledge of any recent graduate. A few pointed questions will quickly reveal what he knows and where he stands with regard to the Church and her teaching. Finally, if the university harbors any well-known "dissenter," the case is closed.

A Catholic university should have a philosophy of education that emphasizes a well-rounded liberal arts education centered on a core curriculum. Legitimate debate over the exact contents of a core curriculum is to be expected, but certainly a well-rounded program of study of the Western intellectual and cultural tradition includes literature, philosophy and the arts. The university also must recognize the existence of objective Truth and our duty to submit to it. Without this affirmation and the belief that our Faith has a truth-claim that is universal in its ambit, there simply cannot be any mission to carry that truth to others. Pope John Paul II made this point in a 1998 *ad limina* address:

> The greatest challenge to Catholic education in the United States today, and the great contribution that authentically Catholic education can make to American culture, is to restore to that culture the conviction that human beings can grasp the truth of things, and in grasping the truth can know their duties to God, to themselves, and their neighbors....The contemporary world urgently needs the service of educational institutions that uphold and teach that truth is "that fundamental value without which freedom, justice, and human dignity are extinguished."

A Catholic university should teach Catholic philosophy, building on the Thomistic foundation of moderate realism. How can a student, or a professor for that matter, engage our neo-pagan, post-modern culture without a firm grounding in metaphysics, epistemology and nature? Philosophy alone is not enough, but it is indispensable as a preparation for theology.

Philosophy, theology and the liberal arts are all essential parts of a Catholic college education. If the university views itself merely as a place that prepares students for a career rather than a place that prepares them for life and gives them a deep appreciation of knowledge as an end in itself in the natural sphere, then it disqualifies itself as anything other than an academic supermarket.

Spend some serious time with the college catalogs of the schools you investigate. Examine their educational philosophy along with their curriculum and requirements. Be sure to read the colleges' mission statements. The more you encounter words like belief, maturity, conviction, commitment, marriage, family, evangelization, culture, character, truth and knowledge, the closer you may wish to continue looking.

An important concern for the Catholic student and family will be the emphasis on religious practice and formation in a particular school's campus life. I am not referring here simply to religious statuary or saints' names on buildings, which may simply be relics of a bygone age. What percentage of the faculty is Catholic? What percentage practices their faith in the traditional sense? Does anyone on campus know or care? Do not underestimate the impact that fully formed and committed Catholic faculty can have upon students. Their influence may easily dwarf that of the chaplain.

Naturally, a college will be as Catholic as the people who direct it. If it is directed at least nominally by a religious congregation, what is its condition? Are there vocations? What percentage of the faculty is made up of members of the institute? Are they noted for their loyalty to the Church? Is there an openness to the variety of spirituality in the present-day

Church, particularly to the lay movements and institutions that are providing so much life in this historical moment? Or does there exist a "turf" mentality or downright hostility to other spiritualities and institutions approved by the Church? There should be no monopoly on providing spiritual help to the students and a great respect for the freedom of the student to find his way.

The state of the college chaplaincy can be a strong indicator. Piety, reverence for Catholic liturgy, the encouragement of personal prayer, frequent confession and communion, the presence of the Blessed Sacrament and the availability of sound experienced spiritual directors should be part of any truly Catholic university experience. My experience with the work of a Catholic chaplaincy has convinced me that an energetic faith-driven campus ministry is a necessity to create a Catholic culture on campus that is capable of forming modern day apostles. Try to determine whether a Catholic college you are considering emphasizes catechesis, formation, practice and evangelization.

Take a look as well at the group activities sponsored by campus ministry. Are there courses or talks covering Catholic teachings and Catholic Bible study, to educate students in their faith? Is volunteer work with the poor, elderly or ill seen in the context of the Gospel and as a logical consequence of the student's adherence to the practices of the faith? In our affluent society, it is very important that the Catholic be exposed to the misery that lies around us and is very often hidden. The joy of unselfish giving for the sake of Christ can help affect a serious change in students who heretofore have been gravely affected by selfish consumerism.

The most important group activity that campus ministry can offer is retreats. A silent retreat with plenty of room for prayer and direction can help a student progress more in his Christian life than a year of other types of activities. It may well be the first time that the student has been left alone in reflective conversation with Christ. There, the meaning and purpose of his life become clearer.

The Sense of Home

Take a look at the quality of the social and moral environment of campus life. For non-commuters, living arrangements are of the highest importance. Do the college dormitories have basically the same rules and regulations, moral tone and adult supervision that you would wish for your college-age child if he were living at home? Are the dormitories places where character can be built and where virtue can grow and, if need be, protected? This is not a question of turning a college residence into a cloister, but rather of assuring an environment where young men and women can live as Christians without being subject to unnecessary temptations and provocations. Are the dormitories single-sex? Or is that at least an option?

Throwing hundreds of young men and women together in close quarters produces inevitable and natural results, most of which at best do not prepare them well for Christian marriage and at worst cause irreparable damage. If you dare, spend the night or even a day or two living in a dormitory. In my experience, most parents do not want to believe the atmosphere of hedonistic immaturity and boorishness that reigns in these places. High spirits are one thing; animal behavior raised to an art is another. Remember, it is your child that you may be placing at moral and physical risk.

Are abortion referrals and contraceptives dispensed on campus? Is the college unequivocally pro-life, or is there waffling and double-talk on the most important question of our time, the sanctity of life from conception to natural death?

How is leisure time used on campus? Are there healthy and uplifting social, recreational and cultural opportunities? Leisure time in today's culture is too often spent watching television or films and reading magazines and novels that make a mockery of the faith and portray the goal of life as basically hedonistic self-fulfillment. On too many but fortunately not all Catholic campuses, there are pressures to conform to the secular *zeitgeist*, which places a premium on "growth" in which the abuse of alcohol, drugs and sexuality is at least condoned if not promoted.

Take a cross-section of recent graduates of a college you are considering. Are they well-educated by your standards, with an appreciation for the finer things of mind and spirit? Are they the type of young adults (and not arrested adolescents) that you would like your children to emulate? Does the practice of the faith give central meaning to their lives, or is it simply accidental and to be sloughed off when convenient? In short, are they Catholic first and American second or vice-versa?

Some of the above criteria should help in identifying authentic Catholic colleges and universities. You may have additional criteria of your own. In a society as caught up in secular goals and ambitions as our own, it is easy even for good Catholic parents to feel the tug of considerations such as selectivity, earning potential and bragging rights. However, your children, who are negotiating the years between youth and adulthood in the Perfect Storm of a permissive and materialistic culture, need more and better guidance than that. If they spend their college years exposed to good influences, set on fire by inspiring examples and informed by confident and clearly orthodox teaching, they will be fortified to form healthy Catholic families and function as humane Christian leaders of a society starving to be fed bread and not stones.

The schools profiled in this *Guide* deserve your consideration as Catholic institutions where students can receive an integral education to prepare them for their God-given vocations. And since this springtime of the New Evangelization is infiltrating Catholic higher education too, we can expect the future years to add more to their number.

Why Study Philosophy and Theology?

Peter Kreeft

Here is one of the clearest criteria for choosing or judging a college: you can be almost certain that any college that has dropped philosophy and theology from its core curriculum is not serious about a liberal arts education. And in my experience I find that this is true of many of the colleges in America.

This raises two questions: (1) What are philosophy and theology, and why are they crucial to a young person's education today? (2) Aren't they outdated, impractical, abstract, irrelevant, elitist, superfluous and even dangerous to faith and sanity?

Some Definitions

"Philosophy" means "the love of wisdom." Wisdom is the knowledge of ultimate causes, explanations and principles. It includes knowledge of values, not just facts. It gives you a "big picture," a "world-view" and a "life-view." It explores such questions as these: What is the essence of a human being? What is the meaning (value, goal, purpose) of human life? What is a good life? What is a good society? Are there higher laws than man's laws? Are we here by chance or design? Are we fated or free? How do we know what is good or evil? How do we know anything? Is anything certain? Can reason prove (or disprove) the existence of God? Why do we suffer? Why do we die? Is there life after death?

Anyone who is simply not *interested* in these questions is less than fully human, less than fully reasonable. Reasonable persons,

even if skeptical about the possibility of answering them, will not dismiss them as unanswerable without looking (that is not reason but prejudice) but will examine the claims of philosophers to have given reasonable answers to these questions before settling into a comfortable, fashionable skepticism.

Theology comes in two forms, philosophical and religious. Philosophical theology ("natural theology") is a subdivision of philosophy. It uses natural human reason to explore the greatest of all questions, the questions about God. Religious theology (or "revealed theology") is a rational exploration of the meaning and consequences of faith in a revealed religion—in our case, the "deposit of faith" or "Sacred Tradition" of the Catholic Church which comes from Christ and His apostles, and the scriptures they wrote.

In most Catholic universities today, Sacred Tradition is no longer sacred. It is treated as something to be "dissented" from ("diss" is the first part of "dissent"), as an enemy to enlightenment, progress, maturity and liberation, or at least as an embarrassment to be "tweaked," "nuanced" or "massaged" rather than as a gift to be gratefully, faithfully and lovingly explored.

Most Catholic universities today have philosophy departments that are excellent spiritually as well as academically, but have deeply compromised theology departments. Their effect on students is much more often to weaken their faith than to strengthen it, not only in controversial moral issues such as abortion, contraception, cloning, euthanasia and sexual morality, but even in fundamental doctrines such as Christ's divinity and resurrection and the historical truth of the Gospels.

We badly need good philosophy and theology. But why? To answer this question, look at *where* they are taught. They are taught in colleges and universities. So to find the "why" of philosophy and theology, we must find the "why" of colleges and universities.

The Goal of Education

Considering the trillions of dollars spent on universities by parents, governments and foundations, it is amazing that most of the people who go there (the students) and most of the people who pay for them (the parents and the government) never even ask, much less answer, this question: What is the purpose of the university? It is the most influential institution in Western civilization, and most of us don't really know exactly why we entrust our children to them.

The commonest answer is probably to train them for a career. A B.A. looks good on your resume to prospective employers. That is not only a crass, materialistic answer, but also an illogical one. Consider what it means. It means that the reason students should study in universities is so that they can get high grade-point averages and thus get better jobs when they graduate.

What does "better jobs" mean? It means first of all, to most of them, better-paying jobs. But why do they need better paying jobs? For the money, of course. Silly question. But why do they need money? That is an even sillier question. Life has expenses. *What* life? Most of them hope to marry and raise families, and it takes a lot of money to do that. Why does a family need a lot of money? The two most ex-

pensive things a family needs money for are a house and a college education for the kids.

Ah, so a student should study to get high grades to get an impressive resume to get a good job, to finance his family when it sends his kids to college to study, to get high grades, et cetera, et cetera.

This is arguing in a circle. It is like a tiger pacing round and round his cage in a zoo. Is there a better answer? There is if you know some philosophy. Let's look.

Probably the most commonsensical and influential philosopher of all time was Aristotle. Aristotle says that there are three "whys," three purposes, ends or reasons for anyone ever to study and learn anything, in school or out of it. Thus there are three kinds of "sciences," which he called "productive," "practical" and "theoretical." (Aristotle used "science" in a much broader way than we do, meaning any ordered body of knowledge through causes and reasons.)

The purpose of the "productive sciences" (which we today call technology) is to produce things, to make, improve or repair material things in the world, and thus to improve our world. Farming, surgery, shipbuilding, carpentry, writing and tailoring were examples in Aristotle's era as well as ours, while ours also includes many new ones like cybernetics, aviation and electrical engineering.

The purpose of the "practical sciences" (which meant learning how to do or practice anything, how to act) is to improve your own behavior in some area of your own life. The two most important of these areas, Aristotle said, were ethics and politics. (Aristotle saw politics not as a pragmatic, bureaucratic business of running a state's economy, but as social ethics, the science of the good life for a community.) Other examples of "practical sciences" include economics, athletics, rhetoric and military science.

The third kind of sciences is the "theoretical" or "speculative" (contemplative), i.e., those that seek the truth for its own sake, that seek to know just for the sake of knowing rather than for the sake of action or production (though, of course, they will have important practical application). These sciences include theology, philosophy, physics, astronomy, biology, psychology and math.

Theoretical sciences are more important than practical sciences for the very same reason practical sciences are more important than productive sciences: because their end and goal is more intimate to us. Productive sciences perfect some external thing in the material world that we use; practical sciences perfect our own action, our own lives; and theoretical sciences perfect our very selves, our souls, our minds. They make us bigger persons.

And that is the reason for going to college in the first place: not to make money, or things, or even to live better, but to *be* better, to be more, to grow your mind as you grow your body.

The Big Picture

What we have been doing for the last several paragraphs is philosophy. We need philosophy because we need to explore such reasons, reasons for studying, reasons for universities' existence, even (especially) reasons for your own existence. For one of the primary questions all great philosophers ask is: What is the meaning of life, the reason for being, the point and purpose and end of human existence in this world? If you don't know that, you don't know anything because you don't know the point of everything. If you don't know that, you may get all A's in all your subjects, but you flunk Life.

The answer to that question for any intelligent, honest and serious Christian, Jew or Muslim is God. Supreme wisdom is about knowing God. And philosophy is the pursuit of wisdom. So philosophy is ultimately the pursuit of God, using the tools of natural human reason and theology by faith in supernatural divine revelation.

The "wisdom" philosophy pursues is not a factual knowledge like physics or history; but a knowledge, and understanding, and appreciation, of values, of what ought to be rather than merely what is. For instance, we need to know whether career (work) or family is more important, because most of us will invest enormous emotional and physical energy in both, and they will always compete and conflict to some extent.

We want to know the meaning of falling in love and romance and sex. What is its meaning, its purpose? For two generations now we have been asking every conceivable question (and many inconceivable questions, too), but not this one, not the very first and most basic one.

You see? Philosophy and theology raise the mind's eyes to The Big Picture. If we can't see that, we miss the forest and see only the trees; we count the syllables in the book of life but don't know what kind of a story we are in.

Good Philosophy, Good Theology

One philosopher tells this story. (I paraphrase.) I was raised in a New York City slum. There were no books in my house. No one in my high school cared about education. I found an escape in the great 42nd Street library, where I devoured books indiscriminately. One day, I happened to read the famous "allegory of the cave" from Plato's *Republic*. It changed my life. I found my identity. My life was that cave, and philosophy was the way out into another, bigger world. My mind was born that day. For the rest of my life I have explored the world outside the cave, the world of ideas, and taught others to do so. The biggest thrill in my life is finding among my students someone like me whom I can show that there is a way out of the cave, and that there is a bigger world outside.

That is why we all need to study philosophy (and, even more obviously, theology): because it is the discovery of another world, another *kind* of world, another kind of reality than the material world: the discovery that ideas are real, and that (in the words of a great book title) "ideas have consequences."

The only alternative to good philosophy is bad philosophy. "I hate philosophy" is bad philosophy, but it is a philosophy: egotism. "Philosophy isn't practical" is a philosophy: pragmatism. "Philosophy doesn't turn me on" is a philosophy: hedonism.

Everyone has a philosophy, just as everyone has an emotional temperament and a moral character. Your only choice is between "knowing yourself" and thinking about your philosophy, or hiding from it and from yourself. But what you do not think about will still be there, and will still motivate you, and have consequences, and those consequences will affect all the people in your life up to the day of your death and far beyond it.

Your philosophy can quite likely and quite literally make the difference between heaven and hell. Saint Francis of Assisi and Adolf Hitler were not professional philosophers, but both had philosophies, and lived them, and went to heaven or hell according to their philosophies. That is how much of a difference thought can make: "Sow a thought, reap an act; sow an act, reap a habit; sow a habit,

reap a character; sow a character, reap a destiny." Buddha said, "All that we are is determined by our thoughts: it begins where our thoughts begin, it moves where our thoughts move, and it rests where our thoughts rest."

Philosophy can lead you to God, and theology can lead you further into God (or away from Him). And God is the source of all truth, all goodness and all beauty; that is, of everything we value. (If that is not true, then God is not God.) All truth is God's truth; when an atheist discovers some scientific truth, he is reading the mind of God, the Logos. All goodness is God's goodness; when an agnostic secularist loves his neighbor, he is responding to divine grace. All beauty is God's beauty; when a dissipated, confused and immoral artist creates a thing of beauty, he is using the image of God in his soul, being inspired by the Holy Spirit, however anonymously, and participating in God's creative power.

Philosophy is a necessity if you want to understand our world. Bad philosophy is the source of most of the great errors in our world today. Errors in philosophy are devastating because they affect everything, as an error of an inch in surveying the angle of a property line will become an error of ten yards a mile down the line.

Most of the controversies in our world today can be understood and solved only by good philosophy and theology; for instance, the relation between world religions, especially Islam and Christianity; human life issues such as abortion, euthanasia and cloning; the justice of wars; the meaning of human sexuality and of the "sexual revolution"; the relation between mind and brain, and between human intelligence and "artificial intelligence"; the relation between creation and evolution; how far we are free and responsible and how far we are determined by biological heredity and social environment; the relation between morality and religion, and between religion and politics; and whether morality is socially relative or universal, unchanging and absolute.

Revealed theology claims to have the answers, or at least the principles that should govern the answers, to many of these questions. So theology is even more important than philosophy, if answers are more important than questions. And of course they are, for the whole point of asking a question, if you are honest, is the hope of finding an answer. It is nonsense to believe that "it is better to travel hopefully than to arrive," and good philosophy refutes that self-contradiction. If it's not better to arrive at your goal of truth than to strain after it, then truth is not really your goal at all, and the straining after it is a sham.

That is not, of course, to say that it is easy to arrive at the goal of truth, or that all we need is a set of answers we believe on the Church's authority but do not understand. The truly respectful attitude toward the authority of the Church—which is an extension of the authority of Christ—is to let revealed truth permeate our minds and our lives like light, not simply to preserve that light by hiding it under a bushel basket. All "ideas have consequences," especially divinely revealed ideas; and it is our job to lovingly draw out those consequences, like philosophers, and not to fear them, like heresy hunters, or to claim them as our own in a spirit of superiority to our divine teacher, like heretics.

Answering Objections

But there are objections to philosophy and theology out there. If this were not so, the teaching of these subjects would not have declined so precipitously. Let us briefly consider and answer some of them.

❖ **What can you do with philosophy and theology anyway?** We have already answered that question by noting that it is the wrong question. The right question is what they can do with you.

❖ **But they're so *abstract*!** Yes, and that is their glory. To be incapable of abstraction is to be less than human, or a less than fully developed human. Animals and small children, for instance, are incapable of abstraction. They do not talk about Fate and Freedom, or Good and Evil, or Divinity and Humanity, or Life and Death (all abstractions). They talk only about hamburgers and French fries, boo boos and bandages, malls and cartoons. These things are not "the real world." They are the shadows on the walls of Plato's cave. Philosophy and theology are not fantasy. They are the escape from fantasy.

❖ **But philosophy is a dinosaur—it isn't up to date, modern, popular, etc.** No. Neither is wisdom, virtue, happiness, piety, fidelity, courage, peace or contentment.

❖ **What does philosophy have to do with real life?** Everything. It is more important to know the philosophy of a prospective employee or employer, landlord or renter, friend or enemy, husband or wife, than their income, social class or politics.

❖ **Philosophy is elitist. It speaks of "Great Books" and "Great Ideas" and "Great Minds."** Yes, it does. At least good philosophy does. If you prefer crummy books, stupid ideas and tiny minds, you should not waste your money on college. If you believe that all *ideas* are equal, rather than all *persons*, you are confused and need a philosophy course. (Is the idea that all ideas are equal equal to the idea that they are not?)

❖ **"Philosophy bakes no bread." It does not make you rich. It is contemplative, like monasticism.** True. But why do we make money and bread? Is money our means (of exchange) to our end? Money is for bread, and bread is for man, and man is for truth. The ultimate end of human life is contemplative: knowing and appreciating the truth. We will not be baking bread or making money in Heaven, but we will be philosophizing.

❖ **Religion makes philosophy superfluous. If you have faith, you don't need reason.** Yes, you do: you need reason to understand your faith. And you need reason to know whether your faith is the true faith. There are many fakes. And how do you know that unless you think about it? And if you don't want to think about your faith, then either you aren't really very interested in it, or you are afraid it is so weak that it will not endure the light. In that case you need a faith-lift.

❖ **But philosophy can be a danger to faith. Many have lost their faith through philosophy.** Yes, and many have gained it, too. Of course, philosophy is dangerous. So is love, and trust, technology and money. Bad things are always misuses of good things. Wherever great harm is done, great help could have been done.

Final Things

This is especially true in theology. I know a chaplain who was ministering at the bedside of an old, dying man who had "lost his faith" and left the Church decades ago. The chaplain asked him what he believed about life after death, and the man replied that he had no idea where he was going and he didn't think anyone else did either, because no one had any idea where they came from in the first place or why they are here.

The chaplain disagreed. He said, "You know the answers to those questions. You learned them as a little boy. You forgot them. But you can remember them now. It's not too late. You learned the Baltimore Catechism, didn't you? Yes, you did. Do you remember how it begins?"

The man wrinkled his brow, retrieving an old memory. "Yeah. It went like this: 'Who made you? God made me. Why did God make you? God made me to know Him, to love Him and to serve Him in this world, and to be happy with Him forever in the next.'" The man paused, lifted his eyes, and said, "You're right. That's true!" And a smile appeared on his face. And then he died.

You need philosophy and theology now because you will need it on your deathbed later.

The Value of a Catholic Education

Eileen Cubanski

As founder and executive director of NAP-CIS, a national association of private schools committed to faithful Catholic education, and an educator for 42 years, I have long appreciated the special value of Catholic education. It is exciting to witness the revival of serious Catholic colleges, those institutions profiled in *The Newman Guide*.

For many people, education—and most especially Catholic education—does not and should not end upon graduation from high school. The value of a Catholic education is most profoundly realized in post-secondary education, an essential stage in the formation of a mature Catholic mind.

Catholic education forms the human person in right order with God; what is at stake is the very meaning of the human person. During the years of vital discernment, a young adult needs to involve the whole person, body and soul, marrying faith and reason in the pursuit of truth and in the governance of his education and future.

A Catholic liberal arts education, during this crucial time in the formation of the person, is essential to understanding the unity of all truths. This is the special contribution of the Catholic intellectual tradition, which even for non-Catholic students ought to be an essential component of the study of Western culture—yet too often is entirely ignored at non-Catholic colleges.

In addition to providing an essential foundation in the Catholic liberal arts, a faithful Catholic college helps the student understand that knowledge learned in the pursuit of a specialized academic discipline does not conflict with faith. Instead that knowledge is enhanced and clarified by Catholic theology, and the student's faith is deepened and enriched. According to the Vatican II declaration on Catholic education, "a true education aims at the formation of the human person in the pursuit of his ultimate end and of the good of the societies of which, as man, he is member, and in whose obligations, as an adult, he will share" (*Gravissimum Educationis*).

Treasure to Be Protected

Because of this, I am rightfully proud of my own 16-year Catholic education, which culminated in 1965 with my graduation from a Catholic college in the Northeast. Unfortunately, not everyone shares the Church's appreciation of Catholic education—including, it seems, the current leadership of my alma mater. The contrast between what I experienced and what passes today as a Catholic college is striking.

When I attended college, theology was a required study in every semester. Every class began with prayer. Mass and the Sacraments were available daily; the noon Mass, in fact, was always standing room only. Yearly retreats were required, sending the message loud and clear that prayer and contemplation were essential for proper Catholic formation and for maintaining a personal relationship with God. The entire campus life was a reminder of the school's Catholic mission, from the statuary and artwork displayed in every building, to the code of dress and behavior that held us all to the highest standards of virtue and morality.

It was in my final-semester theology class, senior year, that I heard a statement which alarmed me and foreshadowed the changes to come. It was from the respected college's chaplain and most-feared theology professor, who told us that, as Catholics, we had a responsibility to develop our own consciences independent of the Church's moral teaching.

The implication was clear. One's conscience must be formed through learning and contemplation of Catholic teaching, and a Catholic education can be invaluable to this process. But my professor's statement was a declaration of independence from Catholic teaching, rather than a call to fidelity. I was terribly naïve to the consequences of this novel idea (at least so it was to me), considering the cultural context of the 1960s.

Little did I know, or possibly suspect, that the door to dissent was open, and the next few decades would witness the slippery slope of declining Catholic identity. At my alma mater, the course is complete. The college is now "Catholic" in name only. Notorious dissenters, such as Father Richard McBrien and Sister Joan Chittister, are invited guest speakers. Cultural programs include the yearly presentation of *The Vagina Monologues*. The list of commencement speakers is a "who's who" of advocates for abortion and women's ordination.

Just as the wonderful nuns who founded the college decades ago eventually shed their habits, the college shed its Catholic identity and, with that, gave up its treasure. Although it consistently makes the *U.S. News & World Report* list of recommended colleges, it is also frequently cited by the Cardinal Newman Society for a lack of Catholic identity.

Victory of the Spirit

Is Catholic education everywhere in such a sad state? Absolutely not! Catholic education is thriving on all grade levels—elementary, secondary and post-secondary—but families have to choose schools and colleges carefully.

In *The Idea of a University*, the Venerable John Henry Cardinal Newman wrote that a college or university is "a place that teaches universal knowledge. ...Since knowledge is limited only by truth, if the Catholic faith is true, a university cannot exist externally to the Catholic place, for it cannot teach universal knowledge, if it does not teach Catholic theology. Hence a direct and active jurisdiction of the Church over it and in it is necessary, lest it should become the rival of the Church."

The crisis of Catholic colleges has been followed with great interest and concern in the last 40 years. There are Catholic colleges that declare and demonstrate their institution as founded on the principles as expressed in *Ex corde Ecclesiae*, the Apostolic Constitution on Catholic higher education, but identifying them can be difficult. This *Guide* will help.

Parents must be just as vigilant in their process of review and selection of a Catholic college as they are in making choices about elementary and secondary education. Parents and their college-bound children must spend a lot of time in prayer, research and observation, and they should ask a lot of questions before making any decisions about a particular school.

Can a Catholic student get a good education at a non-Catholic college? Sure, as far as it goes. But a Catholic college looks beyond learning a profession and preparing to be a good worker of the 21st century. It offers a more complete education, the free pursuit of truth. That is because a faithful Catholic college or university teaches from the source of truth, which is Jesus Christ, and, therefore, possesses the fullness of truth.

A Catholic college protects and nurtures a student's faith. It rejects the disordered secular "theology" that posits man as the supreme being and deprograms a person's faith from any part of daily life. Instead of compartmentalizing life and identifying himself by what he does and not who he is—so that he is a doctor, lawyer, teacher or parent who happens to be Catholic—a Catholic college prepares the student to be a Catholic doctor, a Catholic lawyer, a Catholic teacher or a Catholic parent.

Fortunately the increasing variety of faithful Catholic colleges offers many options to students. It is one important sign of the "Springtime of Hope" in the Church of which Pope John Paul II spoke. Catholic education in all its venues—homes, elementary and secondary schools, colleges and universities—leads the renewed vitality in the Church and is the hope to restore all things to Christ in the Church and society.

This could not be more important. The source of salvation is Jesus Christ, teaching us how to know, love and serve God through the Catholic Church. Catholic schools and colleges are the formal expression of the Church's teaching mission.

Young people rely on Catholic education to teach not only the skills and knowledge that are necessary for responsible citizenship, but also the truths of the Catholic faith. By forming the hearts, minds and wills of students, Catholic education helps them discern their secular and religious vocations in life, witness to their faith in the world and pursue their ultimate end in Heaven.

Catholic education is essential to the growth of the Church and is thriving with the Holy Spirit's loving intervention. It is by Catholic education that He protects and preserves the Church. The Holy Spirit is in control within the Church to bring faithful Catholic education to every soul, from early childhood to aspiring adults ready to become the future leaders of the Church and society.

For educators like me and those you will find at the colleges in *The Newman Guide*, all our successes and failures are cast in the shadow of the Cross. From the heart of the Church to the heart of our schools, we celebrate the activity of the Holy Spirit and our part as His instruments in Catholic education. We look to the Cross to show us most powerfully the vertical dimension to the tasks, challenges and opportunities that lie ahead for Catholic education. We can do no less than to help carry that Cross and share in the celebration of its ultimate victory—the salvation of souls.

Contributors

Joseph A. Esposito is editor of *The Newman Guide* and director of research at the Cardinal Newman Society. He served in three presidential administrations, most recently as Deputy Under Secretary for International Affairs at the U.S. Department of Education. He also was a working group chair for the Commission for Assistance to a Free Cuba. Esposito has been a full-time writer for Catholic publications and an adjunct professor of history. He has four graduate degrees and is a member of Phi Beta Kappa.

Father Benedict J. Groeschel, C.F.R., is a much-loved author, preacher, and servant to the poor. He is perhaps best known as host of *Sunday Night Live* on EWTN. Father Groeschel also is director for the Office for Spiritual Development and founder and director of Trinity Retreat for the Archdiocese of New York, and cofounder of the Franciscan Friars of the Renewal. He earned his doctorate in psychology from Columbia University, is a professor at St. Joseph's Seminary and the author of many books.

His Excellency Most Rev. Elden F. Curtiss has been Archbishop of Omaha since 1993. Previously, he served 17 years as Bishop of Helena, Montana. He also was superintendent of schools for the Diocese of Baker, Oregon, and president-rector of Mount Angel Seminary in Saint Benedict, Oregon. Archbishop Curtiss studied at St. Edward Seminary College and St. Edward Seminary and has graduate degrees in divinity and educational administration. He will celebrate his golden jubilee as a priest in 2008.

Patrick J. Reilly is founder and president of the Cardinal Newman Society and a senior fellow at the Capital Research Center. Reilly has commented and written extensively, including co-editing *Newman's* Idea of a University: *The American Response*. He previously served as executive director of Citizens for Educational Freedom and worked at the U.S. House of Representatives and U.S. Department of Education. He is a Fordham University alumnus and received a graduate degree from The American University.

Father C. John McCloskey III, a priest of the Prelature of Opus Dei, is a research fellow at the Faith and Reason Institute. He served 13 years as a chaplain for Princeton University students and five years as director of the Catholic Information Center in Washington, D.C. He has hosted several EWTN series. In 2007 he co-authored *Good News, Bad News: Evangelization, Conversion, and the Crisis of Faith*. He is a Columbia University alumnus and holds a doctorate in sacred theology.

Peter Kreeft has been professor of philosophy at Boston College since 1965. He previously taught at Villanova University and has been a visiting professor at many colleges and seminaries. A Catholic apologist who converted from Calvinism, Kreeft has written more than 50 books on philosophy, theology and apologetics. He received his doctorate from Fordham University and is the recipient of many honors.

Eileen Cubanski co-founded and serves as executive director of the National Association of Private Catholic and Independent Schools, a national accrediting agency and teacher certification program for private Catholic and independent schools. She also founded St. Maria Goretti Academy, in Loomis, California, in 1993. She has an undergraduate degree in child study and elementary education and a master's degree in education administration.

Answers to Some Questions About Selecting a Catholic College

1. What is the special value of a Catholic college education?

A sincerely Catholic college provides a free but healthy environment for serious consideration of ideas without the tyranny of harassment, political correctness or enforced relativism. The same cannot be said for many secular institutions.

At the colleges featured in this *Guide*, students will also find a vibrant Catholic culture on campus that respects Catholic moral teaching and offers numerous opportunities for spiritual development. Although every campus varies, differences from the typical Catholic secular campus might include a more active Catholic campus ministry, respect for Catholic values in areas including residential life and campus programs, active pro-life and social justice efforts, community outreach programs, Catholic study groups, etc.

2. Can Catholic colleges appeal to non-Catholics?

Non-Catholics will find great value. The Catholic intellectual tradition taught at faithful liberal arts colleges embodies much of Western thought and is not well presented at many non-Catholic colleges. A campus culture built upon Christian morality is also a welcome departure from much of American higher education.

3. Can I get a good education at Catholic colleges and universities that are not included in this guide?

This *Guide* represents approximately the ten percent of Catholic colleges that place a premium on their Catholic identity in all aspects of campus life. They also provide a good education. Among those colleges not included in the *Guide* are some with strong academic credentials but that do not have, in our opinion, the same commitment to Catholic identity.

The opportunity for strengthening spiritual formation during the college years is enhanced where Catholic teachings are constantly reinforced. We believe that the best combination of spiritual and academic commitment is reflected in these 21 colleges.

4. What is *Ex corde Ecclesiae*?

It is the Apostolic Constitution on Catholic higher education issued by Pope John Paul II in 1990. The document, which is reprinted at the back of this *Guide*, identifies what constitutes Catholic identity at Catholic colleges and universities and specifies General Norms to achieve a Catholic mission. These Norms are binding on Catholic colleges as an application of Canon Law.

In 1999 the U.S. bishops approved guidelines to implement *Ex corde Ecclesiae* in the United States; these became effective in 2001. Compliance by the U.S. Catholic colleges and universities varies widely. Clearly, a Catholic institution that minimizes or subverts *Ex corde Ecclesiae* has serious problems with its Catholic identity. All colleges recommended in this *Guide* support *Ex corde Ecclesiae*.

5. What is a core curriculum?

A core curriculum is a body of courses that is required for all students. Generally, these reflect a traditional liberal arts perspective. Some colleges' core curricula encompass the entire four-year program, while others reflect only a limited number of courses.

The importance of a core curriculum, in our opinion, is to ensure that students are adequately exposed to the Catholic intellectual tradition through theology, philosophy and other disciplines. As a rule, the larger the number of such required courses, the better the curriculum is likely to be in forming the student's thinking as a Catholic.

Sometimes a college may allow some flexibility within the core curriculum, allowing, for example, a student to choose among various theology courses. This may or may not be desirable depending on the choices available. In the main, we prefer a situation where students are exposed to as large a number of strong, orthodox Catholic courses as possible.

6. How is a core curriculum different from a Great Books curriculum?

A Great Books curriculum prescribes that students be extensively taught the classical works of Western Civilization, generally through the texts and discussing them and writing about them. A Great Books program can be secular in nature, but those identified in this *Guide* are not.

Those who promote a Great Books approach at Catholic colleges see it as an unfettered way to present the Catholic intellectual tradition, because they take the position that the great classics are intertwined with Catholic thought.

A Great Books program tends to be rigorous and can be an outstanding opportunity for serious students seeking a broad liberal arts degree. Such an approach, however, is not for everyone—for instance, a student who is seeking specialized courses in a traditional college major.

7. I consider myself more a "doer" rather than a "thinker." Should I avoid colleges that place a premium on theology and philosophy courses?

No, that would be a mistake. Everyone should be concerned with "First Things"—the natural and supernatural truths that lie at the root of all knowledge and activity—and the best way to do so is to understand what they are and how to address them. You would shortchange yourself by avoiding these academic areas. For a fuller discussion of the importance of philosophy and theology, please read Professor Kreeft's essay at the beginning of this *Guide*.

8. In identifying a college, should I place a greater emphasis on a well-rounded education or on training for a career?

This is a raging debate in education circles. Historically, colleges were established to teach people to read the Bible, perhaps even to become clergymen. Another consideration was that students be taught enough of the classics to be good, productive citizens.

The focus on education, including higher education, has shifted. There is a certain enthusiasm for courses and majors to be "relevant." To a large extent, we as a society are the poorer for it.

We encourage students to direct their educational priorities in this order: (1) broaden your understanding of the Catholic intellectual tradition; (2) develop a greater appreciation for writers and thinkers who have influenced Western thought, including prominent Americans; and (3) sharpen your reading, writing and other intellectual skills to eventually take an active role in society.

That's why a core curriculum is valuable; it helps direct you toward learning what is essential for you to lead a rewarding life as a Catholic in a democratic society. If you don't learn these basics in college, you are unlikely to learn them later in life.

9. How important is accreditation?

Accreditation is very important. Problems can result down the road if a student graduates from an unaccredited college. In applying to graduate school, for example, they may find that their undergraduate work is not fully acceptable at the college to which they are applying.

A few colleges in this *Guide* are not yet accredited because they are new and accreditation takes several years. There is a standard process that an aspiring college must follow. The good news is that once accreditation is granted, it applies retroactively. We are impressed by the progress that the not-yet-accredited colleges in this *Guide* have made, and we are confident that that the key question is "when" not "if" they will be accredited.

Nevertheless, students should discuss this matter with the admissions office at each college and feel comfortable with the accreditation status of the college that is finally selected.

10. Can a Catholic college have a lay board or lay officials and be committed to Church teachings?

Absolutely. It is not unusual for dedicated, orthodox Catholic laypeople to found or direct a college.

The key is how closely the college embraces *Ex corde Ecclesiae*. Does it, for instance, require the theology professors to receive the *mandatum* from the local bishop? Is the college's commitment to Church teachings reflected in the spiritual life, the curriculum, the outside speakers who appear on campus, the types of groups that flourish on campus, etc.? What is the college's relationship with the local bishop?

11. What is the *mandatum*?

According to the U.S. Conference of Catholic Bishops, "The *mandatum* is fundamentally an acknowledgement by church authority that a Catholic professor of a theological discipline is teaching within the full communion of the Catholic Church."

According to Canon Law, every Catholic theology professor must receive the *mandatum* from his local bishop. Catholic colleges, however, are not obligated to require the *mandatum*, and most colleges will not reveal which professors have received it.

Students seeking assurance of the orthodoxy of theology professors should consider colleges that voluntarily require the *mandatum* for employment and tenure. Many colleges in this *Guide* do so.

12. Do requirements such as the *mandatum* or prohibiting appearances by pro-abortion speakers curb academic freedom?

No. A college that identifies itself as Catholic should be expected to reflect Church teachings. A college's purpose is to seek and teach truth; at a Catholic college, the Catholic faith is recognized as truth from God, revealed to us through Scripture, Christ and the Church.

Academic freedom protects faculty from interference when they seek or teach truth according to the methods proper to their academic discipline. Academic freedom also protects the truths of Faith from those who have no recognized theological expertise but who would publicly undermine Catholic teaching.

13. How important is it to select a college with a vibrant spiritual life?

It is critical. While most people assume that colleges help provide a good education and prepare young people for careers, it is also a time for them to strengthen their spiritual life as they mature into adulthood. The best way to be so formed is to be in an atmosphere where the spiritual life, inside and outside the classroom, is emphasized and nurtured. A Catholic college that does this is fulfilling its role.

14. Is there an ideal residence hall arrangement?

In general, we believe that male and female students should live in separate residential facilities and that visitation rules should be appropriately enforced. We also believe that residential facilities that have strong leadership, sometimes from priests, and which provide a forum for chastity discussions are to be respected and encouraged.

There are some instances where colleges have males and females in the same dormitory but restrict each gender to different wings or even floors. This may reflect a college's space or financial limitations. Such an arrangement, while not ideal, could be workable provided the college maintains strict and careful supervision. These arrangements bear close inspection by parents and students.

15. Alcohol consumption seems to be a problem on college campuses, even at good Catholic colleges. What does this mean for a parent?

Underage and binge drinking are widespread problems and seem to reflect a general permissiveness within the broader society. Good Catholic families are not necessarily immune. It is imperative that parents discuss the issue candidly with their son or daughter. While colleges can and do address the issue through lectures and strict policies, it is ultimately the responsibility of the individual student to do the right thing.

16. Why are there so few larger universities in this guide?

When we evaluated all the U.S. Catholic colleges for inclusion in this guide, we looked for those that actively lived their Catholic identity. We did not screen for size or locale or other extraneous criteria. These colleges are what our research reflected.

Sometimes the larger universities, in an attempt to build a national secular reputation as a research university, feel the need to de-emphasize their Catholicism. Some call it academic freedom or even just diversity, but it often unhinges a college from its traditional moorings.

A large Catholic college can be faithful to its identity if it so chooses. We are hopeful that more will begin to recognize that academic excellence, freedom of inquiry, national reputation and Catholic identity are all simultaneously compatible.

17. Some of the colleges in this guide are small, even very small. Should I be concerned about attending a college with a small student body?

Certainly not. Small colleges can provide great individual attention to student needs. They can help students gain confidence in classroom discussions, develop good relationships with faculty members and forge friendships with other students.

But small colleges are not for everyone. Some students prefer the opportunity to interact with a wider range of students, participate in more activities and take advantage of broader course offerings. A student needs to evaluate whether he or she is comfortable with the size of the college based on such issues as his or her personality and academic needs.

18. What about locale? Suppose I like a college but don't like the town or the area of the country?

Again, this is a personal decision. Keep in mind that you are selecting a college that you are likely to be attending for four years. It helps to be in an area in which you are comfortable. A lifelong city dweller might find it difficult to live in a small, rural area. You would not want to select a college primarily on the basis of its location, but you should factor that into your decision-making.

19. Is a college more likely to have a stronger Catholic identity if it has an historical tie with a religious order?

Alas, it is not. If that were the case, there would be many more orthodox Catholic colleges that we could recommend. The commitment to a Catholic identity on campus varies from order to order, sometimes within an order and from institution to institution. In some instances, the presence of a religious order has a profoundly positive impact and in others it is negligible. Colleges need to be evaluated on an individual basis.

20. College is expensive. What should I know about financing my education?

A college education is, indeed, expensive. Fortunately, there is an array of financial aid that exists at each private college, including those in this *Guide*. In some cases, almost all students receive some assistance.

It is essential that you speak frankly with the admissions and financial aid officials and investigate what help might be possible. We have been struck by the number of substantial scholarships that are available at these colleges, sometimes reserved exclusively for Catholic students whose records indicate great promise.

21. Should I be concerned that a college that interests me is not widely known?

Not really. Some students believe that graduating from a prestigious institution opens certain career doors. And, in some cases, it does. But for most students, such impact will be minimal.

What is important is whether your Catholic faith can be strengthened or at least maintained. Other considerations are whether you will get a good Catholic education, whether you will enjoy your undergraduate experience and whether the college provides you with an opportunity to make some lifetime friends. What more can you ask for?

22. I have found a few colleges in this guide that greatly interest me. What do I do next?

You should first thoroughly investigate the college's website. If you have questions, e-mail them to the appropriate college representative. Read the campus newspapers to learn more about what's happening on campus—what are the issues, what are the problems, what do students seem to care about (most campus newspapers are online).

When you feel you have enough information to winnow down your list, visit each campus that has made the cut. The campus visit is essential. Talk to students there, wander around the campus, explore the town, attend Mass and campus events and speak forthrightly with college representatives. May God bless your search!

1 ⭐ Aquinas College • Nashville, Tennessee
2 ⭐ Ave Maria University • Ave Maria, Florida
3 ⭐ Belmont Abbey College • Belmont, North Carolina
4 ⭐ Benedictine College • Atchison, Kansas
5 ⭐ The Catholic University of America • Washington, D.C.
6 ⭐ Christendom College • Front Royal, Virginia
7 ⭐ The College of Saint Thomas More • Fort Worth, Texas

8 ⭐ DeSales University • Center Valley, Pennsylvania
9 ⭐ Franciscan University of Steubenville • Steubenville, Ohio
10 ⭐ Holy Apostles College & Seminary • Cromwell, Connecticut
11 ⭐ John Paul the Great Catholic University • San Diego, California
12 ⭐ Magdalen College • Warner, New Hampshire
13 ⭐ Mount St. Mary's University • Emmitsburg, Maryland
14 ⭐ Our Lady Seat of Wisdom Academy • Barry's Bay, Ontario, Canada

15 ⭐ St. Gregory's University • Shawnee, Oklahoma
16 ⭐ Southern Catholic College • Dawsonville, Georgia
17 ⭐ Thomas Aquinas College • Santa Paula, California
18 ⭐ The Thomas More College of Liberal Arts • Merrimack, New Hampshire
19 ⭐ University of Dallas • Irving, Texas
20 ⭐ University of St. Thomas • Houston, Texas
21 ⭐ Wyoming Catholic College • Lander, Wyoming

Joyfully Catholic

Christendom College

Front Royal, Virginia

www.christendom.edu

Overview

Nestled in Virginia's Shenandoah Valley amid the breathtaking sight of the Blue Ridge Mountains is Christendom College, a stellar example of a small, orthodox Catholic liberal arts college. For more than a generation, Christendom has been preparing undergraduates to live their faith within families, careers and vocations.

The college started modestly in 1977 when historian Dr. Warren Carroll and several others offered its first classes in a former Catholic elementary school building in Triangle, Virginia, about 45 minutes south of the nation's capital. Two years later, a permanent campus was established at its present site in Front Royal, 70 miles west of Washington, D.C.

From the very beginning, Christendom has sought to address what it saw as deficiencies in existing Catholic higher education. It forthrightly identifies its Catholic mission by emphasizing its role as an educational apostolate, requiring all professors to be Catholic and teach all classes through a Catholic prism, fostering a vibrant campus spiritual life and enforcing college regulations consistent with Catholic teachings. The spiritual emphasis is so comprehensive that the college says that Catholicism represents "the air that we breathe."

Consistent with its Catholic worldview, Christendom has an 84-credit core curriculum that constitutes about two-thirds of the four-year program. All courses in the freshman and sophomore years are prescribed.

QUICK FACTS

Founded: 1977
Type of institution: Small liberal arts college
Setting: Small town
Undergraduate enrollment: 397 (2006–07 academic year)
Total undergraduate cost: $24,090 (tuition, room, board and fees for 2007–08)
Undergraduate majors: Six

FIVE KEY POINTS

1. One of the most strongly orthodox Catholic colleges in the country.

2. It has a solid, integrated liberal arts core curriculum.

3. The spiritual life is vibrant and pervasive.

4. The study-abroad program in Rome attracts most of the college's juniors.

5. The college attracts a highly impressive cadre of orthodox Catholic speakers to campus.

These include four theology courses, including "Fundamentals of Catholic Doctrine I and II." There also are four required philosophy courses during the first two years.

For the junior and senior years, students must take two more theology courses ("Moral Theology" and "Apologetics") and two additional philosophy courses. Two years of a foreign language—Latin, Greek, French or Spanish—are required as are courses in English, history, science and political science (one of which is "Social Teachings of the Church"). All students must write a senior thesis.

Students can select from six majors and work in their concentration in the third and fourth years. The majors are classical studies, English language and literature, history, philosophy, political science and economics, and theology.

President Timothy O'Donnell told us, "The college has a very clear vision. We stress academics and Catholicism. As a result, we attract students who know what they're getting. We end up attracting a person who hungers for what we are providing."

Clearly it is a program that works on a number of levels. Despite its small size, the 397 students in the 2006–07 academic year came from 45 states and two other countries. About half of these students had been home-schooled.

The college works hard to nurture its students, reflected by a solid 90 percent freshman retention rate. This success is even more impressive given that the college and its students accept no federal funds or federal aid, including no federally subsidized student loans.

The college is financially sustained by a devoted national following among many Catholics. Eighty-five percent of its fundraising comes from individuals, which contrasts markedly with the nationwide average of only 20 percent. Similarly, it receives 11 percent of such funding from corporations and foundations as opposed to the 52 percent in the rest of the country.

But a few students, after receiving the benefit of the rigorous core curriculum program of the first two years, choose to transfer to another college that allows them to major in disciplines other than the six at Christendom. The college understands this and awards an Associate of Arts degree to those students choosing to move on. At the 2007 commencement, two of the 70 graduates received an associate's degree.

Christendom, which is fully accredited by the Commission on Colleges of the Southern Association of Colleges and Universities, prepares students for graduate school and various professions. It also has seen about 10 percent of its alumni enter religious life. And, in keeping with its atmosphere of like-minded students and support for family life, approximately 300 "alumnus-to-alumna" marriages have taken place.

The college acquired the Notre Dame Graduate School ten years ago. Located in Alexandria, Virginia, across the Potomac River from Washington, D.C., it awards a Master of Arts in Theological Studies, mostly to adult students. The school holds summer sessions at the Front Royal campus.

Governance

A 13-member board (which includes one priest) governs the college. Founding president Dr. Warren Carroll and current president Dr. O'Donnell are members. Christendom is located within the Diocese of Arlington, and according to the college, "is submissive to the authority of the Bishop of Arlington regarding the orthodoxy of Catholic doctrine taught at the College." Board members take an annual Oath of Fidelity.

Dr. O'Donnell has been at the college for 23 years and was named its third president in 1992. He received both his licentiate and doctoral degree from the Pontifical University of St. Thomas Aquinas, the well-regarded Rome institution known as the Angelicum. Among other honors, Dr. O'Donnell was named by Pope John Paul II a Consultor to the Pontifical Council for the Family to a five-year term (2002–07).

Public Identity

It would be difficult for Christendom to have a fuller Catholic identity. It does truly permeate the campus. All faculty members are Catholic and annually make a Profession of Faith and take the Oath of Fidelity before the Bishop of Arlington. According to one of these professors, "The faculty believes this commitment to the Magisterium of the Catholic Church strengthens our academic freedom, since it frees us from error in fundamental principles upon which our research and teaching are based."

This approach is clearly articulated in the college's vision statement, which notes, "Only an education which integrates the truths of the Catholic Faith throughout the curriculum is a fully Catholic education."

Not surprisingly, Christendom has fully embraced *Ex corde Ecclesiae*. It is refreshing to read of such support from a college president. As Dr. O'Donnell writes: "*Ex corde Ecclesiae* is the call of a parent to her rebellious child. The Holy Father's ardent desire is that those in leadership positions should come to their senses and return to their Father's house lest they perish on the way."

The list of speakers who have appeared on campus represents a veritable "who's who" of Catholic orthodoxy, ranging from prominent cardinals and leading Catholic public officials to distinguished academics, writers and pro-life activists. The graduation speakers, honorary doctorate recipients, *Pro Deo et Patria* Medal awardees and guest speakers represent an impressive grouping of defenders of the faith.

There are no questionable speakers and, in fact, every speaker we could identify actively promoted Catholic teachings. There are no clubs that are at variance with Catholic beliefs. One college administrator put the identity issue in perspective: "The greatest strength of Christendom College is its integral living out of orthodox Catholic doctrine both inside and outside the classroom."

In a move that further emphasizes its commitment to the Church, Christendom sponsored a three-day religious Discernment Weekend in February 2007. Arlington Bishop Paul Loverde celebrated the opening Mass and Father Frank Pavone, national director of Priests for Life, was a featured speaker.

The college also evangelizes to a broader audience through its Christendom Press, which currently has 32 titles in print. Distributed through ISI Books, the press includes works on religion and Catholic-related history from such authors as Dr. Carroll, Father Stanley Jaki, O.S.B., Mark Shea and L. Brent Bozell.

Spiritual Life

The Chapel of Christ the King is at the center of the campus. All activity on campus passes by the chapel several times a day. Time is taken out every class day to allow students to attend the two daily Masses, one at 11:45 a.m. and another at 4:45 p.m. About 75 percent of the student body attends Mass during the week. President O'Donnell and many other faculty members attend daily Mass, providing good role models.

The Mass is always reverently celebrated, and a more solemn *Novus Ordo* liturgy is celebrated in Latin on Wednesdays and Fridays. On Sundays and solemnities, a solemn "high" Latin Mass with Gregorian chant is sung by the *Schola Gregoriana* and sacred polyphony sung by the Christendom College choir.

On Sundays, some students attend the 12:15 p.m. Tridentine Mass at Front Royal's St. John the Baptist parish. Before that Mass was offered, a few traveled to downtown Washington, D.C., where St. Mary, Mother of God Church has long had a Tridentine Latin Mass every Sunday.

There are two very involved chaplains, including Father Seamus O'Kielty, a retired priest who has led a colorful career as an African bush missionary, a temporary chaplain in the Bolivian army and as a U.S. Navy chaplain. Both priests are highly regarded on campus.

These priests hear confessions every weekday, and lines for confession are reported to be long. There is daily adoration of the Blessed Sacrament as well as recitation of the Rosary and the Divine Office of Morning, Evening and Compline Prayers. There are additional holy hours during examination periods.

A student group called Disciples of the Sacred Heart has a special prayer time in the evening before each first Friday in reparation to the Sacred Heart of Jesus. The Legion of Mary is very active at Christendom, with outreach to the town and vicinity.

In the area of social action, students in the Shield of Roses pray the Rosary and offer sidewalk counseling in front of Planned Parenthood in Washington, D.C., each Saturday

morning. Participation in the annual March for Life, also in the nation's capital, is a tradition that includes nearly the entire student body.

All religious ministries at Christendom are specifically Catholic, so the issue of "balance" with that of other faiths is non-existent. In fact, Catholicism is the only faith noticeably represented on campus. One student told us, "We had an atheist a couple of years ago, but I heard that she recently converted."

Catholicism in the Classroom

The college bulletin states: "The Christendom College [84-credit] core curriculum, unlike the 'smorgasbord' general education requirements common in most colleges and universities, is designed to provide the orderly, sequential presentation of fundamental principles of theology, philosophy and mathematical science in conjunction with the historical and literary knowledge which is foundational for an understanding of our civilization."

Because faculty members voluntarily take an annual Oath of Fidelity, orthodoxy in these two subjects is safeguarded. There are no critics of Catholic teaching. As Dr. O'Donnell said to us, "Any public dissent from the Magisterium or the Pope are grounds for immediate termination."

The commitment to Catholic identity and orthodoxy shows itself most in the theology department. In addition to courses on Mariology, the papacy, Church councils and documents, there are broader ones such as "The History and Nature of Modernism" and "Theology and the Public Order." There is a Thomist cast to the theology and philosophy departments.

The most popular majors at Christendom are history, philosophy and political science. From its inception, the college was targeted to eventually reach a maximum number of 450 students, which is about 50 above its current enrollment. As it remains a small college, it lacks certain curricular options. For example, although there is a minor offered in mathematics, there is no major.

But regardless of the major, students are not shortchanged in their religious formation. For one thing there is the integrated curriculum that builds on theology and philosophy with a strong emphasis on Catholicism.

In addition, spiritual values and Catholic tradition are present in all the disciplines. One student said that the college worldview is that "the center of history is Christ becoming man." It is not surprising that there would be a certain intersection of majors.

American history courses look at the role of the Catholic Church in building the country. One student explained that a course on the history of Germany used Catholic values to better critique the horrors of Hitler and Nazism.

An English professor said of the Western classics: "These works, as well as those in the Anglo-American tradition, are critically studied for what they reveal of the human heart and soul, and of our understanding of man's place in the universe."

"This field of study," he added, "including mastery and understanding of the tools of literary analysis and scholarship and their philosophical bases, is an important and legitimate discipline for a Catholic college whose graduates are expected to engage the modern culture and work to transform it."

In the political science department, all students take an introduction to political theory and a Catholic social doctrine class. The latter deals explicitly with Catholic teaching affecting the political order. Major encyclicals and social doctrines are studied.

A dress code is maintained in the classroom, at Mass, meals and special events. Usually this includes a dress shirt and necktie for men and a dress or blouse and skirt for women. A jacket is also required for men at Sunday Mass and for speakers' presentations.

As a way to enhance the curriculum, students have the opportunity to attend the Junior Semester in Rome either in the fall or spring. It is a rigorous five-course semester, which includes one course each in theology, philosophy, art and architecture, Italian and an interdisciplinary course. Eighty of the 90 juniors participated during the 2006–07 academic year. There also is a short summer program available in Ireland.

Finally, Christendom sponsors several summer programs for different populations. For the past 18 years, there has been an adult summer institute dealing with various issues. In July 2007, Father Benedict Groeschel,

C.F.R., former Senator Rick Santorum and others spoke at a "Marriage and the Family" conference.

And each year 100 high school seniors can attend a one- or two-week summer program that includes classes, spiritual programs and recreational opportunities. As is the case with other colleges, such a program allows students to sample life at the campus and determine whether it is a good fit.

Student Activities

Christendom offers many activities outside the classroom. The St. Lawrence Common, where students and staff dine, is the scene for dances and performances sponsored by the Student Activities Council. There are some typical college activities such as orientation weekend, Italian night, Oktoberfest, formals and other dances.

But there also are the unique St. Genesius Night, St. Bridget's Eve Festival, St. Joseph's feast and St. Patrick's Day festivities. In fact, many activities focus on the liturgical calendar or feast days of saints. President O'Donnell told us, "The main motive for celebration is lost on most people. Having things in order, by making faith or saints the focus, there is a proper ordering and [students] end up having a lot more fun."

This focus, not surprisingly, spills over into campus groups, which include the Shield of Roses, Legion of Mary, Holy Rood Guild (assisting with altar vestments and linen) and pro-life club. The Corporal Works of Mercy group ministers to the poor in the Front Royal area by helping out at soup kitchens, delivering meals and visiting nursing homes.

The St. Juan Diego Confraternity assists in the formation of student missionary workers who participate in the college mission pro-

gram. Members pray for the Catholic evangelization of the Americas and participate in trips within the region.

There is an active drama contingent on campus, including the St. Genesius Society, named after the patron saint of actors; the Fine Arts Program; and the Christendom Players. Among recent productions were *A Midsummer Night's Dream* and *You Can't Take It with You*.

Cultural opportunities and lectures also exist through the Beato Fra Angelico Arts Program. One offering in April 2007, for example, was a multimedia presentation on the Shroud of Turin.

Other groups include the Chester-Belloc Debate Society that helps students hone their argumentation and rhetorical skills. Students can write for *The Rambler*, a weekly publication, and discuss spiritual writings with the Oratory. There is a Friday book discussion group and a chess club.

Christendom competes in several varsity sports in the Shenandoah-Chesapeake Conference. Rugby, a very popular campus activity, was added as a varsity sport in 2007. Various intramural sports also are available.

Residential Life

Campus housing is provided for all full-time students. Although 95 percent of students live on campus, some are allowed to make their living arrangements at off-campus college residences because of dietary considerations or a need for a quieter atmosphere.

There are three female and three male residence halls. Intervisitation is never allowed. In addition to eliminating the opportunities for inappropriate behavior, one female student applauded the separated residential policy, saying, "It provides a safe haven, a time for girls to breathe. It's a great place for people to bond and form friendships and to just be you. It encourages girls to have good Catholic friendships."

There is an active religious life within residence halls, where there are group Rosaries and where a Pilgrim Virgin statute migrates from one building to another. Chastity and modesty are strongly promoted by the Student Life Office and others.

Every floor in every hall has either a resident assistant or a proctor whose job it is to promote community life, enforce college behavior policy and assist students. There are weekly room inspections. Neither television nor Internet access are allowed within the residence halls but are provided in campus centers. Students under the age of 21 have a curfew of midnight during the week and 1 a.m. on weekends.

The published rules of student conduct are fully in accord with Catholic moral teaching. Drinking is prohibited in the college residences but some students do seem to get around the policy. There is an effort made to teach students to drink responsibly and, at campus events, students over the age of 21 are provided with alcohol in limited amounts.

Medical needs for students can be addressed at Warren Memorial Hospital, a 196-bed facility in Front Royal that is located about ten minutes from campus. The Washington, D.C., metropolitan area includes nationally respected specialists and hospitals.

The Community

The town of Front Royal, which has a population of about 14,500, is rather plain, although the backdrop of the Blue Ridge Mountains is beautiful. For diversions, students seem content with the campus activities and the rich array of outdoor opportunities in the area. These include the abutting Shenandoah River, which allows for canoeing, tubing and fishing. Hiking is available at the nearby Shenandoah National Park and corresponding mountains.

The nation's capital is only about 70 miles away and it presents historical, cultural, artistic and political opportunities for students. A number of students are from Northern Virginia and quite familiar with the region.

Front Royal is easily reachable via Interstate 66 from Washington, and north-south Interstate 81 is close. Dulles International Airport, a major airport that served 27 million passengers in 2005, is about an hour east of the campus. Closer to the capital city along the Potomac River is Ronald Reagan Washington National Airport, another significant facility with many direct flights to the eastern half of the United States.

The Bottom Line

For 30 years Christendom College has made a vital contribution to American Catholic life through its solid spiritual formation and its liberal arts curriculum. While some colleges in this *Guide* may match its Catholic commitment, it is unlikely that any exceeds it.

One faculty member said to us, "The college exemplifies in small what 'Christendom' means: a society ordered to Christ, our God and King." You can see it, you can feel it on the campus. They are justifiably proud of presenting Catholicism as "the air that we breathe."

Many Catholics are aware of Christendom so we are probably not breaking any new ground in recommending it. But we want to encourage parents and students to look at the college, and for all the right reasons.

The College of Saint Thomas More

Fort Worth, Texas

www.cstm.edu

Overview

Texas may be known for its brashness and outsized image, but one of the state's academic gems is a micro college that reflects quiet civility, a unique commitment to classical education and a firm dedication to orthodox Catholicism. Located in the former cowboy capital of Fort Worth, Texas, The College of Saint Thomas More offers its students an uncommon formation.

The college was founded in 1981 as the Thomas More Institute. The driving force since its inception has been Dr. James Patrick, who has served as provost and is now chancellor. He has worked to ensure that the Western intellectual tradition is taught through the prism of *Ex corde Ecclesiae*.

All 55 students study the College List of Texts, a Great Books-plus curriculum. It includes the great Church fathers and classical thinkers as well as important modern writers. Graduates are awarded a Bachelor of Arts degree in Liberal Arts. The college was accredited by the appropriate regional agency, the Commission on Colleges of the Southern Association of Colleges and Schools, in 1999.

Even more so than Thomas Aquinas College, a somewhat similar institution, Saint Thomas More appeals to non-traditional students; indeed, only about 25 percent of incoming freshmen enter directly from high school. Most of the students are in their 20s while some are in their 30s or older.

QUICK FACTS

Founded: 1981
Type of institution: Micro liberal arts college
Setting: Urban
Undergraduate enrollment: 55 (2006–07 academic year)
Undergraduate cost: $15,780 (tuition, room and board for 2007–08)
Undergraduate major: One (Liberal Arts)

FIVE KEY POINTS

1. Solidly committed to orthodox Catholicism.

2. Very small environment allows for close faculty-student interaction.

3. A unique curriculum includes the Great Books and other influential works.

4. Emulates a 19th-century Oxford University environment.

5. Appeals to mature students who might have been dissatisfied elsewhere.

In the 2006–07 academic year, six of the eight incoming freshmen transferred from other institutions. One student was a physician thinking of entering the priesthood. Two students enrolled after leaving military service. The college attracts students seeking a broad intellectual challenge that they perhaps did not find at their previous institution.

Several have described the college as steeped in a 19th-century Oxford University model with Fellows (professors), seminars and ongoing conversation inside and outside the classroom. There is considerable attention given to English converts such as John Henry Cardinal Newman, G. K. Chesterton and those in the Oxford movement. A particular mark of the school is an institutional commitment to civility and decency.

Students take four years of theology, philosophy, classical languages and literature. According to Chancellor Patrick, "We do more here with literature than almost anyone else." An alumnus who now teaches at the college said, "In one sense every class is the same class. That is, all courses go back to the fundamental questions of truth and of human nature."

Governance

The college is owned and governed by a non-profit, all-lay board of visitors, composed of eight members who serve seven-year terms. Four board members are also Fellows. Board members are to be Catholics but there is an exception to this rule for one member who is a long-time and special supporter of the college.

Bishop Kevin Vann of the Diocese of Fort Worth supports the college and visits it. He also has endorsed the college's current capital campaign.

Dr. Patrick, 74, has clearly been the visionary and leader of the college. A truly Renaissance man, he is an expert on architecture, history, education and theology (he has a doctorate in theology). One 2003 alumnus said of him: "He is the heart and soul and body of the college."

The college is not worried about succession. As one staff member said, "It is not Dr. Patrick's college. It is The College of Saint Thomas More and it is the Great Books that are the teachers. If you have the books and people who have read them, you'll have a school."

Public Identity

Another alumnus we interviewed said, "You couldn't imagine going to a school that is more dedicated to truth, to not just Catholic spiritual life but also to continuing the Catholic intellectual tradition."

While many of the writers on the College List of Texts are prominent Catholic thinkers, just as many are not. But the college makes it very clear what is its priority. The website notes: "More than the great authors, Jesus is the center of the College, and it is the wish of the Fellows and Visitors that His teaching and life permeate the work of the College."

Outside the classroom, such a position is reflected in the speakers invited to speak on campus. Campus speakers have included Father George Rutler, an influential priest of the Archdiocese of New York; Father Joseph Fessio, S.J., currently of Ave Maria University; philosopher Peter Kreeft; and E. Michael Jones, editor of *Culture Wars*. There has been a one-man C. S. Lewis play as well. There have been no speakers, plays or other public events at variance with Church teachings.

Spiritual Life

Mass is celebrated twice daily at the Christ the Teacher Chapel by a retired priest who serves as chaplain. The weekday Masses, with "spectacular sermons," are *Novus Ordo* and on Sundays are the 1962 Tridentine Mass. Adoration is every week from Thursday noon until Tuesday noon. Confessions are scheduled once a week, but informal opportunities are present before each Mass.

There are a variety of religious activities at the chapel. These include a Children's Holy Hour on Tuesday morning, a Young Serrans First Friday's Holy Hour of Reparation and several cenacles including a Scriptural Rosary.

Three-fourths of the students are Catholic, and conversions are common. One alumnus said that such conversions come not from evangelization "but through the curriculum, the personal example of others and through the openness in which non-Catholics are not made to feel alienated."

There is excitement about the building of a new Chapel of Christ the Teacher, for which fundraising is now taking place. When completed, the chapel will seat 120 people with the opportunity to accommodate another 80. This construction of the chapel and a new library will be the first stage of a new campus for the college.

Students also take advantage of two nearby churches, St. Patrick Cathedral and St. Mary of the Assumption, both of which are ten minutes away. The latter has a Latin Tridentine Rite Mass on Sundays at 5:30 p.m.

Catholicism in the Classroom

Every Fellow at the college is Catholic, and each takes an Oath of Fidelity on his or her knees before the Blessed Sacrament. One former student said, "All of the professors at the college stand out as representative of the faith. All are dedicated to the truth."

So it is not surprising that the theology and philosophy courses offered here are solid and taught faithfully. Dr. Patrick teaches theology, and one of his former students said of his teaching: "It is impossible to describe. He has a precise, broad, comprehensive and ingenious grasp of the Western theological and intellectual tradition." Another said quite simply, "He educated me."

Dean Judith Stewart Shank teaches literature and philosophy. According to one alumnus, "She presents literature as a mode of knowledge, a subset of philosophy. Literature, then, reveals truth through beauty, especially the beauty of language."

We were impressed by the entire complement of 12 Fellows and associates. In addition to Drs. Patrick and Shank, interviewees also mentioned Dr. Donald Carlson, who teaches literature, and visiting Fellow and C.S. Lewis scholar Dr. Thomas Howard, who also teaches literature. In addition to English Catholic writers, there is a focus on southern agrarian authors such as Flannery O'Connor.

There is a limit to what disciplines are studied here, but proponents argue that what is taught is what is needed. These are the classical disciplines. We believe that the college is the only American college requiring Latin or Greek all four years. Dr. Patrick, when asked why French or other more modern subjects are not part of the curriculum, said that those are all good things but they are not the most important things to study.

What is studied is often done in an atmosphere reinforcing the image of Oxford. For example, during the period from October to the end of the Easter Octave, Fellows and students dress in shorter versions of academic gowns for Monday night seminars, meals, chapel events and examinations. "Civilization Day" is held from Monday at 6 p.m. to Tuesday at 6 p.m.; during this time students dress well, have more elaborate meals and practice civility.

Also reinforcing the Oxford ambiance is the importance given to lively debate at the daily 12:15 p.m. "common table" lunch provided at The Refectory. Here Fellows and students continue classroom discussions.

Campus intellectual life also benefits from several periodic talks, including the Cardinal Newman Lecture, Thomas More Lecture on Learning, St. Elizabeth Ann Seton Lecture, C.S. Lewis Lecture and the Louise Cowan Lecture in Literature.

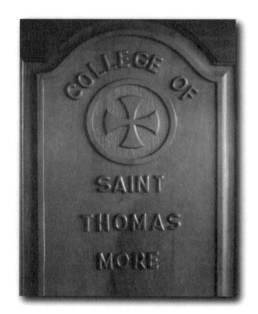

Students are exposed to modern technology. All students have to pass a computer literacy examination by the end of their sophomore year. An ROTC program is offered through neighboring Texas Christian University.

En route to the bachelor's degree, which was first awarded in 2000, students can opt for an associate's degree after two years, but this is not promoted. The college prefers students to finish the whole program and be awarded the B.A. degree. Six bachelor's degrees were conferred in spring 2007.

The college hosts the Cardinal Newman Institute for the Study of Faith & Culture, which offers non-degree, graduate-level theology courses. There also has been an Extended Studies Program (ESP) since 2004, where adult students listen to tapes on their own and periodically visit campus, but this is a program that has not caught on.

The college sponsors study-abroad opportunities. According to one college official, a study session in Rome is intended for January of the freshman year, and a tour of Greece is ideal after the junior year. Neither is mandatory, but they are considered integral to the course of studies.

A study session at Oxford had been encouraged for the summer between the sophomore and junior years. Unfortunately, the program was cancelled in 2006 and 2007. The college expects to offer it once every four years, rather than annually as in the past.

There is a small classical college preparatory school for students aged 12 to 18 on campus. Named after St. Thomas More's daughter, the Lady Margaret Roper School requires Latin and also offers Greek as part of its curriculum. About one-quarter of the graduates eventually enroll at the college.

Student Activities

There are not enough students to have organized clubs. Also, many students have part-time jobs. An attempt to have a student government association that coordinates activities and programs has not resulted in much. Most social events are the result of students getting together casually and talking, playing sports or doing other things.

Residential Life

The campus has two small apartment buildings for residences, which accommodate between 18 to 25 students. Men and women are assigned separate apartments. There is no overnight opposite-sex visitation and violations are reportedly rare.

One interviewee said, "There is a 'nocturnal lifestyle' on campus, with many students staying up very late, and men and women get together for conversation. But you do not have problems with overnight opposite-sex sleepovers. Chastity is encouraged but not drummed into people."

Dr. Patrick spoke to us on this latter point: "The students want to be good. As a college, we have abandoned the notion of making people be good. We instead say, read these books. These books inspire towards the good. If you choose, you can become a romantic fool and die or you can read and be attracted to the good."

Students also are expected to help out around the school with community lunches and other chores.

The Community

The college is located in the university section of southeast Fort Worth next to Texas Christian University and near a few small colleges. Fort Worth, a city of 625,000 people, has an Old West heritage reflected by its historic stockyards.

But it is a city on the move; its population has more than doubled since 1950. The city boasts a number of cultural attractions, including three notable art museums, a zoo and a science center. The sophisticated Baylor All Saints Medical Center is located two miles from campus.

Fort Worth has a crime rate significantly above the national average but relatively low among major U.S. cities. The climate in North Texas is very hot in the summer and moderate in the winter.

The other anchor of the Metroplex area, Dallas, is 30 miles east of Fort Worth and offers additional opportunities. The Dallas/Fort Worth International Airport is between the two cities, and it is a major transportation center. Fort Worth is also reachable via Amtrak and Interstates 20 (east and west) and 35 (north and south).

The Bottom Line

Colleges don't get much smaller than The College of Saint Thomas More. But its size is a benefit as dedicated Fellows and motivated students meet in a community to learn. The college reflects the perspective of one of its principal founders, Dr. Patrick: "The education is the propagation and defense of the intellectual life, rooted in the culture of the West, which is the Catholic Church."

The college appeals to non-traditional students, often attracting those who were dissatisfied with an earlier choice and who are looking for a more rigorous intellectual challenge. Such students do not seem to mind the lack of spacious facilities or extensive extracurricular activities. Those who want to get a foundation in the classics and use it to better understand their faith should find The College of Saint Thomas More an oasis.

Franciscan University of Steubenville

Steubenville, Ohio

www.franciscan.edu

Overview

Located 40 miles west of Pittsburgh on a hill overlooking a small, gritty Ohio city, Franciscan University of Steubenville began with modest goals in 1946. Bishop John King Mussio of the then-new Diocese of Steubenville wanted to develop a Catholic institution that would educate returning war veterans. He turned to the Third Order Regular of St. Francis (T.O.R.) to fulfill his objective.

The university has grown up about one mile from the city that was once an important steamboat port on the Ohio River and now has a population of about 19,000. Perhaps the most prominent local native is the late entertainer Dean Martin. But over the years, the term "Steubenville" has come to represent the university, rather than the city, for many Catholics.

During the Vietnam War era, many Catholic and secular colleges were experiencing challenges. Franciscan University was not exempt as the university lost its moorings. Fortunately, in 1974 there emerged a visionary leader, Father Michael Scanlan, T.O.R., whose 26-year presidency reestablished the vigor and Catholic identity of the university.

Part of that renewal was attributable to its establishment as a prime center for charismatic worship among U.S. Catholic colleges. Although the charismatic focus is less predominant than, say, 20 years ago, it remains an important part of the mix of Catholic religious preferences at the university.

QUICK FACTS

Founded: 1946
Type of institution: Medium-size university
Setting: Small city
Undergraduate enrollment: 1,982 (2006–07 academic year)
Total undergraduate cost: $24,100 (tuition, room and board for 2007–08)
Undergraduate majors: 35 (five in associate programs and 30 in bachelor's programs)

FIVE KEY POINTS

1. Faithful Catholicism permeates every aspect of campus life.
2. Franciscan University has unique ties to the Catholic charismatic movement.
3. The faith-centered household system is strong, supportive and notable.
4. Forty percent of undergraduates major in theology or catechetics.
5. The best example of an enduring Catholic college turnaround.

Today, Franciscan University has an enviable reputation as one of the most outstanding examples of orthodox Catholic higher education in the United States. This commitment has attracted an undergraduate student body that is 98 percent Catholic and comes from 50 states and 16 other countries.

For the first 40 years of its existence, the institution was the College of Steubenville. Its current name was acquired in 1986, reflecting the broadening of its curriculum and its graduate program. The university offers 35 majors in mostly typical liberal arts fields as well three religious-oriented majors in humanities and the Catholic Church, catechetics and theology. A new major in sacred music is planned for the fall of 2007.

Undergraduates are required to complete a flexible core curriculum of 48 credits, of which 15 are in a broad "communications" grouping and another 15 are in humanities. Students choose six credits or two courses of theology. A review of the core curriculum is currently underway.

The university also offers seven different master's degrees, including an M.B.A. and an M.A. in theology and Christian ministry; this latter program offers a study-abroad component in Rome at the Dominican Pontifical University of St. Thomas Aquinas (the Angelicum).

The institution began a $25 million capital campaign in October 2006 entitled "Leading the Renaissance in Catholic Higher Education: The Campaign for Franciscan University." Among the goals for the fundraising program are endowed chairs in bioethics, business ethics and catechetics.

Graduates join a 10,000-member alumni network, which is largely concentrated in Ohio, Washington, D.C., and New York City. One example of the caring nature of this group is that they have formed a Special Needs Net-work to assist alumni who have children with autism and other special needs.

Governance

The ownership of the university and the responsibility for its Catholic identity rests with the Franciscan order, officially known as the Third Order Regular of St. Francis of Penance of the Province of the Most Sacred Heart of Jesus, based in Loretto, Pennsylvania.

A largely lay board of trustees of 25 members reports to the order. Father Christian Oravec, T.O.R., is the minister provincial of the province and chairman of the board, as is the tradition. Seven other members of the board are Franciscans. Among the lay members is the well-respected Notre Dame law professor emeritus Charles Rice.

All five presidents of the university since 1946 have been Franciscan—the president is required to be a friar—with Father Scanlan serving from 1974 to 2000; he is currently chancellor. His successor is the current president, Father Terence Henry, T.O.R. About 20 Franciscan friars are involved in various capacities on the campus.

Public Identity

In explaining its mission, the university includes the following: "The Way, the Truth and the Life are fundamental concepts and guidelines for evaluating University priorities, staffing and budgets and are understood as explicating dynamic orthodoxy." In fact, "dynamic orthodoxy" is identified as one of the pillars of the university.

According to the Vice President of Academic Affairs, Dr. Max Bonilla, Catholic orthodoxy is promoted through the senior management of the university. He said, "The president and board strongly support and encourage faithful following of [Catholic] identity. The board makes sure the senior administration will support the mission. Selection of the board members is done on the same basis. This has maintained a great clarity as far as being faithful to the Church."

The mindset which emphasizes Franciscan, Catholic and Christian mooring does, indeed, permeate the campus. Dr. Bonilla added, "Everything we do is in the context of Catholic identity."

This is worn with a badge of honor. Father Henry, the president, wrote in a 2006 issue of the alumni magazine, *Franciscan Way*: "[P]arents frequently express surprise and heartfelt gratitude for the degree to which a Catholic worldview pervades the entire Franciscan campus—something they noticed was absent at other colleges they had visited."

And according to one theology professor, "Here, more than anyplace else that I've seen, there are a lot of practicing and faithful Catholics, from physical plant staff members to the registrar's office to high administrators in student life and academic affairs and the president himself—they are really good Catholics."

One way they show this pervasiveness to the outside world is through the people to whom they have awarded honorary degrees. Of the more than 80 such degrees granted since the mid-1970s comes a veritable "who's who" of orthodox Catholic leaders in the field of theology, public affairs, journalism, academia and the pro-life movement. It is quite clear that the university seeks to acknowledge those who promote Catholic teachings.

The speakers for the university's May 2007 commencement—which featured the largest graduating class in the university's history—were Archbishop Timothy Dolan of the

Archdiocese of Milwaukee; Dr. Josef Seifert, a noted philosopher and pro-life advocate; and Dr. Edmund Pellegrino, a leading Catholic ethicist and chair of the President's Council on Bioethics.

All guest speakers need to be faithful to the Magisterium and approved by the president. One faculty member told us that in 14 years at the university, there were only two people whose appearance he questioned, one of whom was a scientist who discussed some New Age ideas.

Sometimes debates on issues will occur on campus where, for example, pro-choice and pro-life representatives will participate. One high-ranking university official said to us, "Strong, pro-life students will challenge the pro-abortion speakers. This is a healthy experience for students to understand what the other side thinks."

He added, "Our mission is to prepare students for society, which brings challenges to their faith. So we don't shelter them. Our point is to seek the Truth."

The need for the public appearance of Catholic propriety is taken very seriously. In fact, we were told that when the family of Dean Martin approached university officials about contributing money for an auditorium named after the singer and "Rat Pack" member, the university declined. They did not believe that he was a suitable role model.

One popular campus event is the Festival of Praise charismatic worship program, which was held eight times during the 2006–07 academic year and annually draws 1,500 students, faculty and parents at each. The unique service started in the 1980s.

Finally, the university has presented a monthly program on EWTN for the past 14 years. An illustrative example of the series, which is entitled *Franciscan University Pres-*

ents, is "The Unchanging Heart of the Priesthood," which aired in May 2007.

Spiritual Life

The most prominent building on campus is the Christ the King Chapel, a 39-year-old modern-looking structure noted for a huge steel crucifix atop its roof. The chapel has become somewhat of a trademark of the university, and it is the center of its vibrant campus life.

Twenty Masses are celebrated weekly. Daily Masses are held Monday through Friday at 6:30 a.m., 12:05 p.m. and 4:45 p.m.; they attract about 700 students each day. All three Sunday Masses are filled to the chapel's 300-person seating capacity. There is, according to the chaplain, Father Dominic Scotto, T.O.R., "full, active and conscious participation" by students at the Masses; about 60 percent of students attend daily Mass.

The Masses are reverent. Most are charismatic or contemporary but there also are traditional Latin or chant Masses. The different varieties seem to blend in very well and, as one staff member told us, such diversity seems to reflect the universal nature of the Catholic Church. No other faiths are promoted on campus.

Confessions are held four times each week with seven or eight priests. There are the periodic Praise Festivals and frequent retreats, including silent retreats, for those in music ministry and others in residential households. There also is a Franciscan house off-campus where some young men live in a "mitigated program" of scheduled prayer and quiet as part of the spirituality of the Third Order Regular. There are days of discernment for women who might consider religious life, and friars help out with this.

The university website notes, "Prayer is the heart of our life at Franciscan University, and a place set aside to develop that discipline is an integral part of our campus life." Additional opportunities for prayer exist at a small chapel known as the Portiuncula or the "Port," which is rich in Franciscan heritage; it hosts 24-hour adoration in the spring and fall and a limited program in the summer. There are also a Marian Grotto, outdoors Stations of the Cross and a life-sized Creche. The campus has 14 Eucharistic Tabernacles.

There is a Tomb of the Unborn complete with an eternal flame, which pays tribute to the millions of aborted babies and also reflects the university's strong pro-life commitment. Each week about 175 members of the Students for Life club do sidewalk counseling outside abortion clinics. More than 1,000 students make the five-hour trip to Washington, D.C., for the March for Life each January, where the university's green-and-white banner has become a fixture.

Campus ministry is active and, in addition to the assisting in various ways with Masses, they have community outreach programs such as Project St. Nicholas, which works with needy Steubenville residents. The Works of Mercy group and others assist with food kitchens as well as prison and other ministries. Such outreach "enables us to be part of the world," according to one student. There are international mission trips.

The university also emphasizes its Catholic outreach through a well-known adult summer conference program, which stretches back 40 years. The focus of these three- and five-day conferences is evangelization in the charismatic tradition. Among the many speakers over the years have been Father Benedict Groeschel, C.F.R., Jeff Cavins and Dr. Scott Hahn. Seven adult conferences and a teen conference were held in June and July 2007.

Catholicism in the Classroom

The university reports that 99 percent of the faculty is Catholic. Fidelity is certainly present in the theology department, which was the first theology department to take an Oath of Fidelity in 1989. It has been done with every new faculty member since. Non-Catholics respect the Catholic tradition. Dr. Bonilla said, "The department knows that our work is to support the Church."

The theology department, with a strong reputation among Catholic colleges, has the most majors on campus with 433 students during the 2006–07 academic year.

One senior called the theology department "exceptional beyond words." Among the notable professors are the prolific writer Dr. Scott Hahn and Dr. Regis Martin. Another student said of Dr. Martin, "He shows great acumen in seeing the connection between literature, theology and the beauty of God in everyday things."

The philosophy department also is strong and faithful. According to one philosophy major, "Much of the philosophy done here is in the personalist and phenomenological tradition of Pope John Paul II." There is a great deal of focus on the Franciscan philosophers as well as on Saint Thomas Aquinas, a Dominican.

Among recommended philosophy faculty are Dr. Patrick Lee, a Thomist and bioethicist, and Dr. Jonathan Sanford, a scholar of Aristotle and Greek, ancient and medieval thinkers.

Catholic commitment extends beyond these two key departments. One student provided us with perhaps the greatest compliment to the faculty at large. In addition to academic competence, he said, "You see professors and administrators going to Mass with families, trying to live their faith and be fathers and mothers. You can talk openly about Christ with them and they try to share Christ with you."

And yet another said, "Profs bring faith into the classroom. Faith is alive in them and they want to share it through studies."

They also reflect a commitment to the university. One faculty member said of this: "It can be measured by the fact that, until recently, the faculty and staff had the second or third lowest pay rates for small liberal arts schools in Ohio. Many have either taken a sizeable cut in pay or foregone a better-paying job to come here. Many see working at FUS as a calling, not as a job."

Several faculty members shared their perspectives on promoting "dynamic orthodoxy" in their classes in a 2005 issue of *Franciscan Way*, the university's quarterly publication. Shawn Dougherty of the drama department talked about infusing Catholic ideals into the work of the theatre and other performing arts.

Similarly, assistant professor of biology Dr. Daniel Kuebler talked about the abundance of academic freedom at the Franciscan University precisely because it is integrated with Catholic thought. "In the end," he writes, "any university worth its tuition must answer one fundamental question: Will you pursue the Truth or not?"

These and other committed professors help steer undergraduates through 35 majors and 33 minors, the latter including such less-common pursuits as Human Life Studies and Franciscan Studies. Five of the majors are reserved for associate degree candidates. There also are eight pre-professional programs. Students can pursue an eight-seminar or 32-credit honors program that relies on the Great Books and the Catholic intellectual tradition.

While the most popular major, by far, is theology, the second most popular is catechetics. Together they account for nearly 800 students or about 40 percent of the undergraduates. The other top seven in order of enrollment are business administration, nursing, education, English, philosophy, communication arts and biology.

Franciscan has had a pre-theologate program for 22 years. Sixty-three students were expected to be enrolled in the fall 2007 semester, while 11 former students were moving on to seminaries for the first time.

There also is an impressive study-abroad program. Each year 150 students, mostly sophomores, study for one semester at a former Carthusian monastery in the Alpine town of Gaming, Austria. They share quarters in a 14th-century building with students from more than a dozen other countries involved in similar programs.

Students at Gaming study European history, languages and art amid a Catholic spiritual environment. Also, in May 2007, Franciscan University cosponsored an International Symposium on John Paul II's Theology of the Body at Gaming.

Student Activities

Students can participate in more than two dozen student organizations. The number and range of groups that deal with spiritual and Catholic outreach efforts are impressive. These include the Catholic Womanhood Missions, which encourages young women to study and emulate the Virgin Mary; Latinos for Christ; Ut Unum Sint Society for Christian Unity; Voice in the Desert, emphasizing personal witness for Christ; and the Knights of Columbus.

Students for Life is very active. The Works of Mercy group assists with nursing homes, homeless shelters, prison ministry, mentoring and other programs with local youth. There are at least 20 ministries under the Works of Mercy umbrella. Students also participate in foreign mission trips.

Other groups include The Tolkien Society, a women's a cappella group (The Annunciations), theatre and student government. There are opportunities to work on the weekly student newspaper, The Troubador, and a campus magazine titled Lumen Vincens.

There is an intercollegiate athletic program. Competing as The Barons, Franciscan University participates in men's and women's soccer, cross country and basketball; women's volleyball; men's baseball and women's softball; and tennis. There is a men's rugby club. Although the university does not currently belong to a conference, it was granted provisional status for the NCAA Division III in August 2007. There also are 14 intramural teams, the most popular being flag football.

Residential Life

Franciscan undergraduates largely live on campus. There are 12 residence halls, the largest of which is St. Thomas More, which houses 299 women. With a sole exception, buildings are restricted to one sex. Opposite-sex visitation in student rooms is restricted to Saturdays and Sundays from 1 p.m. to 5 p.m. There is a defined and enforced code of conduct.

A unique aspect of the university is the household system that was launched by Father Scanlan 32 years ago. Three or more students of the same sex can come together as a household to support each other spiritually, academically and in other ways. Each household has an advisor. The university describes the households as "radical, Christ-centered, Spirit-empowered faith communities who seek to do the will of the Father in all things."

In spring 2007 there were 26 women's households, and they had such names as Ark of the Covenant, *Carae Domini* (which extends back to 1975), Daughters of Jerusalem, Handmaids of the Lord and *Veritatis Spiritu*. Among the 23 men's households were The Apprentices of St. Joseph, Fishers of Men, Soldiers Under Command and Watchmen of Zion. There were three households reserved for men in the pre-theologate program.

Students often congregate in the J. C. Williams Center, the student center located near the center of campus, to hear bands and visit the Pub deli. Regarding the dining facility, Antonian Hall, one student told us, "We might not have the largest cafeteria but we have the nicest cafeteria workers! Everyday, they serve you with a smile, get to know you."

A health center staffed by a physician and three nurses treats routine matters. Trinity Health Systems operates two medical centers in Steubenville. There are a number of larger hospitals in nearby Pittsburgh.

As with virtually all campuses, there have been some drinking problems reported, but it has largely been restricted to off-campus incidents. The campus itself is safe, and any crimes committed tend to be petty property-related ones.

The Community

Steubenville is located on the border of Ohio, Pennsylvania and West Virginia. A fairly typical small Rust Belt community, Steubenville has a population of about 19,000 people. The unemployment rate for the past couple of years has been in the seven-to-eight percent range. The city has a higher than average crime index.

The downtown is known for its 25 large art murals. But students are likely to be more attracted to Pittsburgh, about 40 miles away. The second largest city in Pennsylvania, Pittsburgh has a wide variety of sports, cultural and entertainment opportunities.

The Pittsburgh International Airport, about a half-hour away, is a major but manageable airport that serves as a hub for U.S. Airways and a number of other carriers. Steubenville is easy to reach by highway, with Interstates 80, 76 and 70 nearby.

The Bottom Line

Franciscan University began modestly in 1946 with a goal to help provide returning servicemen with an education. Within a generation, it had begun to lose its identity. But, thankfully, a visionary leader appeared in the early 1970s, and Father Michael Scanlan led the university to renewal and prominence over a remarkable 26-year period.

The university stands as a center of charismatic Catholic worship, but it offers other orthodox approaches as it has taken its place as one of the premier Catholic universities in the United States. Its Catholic identity is strong and vibrant as it penetrates everything the institution does. It is a case study of how commitment and leadership can revitalize a university.

For those who want a very strong Catholic environment that will bolster their spirituality while also challenging them intellectually, Franciscan University is certainly worth investigating. There is much here that makes it a "must visit" college for most high school seniors.

Magdalen College

Warner, New Hampshire

www.magdalen.edu

Overview

In the early 1970s a group of Catholics were interested in supporting the call of Vatican Council II for the education of lay Catholic leaders. They approached then-Bishop Ernest Primeau, the ordinary of the Diocese of Manchester, to receive an endorsement to establish a college within his diocese.

The college recounts that the bishop, who had been active in Vatican II deliberations, said to them, "You have my blessing and approval, now let us see how well you laymen will conform to your apostolate."

What they have created over the past 34 years has been very much in conformity to their goal and to the Church's mission. Magdalen College, named for patroness Saint Mary Magdalen, has been a beacon of fidelity to Catholic teaching and a forceful witness to *Ex corde Ecclesiae*.

It also has firmly established a classical liberal arts program that exposes students to an interrelated Program of Studies focusing "on the great questions of life." This curriculum relies on the Socratic method as about a dozen students come together in tutorials. All classes are opened with prayer.

There are no electives and no majors at Magdalen; all graduates receive a Bachelor of Arts degree. The college received full accreditation from the American Academy for Liberal Education in 2004.

Although the college is now firmly established, the early years were challenging and

were a testament to the founders' faith. The first-year class in 1974 met in a motel in Bedford, New Hampshire, a town that hosted the college for the next 17 years.

The campus was then relocated to its present 135-acre site in the small central New Hampshire town of Warner. Bishop Primeau's successor, Bishop Leo O'Neill, blessed the new campus on the Feast of St. Mary Magdalen in 1991.

The college is located about 22 miles from the state capital of Concord and is a 90-minute drive from Boston. But it draws a student body from 23 states and several other countries. Eight of the 11 graduating seniors in the class of 2007 were from Arkansas, Illinois, Minnesota, Missouri, New York, Texas, and Virginia; three were from New England.

To accomplish its objectives of individual attention and fostering a sense of community, the college will continue to be small. Currently, there are 72 students enrolled and the maximum number is pegged at about 85–90. Students conduct themselves with pride: Men wear a coat and necktie and women wear a dress or skirt and blouse to class.

On this issue of size, President Jeffrey Karls told us, "Our charism is our size. Our size is something that at first might put people off, but we intentionally keep it small because we want our students to have a very significant experience of community, of living the faith in community."

Among other data about the student body: more than half were homeschooled; nearly one-third have gone on to graduate study; and about one-quarter of the alumnae are full-time mothers and homemakers.

One of the unique aspects of the college is that students take four years of catechesis focusing on Catholic teaching. Graduates who maintain a "B" average are so well trained in

this area that the college has been empowered to award the Apostolic Catechetical Diploma. We are not aware of any other undergraduate institution that does this.

Such a program supports Magdalen's goal of providing lay leaders. It also encourages vocations; about 10 percent of the college's graduates have become priests or other religious. Although students are not required to be Catholic, all but two of the 2006–07 student body was. All faculty members are Catholic.

To further support its mission, the college announced in May 2007 the acquisition of a property known as Durward's Glen in Caledonia, Wisconsin, about a half-hour from the state capital of Madison. The property, purchased from the Order of Camillus Servants of the Sick, will be used for retreats, other programs and eventually a second campus. Bishop Robert Morlino of the Diocese of Madison has blessed Magdalen's expansion into his diocese.

The New Hampshire campus is located about 40 miles northwest of another small, Great Books-oriented Catholic college, The Thomas More College of Liberal Arts, which is also profiled in this guide.

Governance

Magdalen College is a lay-run, nonprofit institution and is governed by a board of trustees. All 11 members of the board must be Catholic, and all make a Profession of Faith.

The president also must be a Catholic. Karls, the third and current president, is an alumnus of the college and served as executive vice president before assuming the presidency in 1998.

Public Identity

In its founding document known as Articles of Agreement, the college sets forth as its objective "to form the students in the life long pursuit of universal truths; the growth of their baptismal Faith; the adherence to precepts and discipline of the Roman Catholic Church; and the living of the special vocation of a Catholic layman and laywoman in such a way as to benefit society, especially through the family."

President Karls continually weighs in on these issues. In the spring 2006 issue of *The Magdalen Newsletter*, for example, he wrote: "In order to maintain and safeguard our Catholic identity, we must sustain our commitment to be faithful to the teachings of the Catholic Church; we must provide courses for students on Catholic moral and religious principles and their application to critical areas such as human life and other issues of social justice; and we must care pastorally for the students, faculty and staff."

Magdalen lives up to those purposes in all aspects of its public life. There have been no examples of speakers or events that run contrary to Church teachings. Many campus appearances have come about through the H. Lyman Stebbins Colloquium. One of the recent speakers in the series was Dr. Robert Royal, president of the Faith and Reason Institute, who spoke on Dante, his academic specialty.

In April 2007, Chris Graveline, an alumnus and U.S. army prosecutor, spoke about the Abu Ghraib prison controversy and other legal issues. Other alumni have spoken about their careers.

The college launches its school year with an Academic Mass of the Holy Spirit. The September 2006 Mass was celebrated by Bishop John McCormack of the Diocese of Manchester. After the Mass, Bishop McCormack said, "Magdalen College is a great gift to the Diocese of Manchester." He also celebrated the 2007 Mass.

The 2006–07 academic year ended with commencement in May 2007. The celebrant of the Baccalaureate Mass was Bishop Sebastian Thekethecheril of the Diocese of Vijayapuram in southwestern India.

In touring the campus there are several manifestations of its Catholic identity, including the Mary Magdalene Shrine at the entrance and an Immaculate Heart of Mary Shrine.

Spiritual Life

Our Lady, Queen of Apostles Chapel is at the center of the campus and campus life. Mass is offered daily by the two chaplains, both Africans of the Religious Missionary Congregation of the Apostles of Jesus. It is reported that almost all students attend. On Sundays, visitors swell the chapel to capacity.

Masses are reverent and traditional. All students are part of the choir. The choir sings motets, polyphony and traditional hymns for the liturgy. One staff member noted, "Singing is a big part of Magdalen."

Holy days are observed with administration offices closed and classes suspended so, as another college official said, "the entire community can celebrate together." In addition, generally there is a banquet, skit or some other special activity to set the day apart.

There also are special observances to denote liturgical seasons. For instance, there are daily reflections and events associated with the Easter Triduum. In May, there is a May Crowning for the Blessed Mother.

Throughout the academic year, the Rosary is prayed daily in the chapel or residence halls. Adoration is available daily in the afternoons. Benediction takes place on Sundays at 4:30 p.m. There also are annual retreats offered separately for men and women, directed by priests or sisters.

Catholicism in the Classroom

Magdalen's academic program is based on the Program of Studies that was adopted in 1998. It is an integrated curriculum in which students participate in required tutorials that build on each other. All students need to take the four-year program in sequence so that transfer students, regardless of their previous academic standing, start with the freshman regime.

An example of this integrated approach is seen with the study of catechetics. In the freshman year, the tutorials cover the basics of faith. Subsequent tutorials then build on that by focusing on such things as historical and biblical timelines, the Catechism and encyclicals. Seniors take a marriage preparation class.

This intensive, four-year religious training allows students to receive the Apostolic Catechetical Diploma. It ties back to the college's apostolate as well as to its goal of providing a well-rounded education.

"Our mission," President Karls told us, "is to educate the lay people, to provide the foundations of faith so that they will sanctify whatever they do in the future. They will have had the catechesis in faith and learned about living the faith."

He added, "Many of our graduates do go out and teach CCD, either as volunteers at a parish or in full-time, paid teaching positions.

With the Apostolic Catechetical Diploma they receive from Magdalen, they are recognized by those who appreciate the certification as well-prepared catechists."

All tutors request the *mandatum* in front of the bishop and the college. The admissions director said of the faculty: "They all have various degrees and specialties but all in their own way represent the faith in the classroom as well as in their personal life."

Another staff member called President Karls "an exemplary father and a friend." Yet another said of tutor Mark Gillis: "He is an example for all to follow. He practices what he teaches. His family life, academic life and spiritual life all sum up an exemplary Catholic example." Gillis, who is the catechesis coordinator, also has established the Don Bosco Boys Camp in nearby Concord and teaches in the Diocese of Manchester's "Called to Discipleship" program.

All 12 tutors received high marks in our interviews. They teach philosophy, geometry, logic, Latin, English, music and singing, philosophy, astronomy, Newtonian physics, biology, modern science, drawing, comparative writing, comparative cultures, classical literature and other subjects. Seniors need to complete a thesis tutorial now known as a *Quaestio*.

Music, particularly singing, occupies an important place in the curriculum. Every student is in the choir and takes music all four years. The reason, according to one staff member: "We learn so much about the Mass, the feasts and seasons of the liturgical year and the teachings of the Church through learning the musical traditions of the Church."

An unusual aspect of the Program of Studies is that students are evaluated at the end of their sophomore year to determine whether they are making satisfactory academic and community progress. They are required to reapply through a process known as the Junior Re-admittance Procedure. Any student who finishes the first two years is eligible for an Associate of Arts degree.

For those who move on to the junior year, there is the opportunity to study in Italy for four weeks in the summer. After visiting Rome, students move on to the Umbrian town of Norcia, where they live in a one-time convent, interact with Benedictine monks at a nearby monastery and study *The Rule of Saint Benedict* and several other writers from Aristotle to 20th-century writer Luigi Barzini.

Prospective students can sample Magdalen College life through visitor weekends; there were eight such opportunities in the 2006–07 academic year, four in each semester. In 2007 there also were three sessions of a Summer Youth Program for 15- to 18-year-olds in New Hampshire and one two-week program in Wisconsin; and a two-week summer academic program for high school juniors and seniors known as the St. John the Evangelist Summer Program.

Student Activities

As noted previously, a key part of student activities is the mandatory Magdalen College Choir, which has twice-weekly practices in anticipation of Sunday Mass. Select students participate in the Performance Choir, Polyphony Choir or the chant and psalm *schola*. The choir performs at St. Joseph's Cathedral in Manchester, other churches, nursing homes, an orphanage and the local town hall. They have recorded five CDs since 1999.

There is a drama club, which recently performed George Orwell's *1984;* an intramural sports program; and a social club that organizes various indoor, outdoor and cultural activities. There also is an Outing Club. Groups that oppose Catholic teaching are not allowed to form.

The Leisure Activities Program generates informal intellectual and cultural opportunities. The H. Lyman Stebbins Colloquium sponsors visits to concerts and historical sites in Boston and other New England cities.

Students also participate in pro-life activities, attending marches both in Concord, the state capital, and at the annual March for Life in Washington, D.C.

The entire class enjoys the annual one-week pre-Lenten break from classes called St. John the Baptist Winter Rest. Included here are social, cultural, sports and musical events. The festive celebration is concluded by a Winter Ball, which also draws alumni.

Residential Life

There are two residence halls: St. Joseph's for men, which has eight to a large room, and St. Mary's for women, with four to a room. Community life is promoted and, as such, televisions and radios are not allowed. Each hall has a small chapel with a tabernacle.

There is no inter-residence visitation. One alumna and current staff member told us, "Chastity is definitely encouraged, especially by the students. They are willing to become involved in a situation if they feel it necessary. We stress respect for the whole person in all areas, and this fosters healthy relationships beyond college."

All students are also required to participate in the Campus Service Program to provide various chores around campus. This program is considered a natural and integral part of community life.

The Community

Warner is a quaint New England town of 2,800 in the New Hampshire Lake Region that traces its history back to 1735. One popular local event is the Fall Foliage Festival every October. The campus is near Mount Kearsage, almost 3,000 feet high, which provides abundant hiking opportunities. The winters are long and snowy, making skiing a popular local pastime. The area is quiet and relatively crime free.

The nearby city of Concord, with state government offices and a population of 41,000, provides additional services to the Magdalen community. The major metropolitan area is Boston, about 90 miles away, which offers many cultural, sports and entertainment opportunities.

Some out-of-town college students may arrive at Boston's Logan International Airport, which accommodates American Airlines, Delta and other carriers. The Manchester-Boston Regional Airport is another airport option, which is about 45 minutes from Warner. For those traveling by highway, Interstates 89 and 93 intersect at Concord.

The Bottom Line

Magdalen College is part of the wave of small, orthodox colleges that were spawned after Vatican II. Its founders had a vision that they could create an institution that would train new generations of lay leaders for the Church. They have succeeded well.

In the process, they developed a broad-ranging classical curriculum that provides students with the intellectual reservoir to be well-read, productive citizens and parents. But they never forgot the human dimension: An important component of their program has been to integrate students together to foster a sense of community.

Leaving aside the appeal of living in rural New England for four years, Magdalen College offers many attractions for the Catholic high school senior who is looking for both a solid education and an enhanced spiritual formation.

Thomas Aquinas College

Santa Paula, California

www.thomasaquinas.edu

Overview

While there are several solid Catholic colleges that successfully reflect the Catholic intellectual tradition, Thomas Aquinas College is unique. It is the leading Catholic example of a Great Books approach that traces its 20th-century lineage to Columbia University, The University of Chicago and St. John's College of Annapolis.

Located next to the small city of Santa Paula, about an hour northwest of Los Angeles, Thomas Aquinas has a simple yet unified curriculum. The course of study is all prescribed as students participate in seminar discussions of classical works. There are no texts, no lectures, no diversity of majors. All graduates receive a Bachelor of Arts in Liberal Arts.

Among its strengths is its faculty, made up of tutors. All 37 tutors are well-rounded academics that engage students in Socratic dialogue in small classes. Each is expected to be able to teach every course. A 1993 accrediting report quoted students as saying the tutors "'were some of the smartest people' they had ever known."

TAC has been practicing this way of educating Catholics—up to 95 percent of the student body is Catholic—for more than a generation. The campus was originally located at a Claretian order facility near Calabasas, California, in 1971 and moved to its present Ferndale Ranch location seven years later.

QUICK FACTS

Founded: 1971
Type of institution: Small liberal arts college
Setting: Small city
Undergraduate enrollment: 351 (2006–07 academic year)
Total undergraduate cost: $27,000 (tuition, room and board for 2007–08)
Undergraduate majors: One (Liberal Arts)

FIVE KEY POINTS

1. A prime example of a rigorous Great Books curriculum.

2. Solidly wedded to integrating classical Catholic thought with academics.

3. There is collegial student and faculty (tutor) environment.

4. The college has acquired a prestigious national reputation.

5. The chaplains focus on providing spiritual direction.

Despite its small size, the college has acquired a solid reputation, with a national student body coming from 42 states and several other countries. It consistently ranks among the best liberal arts colleges in the country. Forty-five percent of its alumni go on to graduate work.

Both the Western Association of Schools and Colleges, the regional accrediting agency, and the national liberal arts American Academy of Liberal Education have accredited the college. This high quality of education has been maintained without accepting federal government support, including some student loans.

Governance

Thomas Aquinas was founded by lay Catholics and continues to be run by a lay board of governors. The 26-member board includes William Wilson, former U.S. ambassador to the Vatican, and many prominent Catholic business leaders. There are no religious on the board, and the college receives no financial support from the Archdiocese of Los Angeles despite praise from Roger Cardinal Mahoney.

Among governors emeriti is Ralph McInerny, the Thomist philosopher at the University of Notre Dame. William Bentley Ball, a Catholic constitutional attorney, and industrialist J. Peter Grace are listed as some of the deceased governors of the college.

Seven members of the board of governors are tutors at the college, including President Thomas Dillon. Dr. Dillon, who has been at Thomas Aquinas for 35 years, has led the college since 1991.

Public Identity

The founding document of Thomas Aquinas College, "A Proposal for the Fulfillment of Catholic Liberal Education," begins with noting the contemporary "crisis in the Catholic college." Acknowledging that, the document continues: "The first and most pressing duty, therefore, if there is to be Catholic education, calls for reestablishing in our minds the central role the teaching Church should play in the intellectual life of Catholic teachers and students."

Dr. Dillon told us that the college has remained faithful to that promise. "Thomas Aquinas College," he said, "was the first Catholic college to set out for orthodoxy. We've kept to the principles that were part of our beginning and are contained in our founding document."

Tutors explain that classical works such as St. Augustine's *Confessions* reflect the Catholic intellectual tradition. Dr. Dillon said, "There is a dedication to theology as the highest science, and our curriculum focuses on the 'highest things.'" In fact, we were told by the director of admissions that the environment is such that student religious conversions are frequent enough that the number of Catholics usually bumps up from 90 percent at the beginning of the year to 95 percent at the end.

There are no questionable speakers on campus as TAC reflects a strong public witness to the faith. Many of the annual speakers are those who discuss the Thomist tradition. In early 2007, for example, there was an all-college seminar on Aquinas's *Summa contra Gentiles*; a St. Thomas Day Lecture by Father James Schall, S.J., of Georgetown University; and a lecture on Thomas Aquinas by Dr. Paul Gondreau of Providence College.

Among other recent speakers have been two *papabili*, Francis Cardinal Arinze of Nigeria, who delivered the 2004 commencement address, and Christoph Cardinal Schonborn, O.P., the Archbishop of Vienna, Austria. George Weigel, the biographer of Pope John Paul II, spoke at a 35th anniversary event for the college and warmly endorsed it.

The May 2007 commencement speaker was Archbishop Albert Malcolm Ranjith, Secretary for Divine Worship and the Discipline of the Sacraments at the Vatican's Roman Curia. He also was the Baccalaureate Mass homilist.

Spiritual Life

Father Paul Raftery, O.P., one of the chaplains, says that the college's strong Catholic identity is shown by "a full embracing of the Catholic faith, fidelity to the Magisterium, a concern for orthodoxy and reverence in liturgy."

There are three Masses daily offered by three non-teaching chaplains who are of the Dominican, Jesuit and Norbertine orders. These Masses are at 7 a.m., 11:30 a.m. and 5 p.m.; there also are two on Saturdays and three on Sundays. They have been described as "reverent, prayerful and sincere." Tutors participate in the weekly Masses, which take place at the Chapel at St. Joseph Commons. There also is a small Our Lady of Guadalupe Chapel. There is a Mass dress code.

The biggest development on campus today is the construction of the $20 million Chapel of Our Lady of the Most Holy Trinity, which is scheduled to open in the fall of 2008. The noted architect Duncan Stroik has designed the chapel, which will be in Romanesque style and will include a 135-bell tower.

This new structure will further enhance an already vibrant spiritual program. In addition to the 20 or more weekly Masses, the students also participate in an evening Rosary and Eucharistic adoration and frequent op-

portunities for confession. There is a Legion of Mary group.

About 11 percent of TAC alumni have entered religious life. Students have gathered in groups to hold discussions with one of the tutors on the subject of vocations. During Lent in 2007, a group discussed then-Cardinal Ratzinger's *Spirit of the Liturgy*, published in 2000.

Father Raftery gives five reasons for the high number of vocations: chaplains wear religious garb; vocation speakers are invited to the college; vocations are emphasized in homilies and conversations; students are introduced to eminent Catholic theologians in their curriculum; and the tradition of vocations has inspired subsequent seekers.

Catholicism in the Classroom

One tutor tells us, "In the case of the theology courses, the depth and attention given these classical works shows TAC's commitment to theology as queen of the sciences." Although it is the goal at the college for each tutor to be able to teach every great book, those who specifically concentrate on theology are practicing Catholics, are carefully chosen and take an Oath of Fidelity to the Magisterium.

Our interviews indicate great respect for the tutors, nearly a third of whom are alumni of Thomas Aquinas College. Interviewees were reluctant to single out any for special praise. In addition to the tutors' erudition—65 percent have Ph.D. degrees—one staff member speaks of the "personal example of the tutors, who are exemplary role models, humble before the Truth, living their vocations as husbands and fathers, leading wholesome lives that the students actually have an opportunity to see because of our small community and the tutors' involvement in the life of the college."

Further, the tutors have formed a collegial faculty environment. One said, "Since there are no departments, you do not find faculty who think they can only talk to others in their field." The curriculum and the faculty's wide familiarity with it promotes a degree of commonality.

These tutors guide students in the first year through the Bible. In the sophomore year, works by St. Augustine, St. Athanasius, St. Anselm, St. John Damascene and Gaunilo are included in the theology works read and discussed. One staff member says, "Students are often powerfully affected by reading Augustine's *Confessions* and his *City of God*." During the freshman, junior and senior years, Thomas Aquinas is read. In the senior year, four landmark papal encyclicals of St. Pius X, Leo XII, Pius XI and Pius XII are studied.

The Great Books curriculum is structured around six categories each year: seminar, language, mathematics, laboratory, philosophy and theology. All the traditional classical writers are present, including Descartes, Galileo, Newton, Tolstoy, Dostoyevski, Einstein and even the debates of Lincoln and Douglas in 1858.

All students take required classes in each year. There are no electives, no classes that reflect "vocational" training. No transfers are accepted. There are no study-abroad programs because it is deemed to be a distraction from the college's focus. Freshmen, sophomores and juniors participate in biannual evaluations with professors in a process known as the "Don Rags," named after a similar system used by Oxford University dons or professors. Grades mostly come from class participation.

The intellectual environment is rigorous. While sometimes the circumscribed curriculum forces, say, pre-medical students to take

additional coursework before attending medical school, those interested in a broad liberal arts focus can thrive in this Great Books oasis. In fact, about five percent of the students already come with bachelor's degrees. Of those, some are professionals in their 20s who want the undergraduate education they might have missed earlier. There have been some middle-aged students.

As with Mass attendance, weekday meals and formal events, there is a dress code for classes. This means slacks, collared shirts and closed shoes for men and dresses or skirts and tops for women. Modesty is emphasized. The prefects, or student resident assistants, university staff and even the chaplains reinforce the dress code.

According to one tutor, "This underscores the concept that we present ourselves in a more classy and formal way when were are engaged in a higher activity. The students usually come to enjoy this practice, and it fosters a healthy way of living they appreciate."

And yet, students at TAC are diverse as well as motivated. One administrator said, "The criteria important for admission are an ability to do the work and a desire for this education. Many of our students are self-selecting. You have to want to learn."

She added, "In the freshman year, many students are learning how to learn. If you went through high school memorizing information for a test and did little else, you will find the Socratic method and reading primary texts very different."

To help give prospective students a preview of academic life at TAC, the college runs an annual two-week summer program for rising high school seniors. They are exposed to tutors in small seminars where they study Sophocles, Plato, Kierkegaard, Shakespeare, Euclid, Pascal and Boethius. They also participate in the college's spiritual life. About 35 to 45 percent of the attendees subsequently enroll as undergraduates.

The environment, although stimulating, is not intimidating. "At TAC," one tutor said, "people can talk to each other. Students can talk with each other at lunch about what they are talking about in class. The majority of the tutors—and chaplains—eat lunch with students. It is a congenial setting. It is intellectual but not *only* intellectual. It is relaxed and personal, too."

President Dillon said that to ensure this type of intellectual and personal environment, the enrollment will remain at about 350 students. He told us, "You can mass produce graduates—and a lot of colleges do—but we are interested in a community of friends. We are looking for friendships for life from TAC."

Student Activities

Despite its small size, Thomas Aquinas has a number of student activities. They include the student journal *Demiurgus* and the more academic *The Aquinas Review*. There are study groups for four languages; a theater group known as St. Genesius Players, which presents a couple of productions per year; the Bushwhackers hiking club; and intramural sports. There are dances and a variety of informal activities.

The Masses are enhanced by student participation in a choir—which also presents concerts—as well as by the Gregorian chant ensemble, *Schola*. There is an active pro-life group, TACers for Life. The director of admissions, Jonathan Daly, offered us a moving story of how this group began.

"It started in 1997 with a student from Washington state named Angela Baird," he said. "She had prayed and counseled outside of abortion clinics since the age of 14. When she was a sophomore at TAC, she and a small group of her classmates went hiking, a popular pastime for TAC students.

"In a tragic accident, she slipped and fell off a cliff when she turned around to speak with one of her friends walking behind her. She landed 60 feet below onto a rock. Two students [including Daly] found her while others went for emergency help.

"As she was waiting for the helicopter rescue, they prayed together. Her final request was for prayers for aborted babies. She died later that night. Ever since her death, TAC students have made regular trips to abortion clinics. On the seventh anniversary of Angela's death, students arrived at a particular abortion clinic and were surprised to find moving vans dismantling the clinic. It was closing permanently."

Residential Life

All TAC students are housed in six residence halls, three for men and three for women. They are named for Blessed Junipero Serra, the 18th-century Franciscan missionary, and five saints. Each room accommodates two students. There is no visitation at any time at opposite-sex residences. Men and women can get together at the St. Joseph Commons building, which houses the cafeteria.

Two of the men's halls have chaplains in residence. Student prefects monitor the dorms. There is a curfew on weeknights and a later one on weekends. Chastity is encouraged. Although one interviewee reported that some drinking takes place off campus, there does not appear to be a drinking or drug problem at TAC.

Regarding health care, the Santa Paula Memorial Hospital, a small facility, closed in 2003. But there are three medical centers within a 15-to-20-minute drive in the cities of Camarillo, Oxnard and Ventura.

The Community

The college is located six miles from Santa Paula, which has about 29,000 people, five times its 1970 population. About 71 percent of the city is of Hispanic origin, and that heritage reflects some of the town's stores and activities.

A one-time movie center, the region now relies on agriculture, and Santa Paula is known as the "Citrus Capital of the World." One of the features of Santa Paula is a series of eight outdoor murals that chronicle the city's history.

The Pacific Ocean is a half-hour away, and students go to the beach. The two million-acre Los Padres National Forest abuts the campus and offers outdoor opportunities. There are many cultural and entertainment opportunities in Los Angeles as well.

The weather is the pleasant type that can be expected in southern California. The local crime is below the national average and most recently was only about 60 percent of the national crime index.

Out-of-state students who attend at Thomas Aquinas are likely to arrive at Los Angeles International Airport (LAX), the busiest U.S. passenger airport west of Chicago and one of the key world airports. United, American and Southwest airlines make up about half of the passenger traffic but many carriers are represented. There is a Santa Paula bus station.

The Bottom Line

In some ways, Thomas Aquinas College stands by itself among Catholic colleges. It is the only Catholic college that has exclusively focused on the Great Books (although the new Wyoming Catholic College is following this model). There is an impressive intellectual rigor at TAC that is matched by a commitment to orthodox Catholicism.

This combination has attracted a wide following around the country, and TAC's reputation has become international. More than 90 percent of the student body is Catholic, and alumni tend to join the faculty as tutors in significant numbers. There is a certain sense of ongoing immersion in a special adventure at TAC that can last a lifetime—and beyond.

The intensity here, although conducted in a collegial way, is likely to appeal to a certain type of student. Fortunately, the TAC summer high school program exposes students to the college. A prospective student may want to pursue this very practical test drive.

The Thomas More College
of Liberal Arts

Merrimack, New Hampshire

www.thomasmorecollege.edu

Overview

The Thomas More College of Liberal Arts is one of several small, faithful Catholic colleges founded over the last generation. Each was launched to provide alternative options to existing Catholic colleges, both in terms of religious identity and academic rigor.

Despite similarities, each is distinctive. Indeed, Thomas More College co-founder Dr. Peter Sampo launched his college in 1978 because he was looking for something that he had not found elsewhere. In addition to his association with other colleges, he was president of Magdalen College from 1974 to 1978.

What was created was a college dedicated to studying the whole texts of great thinkers as a vehicle for helping transform students. Dr. Sampo referred back to the ancient Greek idea of a *paideia*, a holistic approach to education that molds young men and women to become active and informed citizens.

The college pursues its *paideia* through a unique set of courses, an emphasis on classroom interaction and balance between the academic and non-academic. It also promotes its Catholic identity with guidance from *Ex corde Ecclesiae*.

According to its catalogue, "Catholicism is manifested in the College not merely as one among many religions with unique observances and beliefs, but as an approach to reality that is implicit in all aspects of the institution's life."

QUICK FACTS

Founded: 1978
Type of institution: Micro liberal arts college
Setting: Rural
Undergraduate enrollment: 92 (2006–07 academic year)
Undergraduate cost: $20,500 (tuition, room and board for 2007–08)
Undergraduate majors: Four

FIVE KEY POINTS

1. Curriculum places clear emphasis on Catholic intellectual tradition.

2. Emphasizes a *paideia* approach to transforming students.

3. Has a unique humanities cycle taken by all students at the same time.

4. All sophomores participate in annual spring Rome semester.

5. Spiritual life is faithful but limited; there is no full-time chaplain.

President Jeffrey Nelson, who came to the college in 2006, said, "The Faith permeates everything [here]." He noted the emphasis placed on Christian humanism in the curriculum, particularly as advanced by Saint Thomas More and John Henry Cardinal Newman.

This is done through the integrated curriculum known as the Cowan Program of Liberal Arts, which was devised by Donald and Louise Cowan, both of whom had long associations with the University of Dallas.

The most unusual part of the core curriculum is the humanities cycle, in which all students take the same course at the same time. Literally, freshmen through seniors are reading, writing and thinking about the same classical works.

The eight-unit cycle spans the period from the ancient world to the 20th century. In the fall of 2007, the unit will be on the Renaissance and Reformation and then move to early modern philosophers and writers in the spring.

By the end of their senior year, each student will have taken 48 credits in humanities, spread out over the eight semesters; that accounts for 40 percent of the total credits needed to graduate. And all will have been done so in tandem with every student in the college.

According to college officials, this non-linear approach to studying Western civilization forces students to think in more creative terms while eschewing typical cause-and-effect explanations. It also challenges younger students to mix it up academically with older ones, thereby building self-confidence.

Other requirements in the core include 12 credits for writing, 12 in classical languages (Latin or Greek), 12 in science and mathematics and three in fine arts. There also is a two-course, six-credit requirement in theology,

"Christology and Ecclesiology" and "Sacraments." All sophomores spend their spring semester in Rome.

But despite its Catholic identity, Thomas More does not offer a theology major. It has four majors: biology, literature, philosophy and political science. Students take 24 credits of work in their discipline during the junior and senior years. All students complete a junior project and a senior thesis.

The college prides itself on attracting an inquisitive, yet eclectic group of students. Students hail from all sections of the country, including from the west coast, and have a number of non-traditional, older students.

The 2006–07 enrollment was 92, all undergraduates. Although that number is consistent with recent years, President Nelson has new plans for growth to about 250-300 students, "which would allow it the same spiritual and intellectual formation but round it out more." He also believes that there should be more emphasis placed on history.

According to the college, more than 60 percent of alumni pursue graduate study. A recent survey indicated that they have gone on to 26 different law schools, 68 graduate schools and one medical school.

The college is fully accredited by both the regional agency, the New England Association of Schools and Colleges and the American Academy for Liberal Education.

For the past 26 years, the college has been located in the town of Merrimack, which has about 27,000 residents. It is located in southern New Hampshire near the border with Massachusetts; Boston is one hour away.

Governance

The college is governed by a 14-member largely lay board, which includes retired Notre Dame law professor Charles Rice. The only religious member of the board is Edward Cardinal Egan of the Archdiocese of New York.

Dr. Sampo served as the president of TMC from its founding until 2006 when he became chancellor and a political science professor there. One graduate referred to him as "the patriarch and grandfather on campus." His successor, Mr. Nelson, had previously been a senior official with the Intercollegiate Studies Institute in Wilmington, Delaware.

Another important part of the college administration has been Dr. Mary Mumbach, a co-founder of the college who serves as dean.

Public Identity

According to a 2004 alumna, "Thomas More College affirms the union of faith and reason. It also upholds the understanding of the Church as Mother—generous, welcoming, unwavering in its adherence to the truth but loving in the way it offers the truth."

All faculty members are Catholic and most of its students are, but the college emphasizes that non-Catholics are welcome. Accordingly, the website notes that the institution "is dedicated to providing a Catholic education to students of all faiths."

The public identity is manifested in its choice of campus speakers. The commencement speakers from 2004 to 2006 were former U.S. ambassador to the Vatican Raymond Flynn, Heritage Foundation president Edwin Feulner, Jr., and journalist Robert Novak. All are faithful Catholics.

The 2007 commencement speaker was novelist Ron Hansen, who has written and spoken as a Catholic apologist and is reportedly a daily communicant.

At the 2007 commencement, honorary degrees were awarded to Hansen; Dr. John Lukacs, a distinguished historian; and Rt. Rev. Robert Taft, S.J., a scholar of Oriental liturgies.

Lecturers have included Dr. Alice von Hildebrand, who spoke on "Purity: This Forgotten Virtue"; Dr. Peter Kreeft, whose topic was "What Thomas Aquinas Really Meant"; and Father George Rutler, speaking on "St. John Vianney and the Enlightenment."

According to one of our alumni interviewees, "Usually our speakers were rather heady but very interesting. They were great choices. Most were not expecting to be grilled so intensely by a well-informed student body."

The college also now runs the Vatican Forum, a speaker series for journalists in Rome, as an adjunct to its Rome semester. Andrea Kirk Assaf had earlier launched the forum; she joined the TMC staff in fall 2007. She is the daughter of the late Catholic conservative Russell Kirk.

As another example of a growing interest in expanding its Catholic public presence, the college announced in March 2007 that it had become co-publisher of *Second Spring: An International Journal of Faith and Culture*.

Second Spring, consistent with Thomas More College's mission, is a Christian Humanist publication. This tool for evangelization has included among its writers Joseph Cardinal Ratzinger (now Benedict XVI) when he was the Vatican's Prefect of the Congregation for the Doctrine of the Faith.

Finally, in July 2007 the college announced it was setting up two funds that should help remove one impediment to vocations. The

Saint John Vianney Fund for Future Priests and The Saint Mother Katherine Drexel Fund for Future Nuns will absorb student loans accumulated by its graduates who are going into a seminary or convent.

President Nelson believes the institution has a "duty, as a Catholic college, to make sacrifices of our own and guarantee that no vocation is ever lost because of fear of student debt."

Spiritual Life

The spiritual life is faithful but basic. The college does not currently have a full-time chaplain. Three local priests visit the campus to celebrate daily Mass ("reverent and peaceful," according to one alumnus) in a small chapel that is located in a multipurpose 17th-century building.

There are regular confessions available before Mass and by appointment. There also is Divine Mercy devotion, nightly recitation of the Rosary and exposition of the Blessed Sacrament. There is a voluntary annual retreat.

President Nelson said that although there is no formal campus ministry, "we *are* a Catholic ministry." And yet, students have told us that the existing program needs strengthen-

ing. "Outreach to others was lacking," according to a recent graduate, "and I think somewhat detrimental to overall student life and for later ministry because our focus on prayer and studies was not given opportunity to flourish."

Another graduate added, "Because of the strong intellectual bent on campus, it can be easy for students to think more than pray." She cited the need for regular retreats and the importance of having a full-time chaplain. Finding a full-time chaplain, we are told, is a priority for President Nelson.

Students also have access to two local parishes in Merrimack. The cathedral of the Diocese of Manchester, St. Joseph Cathedral, is located 10 minutes away.

Catholicism in the Classroom

Students are required to take two courses in theology, one on campus and one in a Rome semester. The on-campus theology class supports Catholic doctrine and is taught by a theology professor who has received the *mandatum.*

The Catholic intellectual tradition is woven into other parts of the curriculum. There is the study of patristics such as Saint Thomas More as well as scholastics such as Saints Thomas Aquinas and Bonaventure.

Also, the writing workshops that students are required to take have included books by Josef Pieper and Pope Benedict XVI, but one graduate said that the addition of more contemporary Catholic and Christian writers such as Chesterton, C. S. Lewis and Dietrich von Hildebrand would be welcome.

The Rome semester generally gets high marks. It is not considered to be a semester of tourism, but rather an opportunity, as one said, "to tap into this culture that is our heritage." It also presents an opportunity to bathe in some of the great landmarks of Catholicism, for which many students are grateful.

All Merrimack campus faculty members are reported to be excellent. One 1996 alumna said, "Everyone has invested themselves in their teaching, not just their reputation, ideas or careers."

One who especially comes up for high praise is Dean Mumbach. A 2000 alumna said, "Dr. Mumbach was a role model of faith, intellect and virtue for me as a young student. She inspired thought-provoking dialogue in our literature courses and has devoted her life to God by way of a vocation that only on the surface is expressed in teaching."

Yet another woman, a 2004 graduate, said, "Dr. Mumbach is rather partial to teaching about the authentic feminine and she embodies it beautifully: gracious, interested, ever-patient and there with a motherly shoulder to cry on."

The faculty received a boost by the hiring of two veteran professors from Christendom College for the 2007–08 academic year. Dr. Christopher Blum was chairman of the history department and Dr. William Fahey was founding chairman of the classical and early Christian studies department. Together, they had 20 years of teaching experience at Christendom.

Despite the intellectual rigor, TMC students study in a relaxed and friendly environment. There are not typical Thomas More students. Students clearly emphasize a degree of individuality as a complement to their inquiring minds. The college, according to one graduate, "doesn't mold people in a certain way, and that is a distinction between TMC and other small schools—it authentically teaches a tradition, not a mold."

Prospective students are able to experience Thomas More College life as part of the Collegiate Summer Program for High School Students. There are two two-week sessions that cover literature, philosophy and American political heritage.

Student Activities

Campus organizations are minimal. There is a St. Cecilia's choir and a *schola cantorum*. There is a Theatre Guild, which performed *Much Ado About Nothing* in fall 2006, and a student newspaper. Students have access to the Merrimack YMCA, which is next to the college. There are no groups that are in opposition to Church teaching.

The academic orientation of the campus works to discourage the formation of student groups. One interviewee said, "For TMC your job is to hit the books, and so people who have interests have to suspend them for four years; they don't have the time. People are pro-life but don't have time for picketing, pro-life activities or lobbying."

A winter highlight is the annual celebration of Thomas More's birthday, February 6, with a medieval banquet. There is a Friday night speaker and film series, which is now an institution. So, too, is the annual November Mudbowl football game between the "Saints" and "Sinners." And students enjoy the Christmas dinner dance.

There is, of course, time for informal relaxation. The Student Social Council meets every week to help direct social functions. Social events include excursions to outdoor locales and to cities such as nearby Nashua and Manchester as well as Boston.

All students perform service on campus, including working in the dining hall, participating in snow removal and assisting with security. This is all part of an effort to create a community spirit.

Residential Life

This is primarily a residential campus. There are two residence halls, Kopka Hall for men and Stillman House for women. Students are not allowed into the residences for the opposite sex. Chastity is encouraged by teaching of the Theology of the Body, talks about chastity and peer monitoring. There is a curfew and students may not go off campus without permission.

Drinking is not allowed on campus, but problems do occur periodically, more so in the men's residence hall. A bigger issue, however, is off-campus drinking. Despite the discouragement from faculty, there is a longstanding tradition of drinking in the nearby woods.

The Community

Merrimack is a small New England town, with easy access to the state's two largest cities. Manchester, with a population of 110,000, is nine miles northeast of Merrimack, and Nashua, with a population of 87,000, is eight miles south of Merrimack. New England's largest city, Boston, is about 50 miles away.

Students have access to three regional hospitals, each about 10 minutes away: Elliot Hospital in Manchester and Southern Medical Center and St. Joseph Hospital in Nashua.

Also nearby is the Manchester-Boston Regional Airport, an efficient and rapidly growing airport. And, of course, Boston Logan International Airport is an option for air travelers.

The winters, although harsh, provide opportunities for skiing. There also are many hiking options in the mountainous state.

Crime in Merrimack is about as low as it gets in the United States. The crime index rate was a mere 15 percent of the national crime figure in 2005.

The Bottom Line

The Thomas More College of Liberal Arts provides a rigorous, classical education. Alumni have told us that the college offered a liberating experience that was refreshing and sometimes surprising.

There are some unique aspects of the college, including its humanities cycle that fosters a community learning experience. In its nearly 30 years of existence, the college has lived up to its founders' desire to create a traditional *paideia*.

Thomas More College has long emphasized its intellectual offerings and has recently strengthened its already notable Catholic identity. For students seeking to broaden their minds, this is an attractive institution. It can provide the transforming experience it was designed to be.

University of Dallas

Irving, Texas

www.udallas.edu

Overview

The sprawling city of Irving, Texas is a 200,000-person suburb of Dallas. In it are the headquarters of such giants as ExxonMobil and the Boy Scouts of America as well as the Dallas/Fort Worth International Airport. It also is the home of one of the finest Catholic colleges, the University of Dallas.

Founded in 1956, this liberal arts-oriented institution consistently ranks among the most praised colleges in the United States. In addition to its orthodox Catholicism, the University of Dallas is widely respected for intellectual rigor and quality of teaching.

The driving force behind the establishment of the university was the Sisters of Saint Mary of Namur. They approached then-Bishop Thomas Gorman to expand their junior college, Our Lady of Victory, and give control to a board of trustees under the jurisdiction of the Diocese of Dallas. Among the initial faculty in 1956 were members of the Cistercian, Sisters of Saint Mary and Franciscan orders.

The university draws students from throughout the United States and from 18 other countries with its commitment to a core curriculum, largely based on the classics of Western Civilization. Academic preparation is such that more than 80 percent of the students attend graduate or professional schools. The university has the distinction of gaining a Phi Beta Kappa chapter faster than any other institution in the 20th century.

QUICK FACTS

Founded: 1956
Type of institution: Small university
Setting: Suburban
Undergraduate enrollment: 1,232 (2006–07 academic year)
Total undergraduate cost: $30,836 (tuition, room and board for 2007–08)
Undergraduate majors: 27

FIVE KEY POINTS

1. Strong commitment to a core curriculum, even in graduate study.
2. An orthodox Catholic identity is emphasized.
3. Teachers and students have created a vibrant intellectual environment.
4. A Rome semester is highly popular and impressive.
5. There is a vital spiritual life on and near the campus.

There are 27 majors that are rooted in the typical liberal arts disciplines. Included are classics degrees in either Greek or Latin and a studio arts program. The Braniff Graduate School of Liberal Arts was added in 1966 and offers master's degrees in eight areas and an interdisciplinary Ph.D., which has the unique character of also relying on a core curriculum. The management school offers several M.B.A.s as well as additional master's degrees in management.

To receive an undergraduate degree at UD, students must take half of their courses in the core curriculum. There are 15 required courses distributed as follows: four each in English and history, three in philosophy, two in theology and one each in economics and politics. Students also select an additional 10 courses from several liberal arts fields.

One former faculty member said of the core curriculum: "Its brilliance lies in studying the ancients, medievals and moderns several times during the college years. While there is an historical and sequential study of these eras, students also go back at different points during their years [at UD] to read, for example, Aristotle and Plato again."

Governance

The university is governed by a 30-plus member board of trustees, comprised largely of lay business leaders from the Dallas area, other parts of the nation and alumni. There are a few Catholic religious figures on the board, most notably the Bishops of the Dioceses of Dallas and Fort Worth, but there no longer is any diocesan control.

Dr. Frank Lazarus became the seventh president of the University of Dallas in 2004. All of his predecessors, with one exception, were lay presidents. Dr. Lazarus, a scholar of classical languages, previously held administrative positions at the University of San Diego, Marquette University and the University of Dayton.

Public Identity

As part of its mission statement, the University of Dallas declares: "The University is dedicated to the recovery of the Christian intellectual tradition, and to the renewal of Catholic theology in fidelity to the Church and in constructive dialogue with the modern world."

The emphasis of the university is rooted in a core curriculum because the administration believes that its western tradition is the Catholic tradition. One English professor told us, "The core teaches us that the goal of education is to seek the Truth and that Truth exists."

As a result, one 2006 alumnus said the university is "one of the only universities left that is both Catholic *and* catholic. That is to say, it is orthodox and faithful and is very willing to pursue Truth from whichever avenues it might come."

President Frank Lazarus gives much credit for this Catholic faithfulness to the professors. In his inauguration address in 2004, he said: "The faculty and administration, but especially the faculty, of this institution have from the time of the founding positioned the University of Dallas in the mainstream of the Catholic Intellectual Tradition by virtue of their scholarship, their development and cultivation of the core curriculum, and by the example of their own lives in the form of personal witness to the Faith and fidelity to the teachings of the Church."

Those we interviewed gave high marks to President Lazarus for reemphasizing the university's Catholic identity while proceeding in a balanced way. He places a high priority on *Ex corde Ecclesiae* and stresses the university's Catholic commitment to high school students and their parents in prospective student weekends.

Unfortunately, the administration of Dr. Lazarus's predecessor, Msgr. Milam Joseph (1996–2003), was marked by some controversy. It was reported to us that during his tenure, the university's Catholic identity was somewhat diluted and there were a few faculty departures. However, the university, by all accounts, seems to be back on its solid, historical footing.

This Catholic ethos has a transformational effect on students, according to close observers of the college. For example, Father Philip Powell, O.P., the campus minister, said, "Many freshmen come in looking like conservative Catholics. Over the course of their time at UD, they often become orthodox Catholics."

He adds, "And what is 'orthodoxy'? It's thinking, teaching and preaching with the mind of the Church. Look first to the Church, the presumption being that the Church has the answer, and in 99.99 percent of the time, Her answer is right."

In addition to the curriculum, the university bolsters its Catholic identity by its choice of campus speakers. Among recent commencement speakers have been Archbishop J. Michael Miller, then the Secretary of the Congregation for Catholic Education at the Vatican, in 2006; and former U.S. ambassador to the Vatican Jim Nicholson in 2003.

Other speakers have included Russell Hittinger, the Warren Chair of Catholic Studies at the University of Tulsa, who delivered the first John Paul II Theology Lecture in February 2007; John Millbank, a British academic associated with Radical Orthodoxy, who presented the 2006 Aquinas Lecture; and marriage and family expert Patrick Fagan of The Heritage Foundation.

Some of UD's speakers do not necessarily deal with Catholic issues but rather address a range of intellectual concerns. Robert and John Hollander of the digital Princeton Dante Project and Nobel Prize winner Dr. Norman Borlaug, the Green Revolution pioneer, are examples. We are aware of no objectionable speakers on campus.

The university also reaches out to the broader Catholic community. One example is through the renamed University of Dallas School of Ministry, which held a two-day conference on the U.S. Catholic Bishops' document "Co-Workers in the Vineyard of the Lord," dealing with lay ministry, in March 2007. The interdisciplinary Society of Catholic Social Scientists held their 2006 meeting on campus.

The university has benefited as well from its long relationship with a number of religious orders, including the Cistercians, Franciscans, Dominicans, Sisters of Saint Mary of Namur and School Sisters of Notre Dame.

Spiritual Life

The spiritual life at UD is, in the words of a 2006 alumnus, "extremely robust and alive." One characteristic of it that repeatedly emerged in our interviews is that faculty and their families actively participate in Masses and other religious activities. As a result, one English professor said, "The students can see their professor as a whole person."

About 75 percent of the student body is Catholic, and that helps ensure an active participation in spiritual activities. Two Masses are offered Monday through Friday (12:05 p.m. and 5 p.m.) at the campus Church of the Incarnation; combined they attract about 200 students daily. There are four Sunday obligation Masses, including one on Saturday night.

Confessions are heard five times a week and by appointment.

Father Powell, the campus minister and also known as the assistant chaplain, is highly regarded. His homilies are accessible online through his blog. Father Powell led a group of 19 students to Peru to work in an orphanage as an alternative spring-break mission in March 2007. He said of this and similar trips, "They are open to anyone who wants to apply, Catholic or not. At the same time, it is clear that it is a Catholic trip, with no cutting back on our daily Masses, morning and evening prayers, etc."

The campus ministry has a few programs such as a monthly Theology on Tap social get-together and pro-life work as part of the Crusaders for Life club. But social justice activities are particularly strong. Among these is participation in the Dallas Hearts & Hammer program that refurbishes inner-city houses and serves meals at homeless shelters.

Students have the opportunity to participate in the spiritual life of the on-campus Priory of St. Albert the Great, which includes 15 Dominican friars, and the nearby Our Lady of Dallas Abbey, which has 28 Cister-cian monks. There is also an Opus Dei center, the Wingren Study Center, in the area; one of their service projects is organizing an annual spring-break trip to a school for the poor in Monterrey, Mexico.

Catholicism in the Classroom

As befits a college that, as President Lazarus notes, emphasizes the Catholic intellectual tradition, it is not surprising that the theology and philosophy departments would be strong. Because of the core curriculum, students also encounter this religious heritage "at different times and in different ways in their studies," according to one faculty member.

The theology department is anchored by chair Dr. Mark Lowery, a moral theologian, described by a recent alumnus as "very orthodox and well-loved," by a campus official as "exemplary," and by a former faculty colleague as "a saint." Among the others in the department frequently singled out for praise is Dr. Christopher Malloy, who teaches systematic theology. He told us, "We present orthodoxy clearly and in dialogue with philosophy and science. If a student wants to get Truth, it is very clear here."

Across the board, our interviewees report that the core curriculum integrates the Catholic worldview with the secular worlds of the various disciplines. This sense of interrelatedness is so pervasive that even a Buddhist who teaches in the English department sees the core as strengthened by the Catholic intellectual tradition. One alumnus spoke of him: "He loves the Catholic confidence that there is a Truth we can strive for."

There are many strong Catholic faculty members in the especially rich English department, including Dr. Gregory Roper, a medieval literature scholar, and Dr. Gerard Wegemer, an expert on Thomas More.

Another example of a spiritually engaged and popular professor is the chair of the history department, Dr. Thomas Jodziewicz, the recipient of the campus 2007 King Fellow Award. He started a faculty-student group around the theme of faith and reason. The reading for the first meeting in fall 2006 was Pope Benedict's encyclical *Deus Caritas Est*.

Despite its liberal arts focus, the sciences and mathematics are not shortchanged at the university. Students in these areas get intensive training, undertake research work and go on to graduate study. Among the notable faculty is Dr. Marcy Brown-Marsden, the biology department chair and a bird expert.

In addition to the core curriculum and the solid faculty, UD students greatly benefit from an excellent study-abroad program. In fact, 80 to 85 percent of the students, mostly sophomores, participate in the Rome Program. This rigorous 15-credit semester has hosted thousands over the past 35 years. The current site, known as Due Santi, is a villa with a vineyard outside of Rome, complete with a 108-student residence hall and athletic facilities. The pope's summer residence, Castel Gandolfo, is visible from the campus.

In Rome, too, the core curriculum is emphasized, as immersion in the culture and intellectual tradition merge. "It is not at all uncommon to see students reading Sophocles in the Rome metro on the way to an art and architecture class," one alumnus told us. And as one English professor emphasized, the spiritual dimension is ever present.

He said, "The semester in Rome is a significant opportunity for spiritual growth. We are able to integrate our lives of study, living together and practicing the faith. We have daily Mass, night prayer. The students particularly love that the faculty are there with their families."

"On the whole," we were told by a recent participant, "people grow up during their Rome semester. The challenge of balancing time, the proximity to the heart of Western Civilization and Catholicism and the closeness to some fantastic peers all rub off on people."

The university also sponsors a study-abroad program for high school students in Italy and England. There are similar opportunities for adults and teachers. This emphasis on foreign study has permitted the University of Dallas to be identified as one of the top 20 study-abroad programs according to the Institute for International Education.

Students also benefit from some domestic institutes. One is the Center for Thomas More Studies, which sponsors courses, conferences and publications related to the 16th-century English saint. The department of education sponsors the Dallas Area Network for Teaching and Education (DANTE), which helps prepare and nurture Catholic schoolteachers in Texas.

And since 1986 the Institute for Religious and Pastoral Studies has provided a variety of courses. Recently, the IRPS launched a Master of Theological Studies degree for the Diocese of Tyler, Texas; a Spanish-speaking Deacon program for the Diocese of Dallas; and online courses for nationwide access.

In May 2007, the institute was renamed the University of Dallas School of Ministry. During that month, the school also graduated an unprecedented number of 100 graduates from its Catholic Bible School. The graduates of this four-year program came from 37 Texas parishes. Bishop Vann of Fort Worth celebrated the graduation Mass.

One final note regarding the academic environment at the University of Dallas relates to the student body. About one-quarter of them are legacy students, meaning that parents or other relatives are alumni. According to one 2006 alumnus, "Students hear firsthand from their siblings, parents and relatives how great UD is, and they want to experience it themselves. It is not at all uncommon for siblings to attend UD at the same time. There is a family atmosphere."

Yet, that does not imply a sense of smugness. Perhaps Dr. Roper crystallized this best when he said, "UD tends to have very well-rounded students but not 'grinds.' The ones coming here have been those who in high school were able to excel academically while also balancing their social lives and outside interests. We also have a number of home-schooled students and a few 'funky types' who want the life of the mind."

Student Activities

There are about 50 groups on campus. In addition to typical collegiate groups, there is a popular Chesterton Society and a Best Buddies program that works with children with special needs. Crusaders for Life, the pro-life group, is very active. Every year the junior class sponsors Charity Week, a major fundraiser for charitable organizations.

The student government is reported to be strong and attracts active Catholics to its service. In addition to an executive council, there is a Student Government Senate and an events programming board known as SPUD. One popular annual social event is Groundhog Weekend in February, which includes a concert, rugby match and other activities.

The weekly student newspaper, *The University News*, is impressive. A conservative competitor to the paper, *Justice*, was disbanded

in 2003 for being critical of the administration of then-president Msgr. Joseph. According to the watchdog group Accuracy in Academia, at issue was Msgr. Joseph's support for gun control and racial admission preferences.

Students also have the opportunity to participate in a broad intramural sports program. The University of Dallas fields teams in 13 sports under the umbrella of the NCAA Division III and competes regionally. Local cultural opportunities are presented in an organized program called Dallas Year.

Residential Life

All undergraduate students are required to live on campus. There are eight residence halls and a small number of apartments. All apartments are same sex although married couples can live in the apartments. Students are separated by gender by floor.

The university handbook specifies visitation times throughout the week, and overnight opposite-sex visitation is not allowed. Students reportedly abide by these rules. There are chastity programs promoted in the dorms and by student government.

Despite the university's strictures against it, drinking has been a problem off and on. One former professor told us, "Drinking had an odd heritage in the early days of the university. There developed a sense that it was 'a Catholic macho thing' to drink, sometimes heavily." Drinking today seems to be more of an off-campus issue.

The health clinic at the Haggar University Center addresses routine medical issues. There are several hospitals in the area, including the Las Colinas Medical Center and the Baylor Medical Center at Irving.

The Community

Irving, Texas, is adjacent to Dallas, a world-class city and part of the Dallas-Fort Worth Metroplex area, which includes about 5.8 million people. The cultural, sports and social opportunities in the area are extensive. In sports, for example, the popular Dallas Cowboys of the National Football League currently play in Irving's 66,000-seat Texas Stadium; the stadium is across the street from the University of Dallas campus.

The region's economy is largely based on health care, aeronautics, communications and banking. The region has a pleasant climate most of the year but has scorching summers.

Crime in Irving is slightly above the national average. But the University of Dallas campus is relatively safe and free of violent crime. The most campus police violations, by far, are for alcohol use.

The University of Dallas is easy to reach, especially via Dallas/Fort Worth International Airport, which is a key hub for American Airlines. Amtrak is located in Dallas, and there is an extensive system of roads in the area as well as the Dallas Area Rapid Transit (DART) system.

The Bottom Line

The University of Dallas is a premier Catholic college in the United States. It combines an extensive core curriculum, often emphasizing classical works, with an adherence to the Catholic intellectual tradition. The university prides itself on its quest for knowledge, confident that any inquiry will lead back to the Catholic Truth.

UD has one of the most impressive study-abroad semesters that we have seen with its Rome Program; more than 80 percent of its students take advantage of this wonderful opportunity to immerse themselves in the classics in a region steeped in the antecedents of Western and Catholic thought. Overall, then, it is no wonder that so many commentators and other college guidebooks give the university such high marks.

Dallas has provided service to the Catholic community in Texas and throughout the nation for half a century. It has weathered some storms, expanded and, in the end, remained faithful to its mission. Any Catholic student interested in challenging his or her mind would do well to put the University of Dallas on a list of colleges to investigate.

University of St. Thomas

Houston, Texas

www.stthom.edu

Overview

Founded 185 years ago in France, the Congregation of St. Basil (Basilian Fathers) surfaced in the Houston area at the turn of the 20th century when they founded a high school. The University of St. Thomas was launched in 1947 at the invitation of then-Bishop Christopher Byrne.

Today, UST is providing a solid Catholic liberal arts education to these students and is poised to attract a wider following. Indeed, its vision is simple but powerful: "We have decided that within 25 years we will become one of the great Catholic universities in America."

The university has four schools—arts and sciences, business, education and theology (which is offered at St. Mary's Seminary). Nearly one-third of the students on campus are enrolled in graduate programs; there are 10 master's degrees offered as well as a Ph.D. in philosophy.

Among the 30 majors are an interdisciplinary Catholic Studies, theology, pastoral studies, international studies (the most popular) and studio arts. Many minors are available, including Irish studies and creative writing. There also are many joint majors, and students have the opportunity to pursue a Western Civilization-oriented honors program.

Ninety-four percent of UST undergraduates are Texans, and nearly three-quarters of its alumni have settled in the Houston area. Half of its students are nonwhite (Hispanic,

```
QUICK FACTS

Founded: 1947
Type of institution: Small university
Setting: Urban
Undergraduate enrollment: 1,805 (2006–07)
Total undergraduate cost: $26,200 (tuition,
    room and board for 2007–08)
Undergraduate majors: 30

FIVE KEY POINTS

1.  Continues to be strongly influenced by
    the Basilian Fathers.
2.  High quality liberal arts curriculum.
3.  Catholicism permeates campus, in-
    cluding through several lecture series.
4.  Understands that strong theology and
    philosophy departments are essential.
5.  Lesser-known college seeking to
    develop broader recognition.
```

African American, Asian American and Native American), and many of these are first-generation college students. It is primarily a commuter school. Sixty-two percent of the students were Catholic in the fall 2006 semester.

The university is located near a cultural section known as the Museum District not far from the downtown center. Houston is the nation's fourth largest city and a leading energy, banking and space center.

Governance

Six of the eight UST presidents have been Basilian priests. The last was Father J. Michael Miller (1997–2003), who went on to become an archbishop at the Vatican serving as Secretary of the Congregation for Catholic Education, and later was named coadjustor bishop of the Archdiocese of Vancouver, British Columbia, in 2007.

There are 15 Basilians who reside on the main campus, and the order permeates the life of the university with, as one administrator said, their "quiet orthodoxy." It is not surprising, then, that the university takes its Catholic identity seriously; the text of *Ex corde Ecclesiae* prominently appears on its "Mission and Vision" webpage.

The current president is Dr. Robert Ivany, whose credentials are most impressive. A retired Army major general with tours stretching from Vietnam to Kuwait, he previously headed the U.S. Army War College. He holds a Ph.D. in history. University regulations require the president to be a Catholic.

Also required to be a Catholic is the vice president for academic affairs, who is now Dr. John Hittinger, formerly of the Sacred Heart Major Seminary, Detroit. Several years ago, he worked to expand adherence to *Ex corde*

Ecclesiae at St. Mary's College of Ave Maria University.

The board of trustees first admitted lay members in 1969, and they now constitute a majority. One third are either Basilians or Basilian appointees. Archbishop Daniel DiNardo of the Archdiocese of Galveston-Houston is also a member.

Public Identity

Although 38 percent of the student body is non-Catholic, the University of St. Thomas has a very strong Catholic identity. This is a result of the faithful engagement of the Basilian Fathers and top administrators; the commitment to *Ex corde Ecclesiae*; the presence of a solid core curriculum, anchored by the theology and philosophy departments; an active spiritual program; and an extensive set of Catholic lecture series.

It also is illustrative that crucifixes are prominent and widespread throughout the campus. They are in every classroom, in public places and in most offices. However, there is no requirement for such display; one Baptist staff member, for example, has chosen to hang a cross rather than a crucifix in her office.

Vice President Hittinger talks about sharing John Henry Cardinal Newman's vision of a Catholic university where "free minds pursue the truth." He told us, "We are looking to attract students who are interested in this kind of education. We want to recruit to mission with students. We want more students who value a Catholic university education." Accordingly, he added, "We intend to broaden our recruitment. We are going to offer special scholarships that stem from our mission."

Such a mission is reflected in the university's strategic agenda. The first of the four strategic initiatives states: "Assert our identity, academic brand, and image as a Catholic university imbued with the Basilian tradition."

This mission is also evident in UST's approach to the broader culture. While 22 Catholic universities—including some of the most well known—hosted the lewd *Vagina Monologues* on campus in February 2007, the University of St. Thomas was addressing human trafficking and violence against women in a much more productive way.

Created by English associate professor Janet Lowery, the *Traffic in Women* play provides an alternative series of monologues based on Greek mythology. In addition to six performances, there also was a high-level panel discussion that discussed trafficking in women, a particular problem in the Houston area.

Rather than appeal to senseless sexual exhibitionism, Dr. Lowery argues for a "more solution-based response to the problems facing women on the planet today" and elevating these "to a public concern." Hopefully, this play can be replicated on other campuses in 2008.

UST abounds in orthodox Catholic speakers such as Avery Cardinal Dulles; the prolific philosopher Peter Kreeft; Alasdair MacIntyre, the Notre Dame virtue ethicist; Father Richard John Neuhaus of *First Things*; and Janet Smith. One faculty member told us, "I'm impressed with the speakers—faithful Catholics and champions of the Faith."

Some of these speakers are part of a number of impressive lecture series. The Center for Thomistic Studies sponsors an annual lecture, which has included ethicist Germain Grisez. Others have been part of the Archbishop J. Michael Miller Lecture Series. And for nearly two decades, the university has had a high-level Lenten Lecture Series; one of the six speakers in 2007 was Father Tadeusz Pacholczyk, Ph.D., of the National Catholic Bioethics Center speaking on cloning and stem cell research.

A Planned Parenthood representative did appear on campus in October 2006 but was part of a YWCA self-esteem program. President Ivany said this appearance "slipped through the cracks," and that he would work to prevent a future occurrence.

Spiritual Life

Religious life revolves around the Chapel of St. Basil, an obvious choice of veneration for the Basilian Fathers. The small but attractive stucco chapel was designed by the notable architect Philip Johnson and was dedicated in 1997. Its outside appearance was enhanced in 2006 when the Felicie Babin Gueymard Meditation Garden, including a labyrinth reminiscent of one at Chartres Cathedral, was opened beside the chapel.

It is at the chapel that most of the 19 weekly Masses are offered and where confessions are heard Monday through Saturday. Every semester is opened with a Mass of Saint Thomas Aquinas. There also are periodic French Masses and Masses for people with special needs. Adoration and Benediction are held every Monday, and 24-hour Adoration begins every Wednesday at 8 a.m. Students are looking at initiating a Perpetual Adoration program.

The university chaplain, Father Daniel Callam, C.S.B., is well respected; one faculty member called him "first-rate, with an impeccable sense of liturgy." Father Callam told us that he works to make Masses "solemn and beautiful and to give sermons that are stimulating with intellectual content." Upcoming homilies are announced at the beginning of each semester and have included such topics as "Where in Hell Is Limbo?" Students can meet Father Callam informally every Friday afternoon at "Tea with the Chaplain."

While Sunday Masses are reported to be "bursting at the seams," there is a certain level of general student apathy that also extends into spiritual offerings. It does not appear that is for lack of commitment and initiative on the part of the university but perhaps rather because of the commuter nature of the school and the diverse student body.

The presence of approximately 25 priests on campus, mostly Basilian Fathers, and the Franciscan Sisters of the Eucharist is important in creating the nurturing spiritual environment that does exist. There also is a nearby convent of Vietnamese Dominican Sisters, and these religious participate in campus activities and take classes.

Sister Maura Behrenfeld, F.S.E., directs the campus ministry. Among other activities, the campus ministry offers a variety of retreats although some are not well attended. The campus ministry sponsored a two-week pilgrimage to World Youth Day in Cologne, Germany, in August 2005.

In the 2007–08 academic year, UST is launching a chapter of the Fellowship of Catholic University Students (FOCUS). It is the first one in Texas.

Social justice programs are offered through campus ministry, but the university has a formal program, the Center for Social Justice, which offers internships and other opportunities for service. Also noteworthy is that the political science department offers a minor in social justice. The center sponsors a Social Justice Seminar Series, and the university holds an annual Social Justice Summer Institute, which focused on "Health Care for All" in 2007.

As part of the university's broader outreach, there are ecumenical and interfaith programs such as the Msgr. William Steele Lecture Series.

Catholicism in the Classroom

The university places emphasis on the study of theology and philosophy. Indeed, it proudly notes in its catalog: "The University of St. Thomas gives the place of honor to theology as queen of the sciences."

Philosophy, rightfully, also is given prominence. As a result, 24 credits in these two disciplines are required for graduation: nine are to be in theology, nine in philosophy and another six selected from either department. Even transfer students must take at least six credits in theology as well as in philosophy while at UST.

Father Callam says that in 10 years at the university, he has never heard any non-Catholics—including atheists—protest this theology requirement. "Most of them end up finding the courses interesting," he said. "I tell them that theology asks the most important questions and even has some answers."

These requirements form the basis of the substantial core curriculum, which includes another 48 credits distributed among English, foreign languages, history, social and behavioral sciences, natural sciences, mathematics, fine arts and oral communications. This overall core of 72 hours is perhaps the largest among colleges that offer multiple majors. Professors dedicated to the Catholic intellectual tradition teach many of the core courses.

A university committee was named by Dr. Ivany in September 2007 to evaluate the core curriculum and, if necessary, recommend changes to it. The current core curriculum is 25 years old.

Those who major in theology are given a written exam before they graduate. It assesses whether the student has acquired an understanding of the Creed, moral theology, history of the Church and systematic theology. The major requires study of the major areas of Catholic theology.

Complementing the theology program is an interdisciplinary Catholics Studies program. The director of the program, Sister Paula Jean Miller, F.S.E., told us that the program is an "effort to see how doctrine has and can be infused into the culture, to enable students to integrate professional learning and development with Catholic teaching."

The Catholic Studies program is one of the possible double majors available which draw from the 30 majors. There is also a four-year, seven-course honors program that is heavily weighted toward the heritage of the Christian West. Dr. Terry Hall, an associate professor of philosophy and former FBI agent, has headed this program for the past seven years.

All full-time theology faculty members are faithful to Church teaching and are required to receive the *mandatum*. Among the department's leaders is Father Joseph Pilsner, C.S.B., who also serves on the board of trustees. The philosophy department is also uniformly strong and includes Father Anthony

Giampietro, C.S.B.; Dr. Theodore Rebard; and Dr. Mary Catherine Sommers, the chair and director of the Center for Thomistic Studies.

There are number of notable professors in other disciplines, including Dr. Clint Brand and Dr. Kerry Jones MacArthur in the English department; Dr. Lowery, the producer of *Traffic in Women* and editor of *Laurels*, the literary magazine; and assistant dean of the School of Arts and Sciences and assistant professor of chemistry Dr. John Palasota.

Some departments have few or no Catholics. But most faculty respect the Catholic identity of the school and, as one observer reports, "cases of outright dissent are marginal, even from among non-Catholics."

Dr. Hittinger is working to address any faculty deficiencies. He is recruiting faculty "to mission." Recognizing that "an existing university is an organic entity that can't be changed overnight," he has instituted Faculty Study Days to encourage professors. In one such workshop in January 2007, he emphasized: "We are committed to the Catholic intellectual tradition and dialogue between faith and reason."

One especially notable recruitment success was the luring of Dr. Dominic Aquila, a respected history professor and dean at the University of Saint Francis, to the position of dean of the School of Arts and Sciences, beginning in July 2007. He announced that strengthening the core curriculum and first-year student performance are his early priorities.

Finally, UST has a study-abroad program with classes in England, Ireland, France, Mexico and Argentina. It has exchange programs with 16 overseas universities. The Institute for International Education placed this program at 16th among colleges of its size in a 2006 survey.

Student Activities

At least 70 campus groups provide students with extracurricular opportunities that include the typical clubs as well as those targeted to various ethnics groups. Among the Catholic-oriented groups are Chi Rho, the theology club; a Knights of Columbus council; and a pro-life club. Chi Rho sponsors an annual career and volunteer fair for the Archdiocese of Galveston-Houston.

There also are 10 sport clubs, ranging from coed fencing to men's rugby, and intercollegiate sports are beginning. The *Cauldron* newspaper, which reaches 3,000 students, is a monthly publication, and the literary magazine provides an outlet for student writing.

We are not aware of any sanctioned groups that are in opposition to Church teachings at UST. There has been an effort among some students to get approval for a homosexual-oriented group, but that has been unsuccessful.

Two notable annual events draw considerable student social involvement. One is the Halloween-related event "Neewollah," which essentially is a costume dance. The other is the Crawfish Boil and Zydeco Fest that was launched by the Black Student Union in 2002.

There also is the annual President's Day of Service, begun three years ago. This initiative taps into students' interest in various volunteer projects, including helping with St. Michael's Home for Children, run by Catholic Charities, and a program for young people with special needs called SEARCH. There is additional volunteer work undertaken during the UST Week of Action.

Students also volunteer at the nearby John P. McGovern Museum of Health and Medical Science. They assist with Head Start programs there and with other activities.

Residential Life

Only about 15 percent of students live on campus, so residential life is limited. There is one large building, Vincent J. Guinan Residence Hall, which welcomed its first students in fall 2003. It is coed, but bathrooms are in student rooms, and no major problems seem to exist; a Basilian Father is in residence.

There is a smaller Augustine Hall for a limited number of freshmen seeking a sense of faith-based community. Some students live in apartments surrounding the campus. There are no fraternities.

The campus does not have a health center although a nurse is available for consultation. Students use the facilities of the world-famous Texas Medical Center, a vast complex of hospitals and health care facilities, which is located a short distance from UST.

The Community

Houston is a large, diverse city (population of about 2 million) with a crime index rate about double the national average. Some of this inevitably spills over onto the campus, largely as theft or pranks. But there have been robberies, including one of a professor, who was assaulted in December 2006. Vigilance, as in most places, is recommended.

Students gravitate to the many cultural, sports and social offerings that are available in the adjacent Museum District and within a short distance from campus. These include the Museum of Fine Arts, the Houston Zoo and major shopping areas. The Houston Space Center is the top local tourist attraction.

Houston is a major transportation hub, and students have access to two major airports, George Bush Intercontinental and William P. Hobby; east-west Amtrak service ("Sunset Limited"); several major highways, including Interstates 45 and 10; and an extensive METRO bus service. The sprawling city of Houston is heavily reliant on car transportation.

The Bottom Line

The University of St. Thomas is an excellent liberal arts-oriented institution. Its extensive core curriculum provides graduates with a well-rounded education. But even more notable is the strong emphasis that UST places on its Catholic identity, which is reflected in its faithful theology and philosophy departments and by the way Catholicism permeates the campus.

The university has received too little recognition for its work, perhaps reflecting the modesty of the Basilian Fathers over the years. Unfortunately, this has not helped its limited endowment—a mere $45 million—nor has it helped recruit large numbers of students from outside Texas.

But hewing to its 60-year-old tradition—and building on it—a new group of administrators are poised to lead the university to another level of academic prominence. Local, first-generation college students from the area will continue to benefit, but so will those from around the country looking for a quality Catholic education at a smaller university.

Born from the Crisis

Ave Maria University

Ave Maria, Florida

www.avemaria.edu

Overview

In 1961, a financially strapped 23-year-old named Tom Monaghan and his brother bought a pizza parlor in a small Michigan city. That business eventually grew into the world-famous Domino's Pizza. Monaghan became a billionaire.

The odds in favor of him becoming a successful businessman were long. His father died when he was four, he lived in foster care and at an orphanage, he was kicked out of the seminary and he dropped out of college. But he had a vision and determination.

Three decades after he began his career, Monaghan turned his attention to Catholic philanthropic endeavors, most notably in the field of education. In 1998, he founded Ave Maria Institute, which became Ave Maria College in Ypsilanti, Michigan, not far from his original pizza parlor.

He also launched a Catholic law school and then, in 2003, Ave Maria University in Naples, Florida. The first new Catholic university founded in the United States since Sacred Heart University 40 years earlier, Ave Maria University moved to its permanent site in the new town of Ave Maria, Florida, in 2007. Naples and Ave Maria are about 25 miles apart in southwest Florida.

The university has suffered through a number of problems during its short tenure. Decisions to close the Michigan-based college and relocate the law school to Florida have generated some acrimony among the faculty.

> ### QUICK FACTS
>
> **Founded:** 2003
> **Type of institution:** Small university
> **Setting:** Rural
> **Undergraduate enrollment:** 364 (2006–07 academic year)
> **Total undergraduate cost:** $23,395 (tuition, room and board for 2007–08)
> **Undergraduate majors:** 10
>
> ### FIVE KEY POINTS
>
> 1. The university is strongly committed to the Magisterium.
> 2. It attracts students by its dynamic spiritual life and sense of mission.
> 3. Various programs stress evangelization for lay students and encourage vocations.
> 4. Ave Maria is set in a new town that seeks to reinforce Catholic identity.
> 5. Administrators are working to iron out early internal problems.

Differences over liturgical styles—offering some charismatic as well as traditional worship—have resulted in another controversy.

We can make no predictions whether these are start-up problems or will become prolonged disputes. As with any new education venture, prospective students should monitor the latest developments to make sure they are comfortable with the direction the university is taking.

Our purpose is to examine Ave Maria's commitment to a Catholic identity and to a Catholic intellectual tradition. Assessed on those criteria, AMU fits well with the new crop of Catholic colleges and universities that are helping revitalize Catholic higher education in the early 21st century.

The principal attraction of Ave Maria to Catholic students and their families is—and should be—a strong commitment to the Church's Magisterium and the embracing of *Ex corde Ecclesiae*. The dean of the faculty, Dr. Michael Dauphinais, notes, "As a Catholic institution of higher education dedicated to the Blessed Virgin Mother, our patroness, we know that her son, Jesus Christ, is the divine Teacher who opens our minds and hearts to the fullness of the Truth."

Such confidence comes through in a vibrant spiritual life, commitment to evangelization, encouragement of vocations and exposing students to a regimen of the best in the Catholic intellectual tradition. This last point is reinforced by a liberal arts core curriculum that encompasses one-half of overall course requirements.

Students are able to pursue 10 majors from the traditional liberal arts fields, including theology, sacred music, and classics and early Christian literature. The first group of students able to complete all four years of college at the Naples campus graduated in May 2007.

These were 74 undergraduates and 13 graduate students.

The fall 2007 enrollment figures indicate that the university has significantly increased its enrollment over the previous year, now up to about 600. It is already a national institution, attracting students from more than 40 states and about a dozen other countries. Long-range plans peg future enrollment at 5,500 students, with nearly three-fourths expected to be undergraduates.

Currently, about half of the students come from public schools, while one-fourth are Catholic school graduates and the other one-fourth were homeschooled.

The university also has a campus, Ave Maria College of the Americas, in San Marcos, Nicaragua. Purchased from the University of Mobile (Alabama) in 2000, the campus offers undergraduate degrees in several business concentrations and four other disciplines. All classes are taught in English.

Ave Maria grants a master of arts degree and a Ph.D. in theology. The Institute for Pastoral Theology offers a Master of Theological Studies, largely attracting older, non-traditional lay students.

In anticipation of future growth and with a desire to form a comprehensive Catholic community, the university launched classes at the town of Ave Maria on August 27, 2007. Located near the town of Immokalee, is thought to be the first new planned Catholic university town in centuries.

The buildings that were ready for the fall opening were an academic center, library and a student union, which includes three chapels. There also were three residence halls and athletic fields.

A private Catholic school, Ave Maria Grammar and Preparatory School, opened on campus with 140 students in August. The K–

12 school includes teachers from the Dominican Sisters of Mary, Mother of the Eucharist. The school has attracted students from several communities. Public schools also are anticipated.

The town, which will include housing, businesses, shopping and services, will be linked to the Ave Maria University campus by a town core dominated by an impressive 1,100-seat Oratory of Ave Maria. Among the notable features in the church, which is the equivalent of about 10 stories, will be a massive, 60-foot crucifix.

A formal dedication is anticipated in early 2008, as work on the Oratory is rushing to completion and other transfers from Naples, including faculty residences, continue. Eventually, the town will occupy 5,000 acres, with about one-fifth of it devoted to the campus.

The university has received pre-accreditation from the American Academy for Liberal Arts and has been working on regional accreditation from the Southern States Association of Colleges and Schools.

Governance

Ave Maria is governed by a largely lay board of directors, which includes three priests (among them Father Benedict Groeschel, C.F.R., and Father Mitch Pacwa, S.J.) and theologian Michael Novak.

Monaghan, who serves as university chancellor and chief executive officer, and Nicholas Healy, the president and chief operating officer, also are board members. Healy, a former maritime lawyer, previously had served as a vice president at Franciscan University of Steubenville.

The university also has a 33-member board of regents, which includes Harvard

law professor and Catholic pro-life advocate Mary Ann Glendon and Father Richard John Neuhaus, the influential editor in chief of *First Things*.

Public Identity

Ave Maria was founded upon *Ex corde Ecclesiae* as a direct response to Pope John Paul II's call for a new evangelization. Dr. Dauphinais, the dean of the faculty, told us, "Ave Maria's Catholic identity is palpable in every aspect of its campus life from academics to student activities. The faculty and students enjoy being at a university where they possess the freedom to be Catholic."

Perhaps this exuberance is best appreciated through the observance of a Christendom College student who visited the Naples campus. In Christendom's *Rambler* publication in February 2007 he wrote, "The students at Ave have a deep awareness of why they are going to a Catholic college. They really understand the meaning behind the higher education that they are receiving."

The staff and faculty are an important component of this commitment. One administrator said, "From the top down, starting with the university president, students see faculty and staff who are confident in their faith and love it. Their faithfulness is very appealing to the students."

"When they see the president of Ave Maria hammering for a Habitat for Humanity project," he added, "it makes a deep impression. When they see fidelity to the faith lived out joyfully, they are drawn to it."

We were told by one administrator that "campus speakers must support the Catholic mission of the institution. If they are Catholic, they must be in good standing with the Church. Academic lecturers need not be

Catholic, but they should respect the Catholic identity of the institution."

The 2007 commencement speaker was journalist and author Peggy Noonan, and the celebrant of the preceding Baccalaureate Mass was Father Neuhaus. Both received honorary degrees.

Spiritual Life

Until the Oratory is completed, Masses are being celebrating in three chapels in the Student Union Building. They are plentiful: three daily Monday through Friday, two on Saturday (including one Sunday vigil) and four on Sunday. Several Masses are in Latin under the *Novus Ordo*, including the Sunday Mass at 8 p.m., but the majority are in English. The Tridentine Mass is offered only in two of the chapels and with prior permission.

We read of one Sunday noon Mass in the Ballroom, the largest chapel, which attracted 500 faculty members and students. The writer, who was impressed by the homily, said, "The students that I encountered knew they were a part of something special and they relished the experience."

There are those on campus who prefer the traditional Mass while others support the charismatic Praise and Worship form. Despite some turmoil over this issue, it appears that the university is moving in the direction of both options.

Confessions are held daily, and the Liturgy of the Hours is prayed throughout the week. There is Eucharistic adoration and popular nightly Rosary walks that attract between 40 to 80 students. Retreats (Ignatian, coed and silent) are offered every semester.

The Angelus is rung three times daily, and we were told by one faculty member, "It is not unusual to see people stop a minute for recollection when the Angelus bell is rung." The university also promotes overall Catholic spirituality by a daily "sanctification of time" by starting classes with prayer, perhaps to the saint of the day.

There are nine priests and at least five religious sisters on campus, reflecting several orders and campus responsibilities. The most well-known priest is Father Joseph Fessio, S.J., the Theologian in Residence. Father Fessio, founder of Ignatius Press, is very popular with students and highly engaged with them. He has, for example, weekly study groups for students that discuss such works as Pope Benedict XVI's *Spirit of the Liturgy*. Father Fessio received his doctorate in theology from the University of Regensburg (Germany), where he studied under then-Professor Joseph Ratzinger.

The university is strongly committed to vocations. It has a pre-theologate program, which includes a Program of Priestly Formation. This initiative is run by the Center for Discernment. There currently are about 50 men in the program who take undergraduate theology and philosophy courses. Some are students who started at Ave Maria and decided to enter, while others were sent to the program by their bishop.

There also is a unique Women's Discernment Program that is run by the Servant Sisters of Hogar de la Madre with added participation of Benedictine nuns. Interested women are able to reside in a special household in a residence hall. The Servant Sisters have a special relationship with Ave Maria.

Catholicism in the Classroom

A university vice president told us, "We are seeking 'orthopraxis,' to help our graduates develop big heads, big hearts and big chests." (This is a reference to C. S. Lewis's *Abolition of Man*, where we are warned about smart men with giant heads but tiny, concave chests.)

The university's bylaws stipulate that at least one-half of the 128 credits required for graduation be within the core curriculum. Sixty-four credits come from 16 specified core courses. The liberal arts disciplines of literature, history, the natural sciences, math and classical languages are studied as well as theology and philosophy.

The three core courses in theology taken in sequence are in scripture, doctrine and moral theology. All students take three foundational philosophy courses, including metaphysics. The core requires one year of Latin and two non-credit *practica* (hands-on activities) courses in fine arts, one of which is Gregorian chant.

One official said, "The theology courses seek to present the theological wisdom of the Church found in Scripture, the Fathers, St. Thomas Aquinas as well as later theologians and the Magisterium."

All theology professors make a profession of faith, take the Oath of Fidelty and hold the *mandatum*. Non-Catholic faculty members do not teach theology or philosophy, although there is no policy prohibiting it.

One theology professor whose name consistently surfaced as an exemplary teacher is Dr. William Riordan, who serves as the department's director of undergraduate studies. In addition to being identified by a university official as a dynamic teacher with "deep fidelity" in the classroom, he is noted for his study groups that read texts from thinkers such as Euclid and other classical writers.

The philosophy department also is strong. It bases its curriculum on philosophy's "orginal meaning as the love and pursuit of wisdom." All philosophy majors must take a comprehensive examination that is so substantial that it carries two credits. One area that is tested is the relationship between theology and philosophy.

In the spring 2007 semester, the philosophy department held a four-session "Christian Philosophy and Metaphysics" lecture series. The focus was on the papal encyclical *Fides et Ratio*, which Pope John Paul II issued in 1998.

Even in departments such as mathematics or economics, the connection to Catholic teaching is evident. Dr. Michael Marsalli, professor of mathematics and chair of the department, "sees numbers as revealing order and beauty," according to one of his colleagues. Dr. Gabriel Martinez, assistant professor of economics, included Catholic social teaching in his classes.

One campus priest pointed to both these men, among others, as examples of faculty members being notable "personal witnesses" to the Catholic faith. Dr. Marsalli, for example, is seen at Mass with his wife at the organ and his 15-year-old daughter playing the violin.

Such commitment continues. Dr. Daniel Dentino, vice president of student affairs and dean of students, told us that he looks for ways to inculcate Christian principles throughout campus life. He said, "We aim to create a culture where faith informs the whole of life—in the residences, the activities, social events and academics."

No member of the faculty is reported to be a dissenter from Church teachings, although about 10 percent of the faculty is non-Catholic. The Protestant faculty, according to one priest on the faculty, is committed to the Church's mission. Dr. David Dalin, an ordained Jewish rabbi, is professor of history and political science. He is the author of the 2005 book *The Myth of Hitler's Pope: How Pope Pius XII Rescued Jews from the Nazis.*

Among other notable faculty is Joseph Pearce, a writer in residence and professor of literature who has written a number of recent biographies of Catholic thinkers, including G. K. Chesterton, Hilaire Belloc and J. R. R. Tolkien. The British-born Pearce also is the author of *Literary Converts: Spiritual Inspiration in An Age of Unbelief,* about several prominent British writers who became Catholic.

Amid this academic background, Ave Maria University offers 10 majors. Theology, with the largest number of professors, also attracts the largest number of majors. Philosophy, literature, politics and economics are ranked not far behind. Minors can be earned in some departments that do not presently grant majors, such as chemistry and physics. There is a pre-med program.

The Institute for Business offers liberal arts students the opportunity to take courses to receive a certificate in business. According to the university, the program "is infused with Catholic teaching in order to inspire the students of the Institute to become Christian business leaders who will help to transform the countries in which they live."

There is a study-abroad program. Students are able to spend one semester at the International Theological Institute in Gaming, Austria, where they live in a 14th-century monastery known as Kartause Maria Thron. There also is an opportunity to study at Ave Maria's San Marcos, Nicaragua, campus. Plans are being made to offer a Rome program.

The university is committed to helping ease the financial burden of students, particularly those coming from large families. In the fall 2007 semester up to 30 full tuition scholarships, known as Magnificat scholarships, were to be offered to freshmen. They hope to continue this program for future entering classes.

Among other features of the campus is the Aquinas Center for Theological Renewal, which sponsors conferences, lectures and publications. One upcoming conference is *"Humanae Vitae*: 40 Years Later," which is scheduled for February 1–2, 2008.

The center also gives several awards. The Veritas Medal for Catholic intellectual contributions was given to papal biographer George Wiegel in 2006 and Avery Cardinal Dulles, S.J., in 2007. The 2007 Charles Cardinal Journet Prize for a notable manuscript was presented to University of Notre Dame philosopher Ralph McInerny. Other awards are the *Ex corde Ecclesiae* Medal and a dissertation prize.

Ave Maria houses the Sapientia Press, which lists 27 titles in its current catalog in the areas of Catholic social science, literature, philosophy, science and theology. They also publish two journals, *Nova et Vetera,* a Thomistic publication, and *StAR,* a Catholic bimonthly featuring well-known authors.

As with many other Catholic colleges, Ave Maria has a summer program for high school students, which allows them to sample the academic environment. In 2007, Father Fessio and Joseph Pearce taught one-week programs that focused on Tolkien and C. S. Lewis. There also are summer intensive language programs in Greek, Latin and Hebrew for current students.

Student Activities

There are more than two dozen clubs and organizations on campus. We were told by one faculty member that the largest ones are the Chastity Team, which encourages students and evangelizes, and the Students for Life, which undertakes sidewalk counseling, prayer at Planned Parenthood sites and participates in the annual March for Life in Washington, D.C.

Among other faith-oriented groups are the Knights of Columbus; *Sodalitas Pontificis Sancti Gregorii Magni*, which promotes the Roman liturgy; Communion and Liberation, dedicated to studying the works of Monsignor Luigi Giovanni Giussani, an Italian who founded the *Comunione e Liberazione* movement; and Operation Prayer Packages (OPPS), which provides prayers and packages to our soldiers overseas.

Other groups cover fine arts, hiking and mountaineering, poetry, swing dance and tennis. The drama club has produced the play *Harvey*, made famous by the James Stewart film, and the musical *My Fair Lady*.

Father Fessio founded AMOR, which stands for Ave Maria on the Road, with some support from Ignatius Press. It involved students traveling to present dramatic skits to parishes and elsewhere. It is expanding to become an independent organization that will be near the university and reconstituted as Theater of the World Incorporated. Ave Maria students are expected to continue to be involved in this evangelization effort.

Ave Maria students also enjoy several formal dances each year. The spring 2007 ball had a 19th-century theme, and students were to dress and dance to reflect the style of the period. That same semester, there was a fashion show, "Image," which emphasized modesty in dress.

The university has seven intercollegiate club sports: men's and women's basketball, which will have a six- and eight-game schedule, respectively, in fall 2007; men's and women's soccer; women's volleyball; men's golf; and cross country. Ave Maria is anticipating eventually competing at the varsity level through the National Association of Intercollegiate Athletics (NAIA).

There is an intramural program consisting of coed opportunities in frisbee, soccer and volleyball as well as men's and women's basketball leagues and flag football for men during October through December.

There also are several opportunities for community outreach. These include the Habitat for Humanity (every Saturday in Immokalee), Big Brothers and Big Sisters, spring break mission trips to Texas and Mexico and general outreach to the economically challenged Immokalee community.

Residential Life

Students live in two women's residence halls and one for men; nearly 600 students can be housed here. With a few exceptions, it is university policy for all students to live on campus. Chastity is strongly promoted in the residence halls. Opposite-sex visitation is restricted to certain times and limited to common areas.

Like Franciscan University of Steubenville, which pioneered the wide use of student households, Ave Maria created several on its Naples campus. In the 2006–07 academic year, there were four women's households—Daughters of Divine Mercy, *Esto Femina*, *Rosa Mystica* and St. Gianna Berretta—and five men's households—Brotherhood of Divine Line, Brothers of the Sacred Heart of Jesus, *Esto Vir*, *Filii in Filio* and *Totus Tuus*.

The university notes, "These Christ-centered groups strive for balanced, healthy, interpersonal relationships while they support and challenge a member to develop spiritually, emotionally, academically and physically."

The Community

One blogger said of his August 2007 visit to the Ave Maria campus, "I am still in shock at what was pulled off in the middle of a sod farm, orange grove and tomato field in rural Florida." The university, particularly with its striking Oratory, stands out like a spiritual oasis.

The town of Ave Maria, once completed, will offer all the amenities of life in an atmosphere that sustains Catholic identity. Plans for the town have been criticized by some groups, including the American Civil Liberties Union, for restricting certain services and products inimical to Catholic teachings. There have been some adjustments, but the town still promises to provide a safe haven for Catholic families and children.

The city of Immokalee is five miles away and has about 20,000 residents, 71 percent of whom are Hispanic. The major industry is agriculture. Immokalee does not have a hospital, and the closest one to Ave Maria is the Le-high Regional Medical Center, which is about 20 miles northwest.

Immokalee has a Seminole reservation and a casino. It is also the home of the National Aubudon Society's Corkscrew Swamp Sanctuary, which protects rare Cypress trees.

Students have access to Collier County parks and can view sporting events, mostly minor-league teams, in nearby cities of Estero, Fort Myers and City of Palms. The beaches along the Gulf of Mexico are close.

Southwest Florida International Airport in Fort Myers is a rapidly growing airport located one hour northwest from Ave Maria. Many major carriers fly in and out of there, and service is provided to the United States, Canada and Germany.

The nearest major highway is Interstate 75, which is the main artery from the campus to Miami, which is about two hours east.

The Bottom Line

Ave Maria University has experienced some growing pains as it has begun a noble experiment to create the first new Catholic university since 1963. Despite some negative publicity, the institution has suffered few disruptions and has continued to increase its enrollment. It also has moved to an impressive permanent home.

One administrator told us, "The overall ambiance of the Catholic faith integrates the campus life by providing a common sense of mission as opposed to the impersonal and fragmented character of many universities today."

That alone is a strong argument for this institution. But when you take into account the unswerving fidelity to the Magisterium, the strong core curriculum, the nurturing of vocations and the presence of an impressive and faithful faculty, Ave Maria stands as a university which must be considered one of the most notable available to American Catholics today.

Holy Apostles College & Seminary

Cromwell, Connecticut

www.holyapostles.edu

Overview

Ranney Hall, the oldest house in the small central Connecticut town of Cromwell, has been a focal point of service to the community for one and one-quarter centuries. In various forms, this building and subsequent additions have formed a sanatorium for the emotionally disturbed, a Catholic seminary and then a Catholic college and seminary.

Holy Apostles Seminary began as a minor seminary in 1957, founded by Father Eusebe Menard, O.F.M. It was originally operated by the Society of the Missionaries of the Holy Apostles, an order of priests also founded by Father Menard. An undergraduate college was opened for lay students in 1972, and the seminary became a major seminary in 1978.

Later, graduate, distance-learning and non-degree graduate programs were added. Today, Holy Apostles College & Seminary is a unique, small-scale Catholic college with modest university components. It also is one that is firmly rooted in the Church.

The seminary has long had strong historic ties with the Bishop of the Diocese of Norwich, who still serves as chancellor of the expanded institution. And for more than two decades, he as well as the Archbishop of Hartford and the Bishop of Bridgeport have served on the board of trustees.

As one staff member told us, "This expansion of the board gave the college and seminary the benefit of episcopal oversight, along with ecclesial and professional expertise." As

QUICK FACTS

Founded: 1972
Type of institution: Micro liberal arts college
Setting: Suburban
Undergraduate enrollment: Six full-time and 22 part-time lay students (2006–07 academic year)
Total tuition cost: $7,800 (for 2007–08)
Undergraduate majors: Four

FIVE KEY POINTS

1. The college is solidly faithful to the Magisterium.
2. Connecticut's three bishops sit on the board of trustees.
3. It has a 97-credit, philosophy-based core curriculum.
4. Lay students benefit from studying alongside seminarians.
5. Holy Apostles is very affordable.

---

a result, Holy Apostles is a solid example of orthodox Catholicism.

The seminary has been thriving. Enrollment has been growing in recent years and reached 82 men in the fall 2007 semester. Nineteen dioceses are represented, the most coming from Sioux Falls, South Dakota, and Santa Fe, New Mexico. Six religious communities also are present.

But it was not until about four years ago, according to Father Douglas Mosey, C.S.B., Holy Apostles' president-rector, that new attention was directed to the undergraduate lay program. He said, "We realize the desire and need for truly Catholic colleges. We have right here in our immediate area a number of Catholic high schools, and we are recruiting there for students and families who want a faithful Catholic education."

The college remains a commuter school—there are no residence halls for lay students and no plans to build any. Father Mosey added, "There also are a number of homeschooling families who might want their sons and daughters to receive higher learning and perhaps continue living at home."

In the fall 2006, there were six full-time and 22 part-time undergraduate lay students. There also were 149 graduate lay students who were studying on campus or through distance learning. The recruitment of undergraduate students is a critical element in the college's long-range plan.

The opportunity to study in a Catholic environment with seminarians is compelling to these students as is the strong core curriculum, which covers 97 credits or about three-fourths of the graduation requirement.

Also attractive is its affordability. Tuition for the 2007–08 academic year is $7,800. According to the college's director of student recruitment, "We are the lowest-priced private college in New England, a fact that I think many parents and students would want to know because, at that cost, it is possible to graduate without incurring college-loan debt."

Yet another appealing aspect of Holy Apostles is the opportunity to study at an historic, picturesque and peaceful campus. Its oldest building was erected in 1751. There are so many trees that students and visitors enjoy a guided trail tour known as the Tree Walk. Many of these trees were planted by representatives of the firm of the noted 19th-century landscape architect Frederick Law Olmstead, who was a native of nearby Hartford.

Students have the option to major in four areas: philosophy, theology, English in the humanities and history in the social sciences. An associate of arts degree in theology also is available. The college is accredited by its regional agency, the New England Association of Schools and Colleges.

Governance

In addition to the three Connecticut bishops, the Holy Apostles board of trustees includes five priests of the Missionaries of the Holy Apostles and nine lay members. One of the lay members is Dr. Marie Hilliard, former executive director of the Connecticut Catholic Conference. The Missionaries of the Holy Apostles turned over the seminary and college to the board of trustees in 1984.

Father Mosey, who holds a Ph.D., is the seventh president of the college and seminary. He is in his 12th year as president. All presidents have been priests.

Public Identity

Given Holy Apostles' commitment to its mission to cultivating ordained, consecrated and lay Catholic leaders for evangelization, it is not surprising that its Catholic identity is strong. One of the college's five goals—all related to faith—is: "To animate the entire college and seminary experience in a recognizable, distinctive, and unambiguously Catholic spirit."

All interviewees emphasized the college's Catholic identity with enthusiasm. One philosophy professor, for example, said, "I have taught in a number of colleges over the years, and Holy Apostles College by far has the best atmosphere for orthodox teaching, camaraderie and friendship. These are reinforced with an integrated liberal arts education. It has the complete package."

And a full-time student told us, "The college has the strongest Catholic identity I've ever seen. When you're hanging out with seminarians in class and on campus all day, you can't get much more Catholic identity than that."

Among the limited number of college speakers has been Father Benedict Groeschel, C.F.R., who delivered the commencement address in 2007.

Spiritual Life

Two early morning Masses are held daily at the 120-seat chapel. Students are welcome, but due to the early hour at the commuter school (7:15 a.m. and 9 a.m.), we are told that not many students attend; most of the attendees are seminarians. More students attend 5 p.m. Evening Prayer.

Masses are reported to be "very solemn and absolutely beautiful." Music is provided with the work of a choir director. Confessions are available. Masses attract some people from the community, and there are plans to build a new chapel that will double the current capacity.

One professor said, "It is not unusual to see lay students at the chapel or meeting elsewhere to say the Rosary together. Catholic spiritual life is a major focus at Holy Apostles College."

Lay students are clearly influenced by the presence of the seminarians. Sean Forrest, a student and administrator at Holy Apostles as well as a Catholic contemporary musician, said, "We have the chance to see the seminarians' strong desire to study and to serve others. Having this exposure to the seminarians makes me love the priesthood even more when I see their commitment."

When Father Frank Pavone, national director of Priests for Life, gave a retreat for seminarians, it was open to all students. Lay students and seminarians work together on pro-life activities, which includes going to an abortion clinic in nearby Hartford on Saturdays and participating in the annual March for Life in Washington, D.C. There is a tomb on campus marking the grave of an unborn child, a victim of an abortion.

Holy Apostles, along with the Cromwell Christian Clergy Association, sponsors the Cromwell Ecumenical Lay Theology School (CELTS), which offers informal courses.

Students have the option of participating in Mass and other spiritual activities, including perpetual adoration, at St. John Church in Cromwell. The parish is staffed by Coventual Franciscan Friars.

Catholicism in the Classroom

The college emphasizes that the curriculum is philosophically based and in the Catholic liberal arts tradition. The 97-credit core includes six Catholic theology courses, which range from "Catechism I and II" to "Liturgy." There also are eight specific philosophy courses, including "Philosophy of God." The philosophy requirement is only two courses short of a major. One student said, "The strength of [the college] is in the theology and philosophy courses."

Other required courses include three in Latin and work in the traditional liberal arts disciplines, especially in literature and history (together accounting for 10 courses). All students need to complete a senior project. The core curriculum helps satisfy the college's objective: "To prepare college seminarians for the study of theology and to prepare lay students for graduate study and most especially for life."

Accordingly to Father Mosey, the president-rector, the college developed its curriculum, with an emphasis on philosophical foundations, after studying a 1961 college catalogue that described Fordham University's Jesuit approach to the curriculum. Fordham has long since abandoned it.

Some of the courses are taught in an interdisciplinary manner, which fits well at a school of such small size. One example of an interdisciplinary, team-taught course is one offered on the Middle Ages by Dr. Angelyn Arden, assistant professor of humanities. She is a licensed clinical psychologist who previously taught in the Great Books program at the University of Dallas.

Faculty members teaching philosophy and theology make a profession of faith and also promise obedience to the bishop and the Magisterium. This is done annually when Bishop Michael Cote of the Diocese of Norwich comes to campus to celebrate the Mass of the Holy Spirit at the beginning of the academic year. All members of the academic and formational faculty of the seminary are approved by the bishop on the recommendation of the rector of the seminary.

One professor praised the scholarship at the college, but said, "Everything is subordinated to spiritual formation. You need a school where you can maintain your faith and receive the intellectual component as well, and Holy Apostles College does this."

Students especially praised two professors. Father Peter Girard, O.P., called by one student a "dynamic teacher," offers courses on Christology, Church Fathers, Saint Paul and the Doctors of the Church. Sister Mary Ann Linder, F.S.E., an associate professor of catechetics, teaches courses in humanities.

The college has attracted a wide range of students, from traditional recent high school graduates to senior citizens. Some come for two years to get the personal formation, we are told, and then move on. Some opt to take the two-year associate of arts degree and return later to Holy Apostles or elsewhere to complete a bachelor's degree.

There are some undergraduate seminarians who take courses with lay college students. The lay students we spoke to considered this to be an important benefit. A college administrator said, "Because seminarians and lay students study, pray and interact in class, they are able to share their unique perspectives and thus deepen each other's overall learning experience."

The college also has hosted the Pope John Paul II Bioethics Center for the past 25 years. The center sponsors lectures and publications.

Student Activities

There are no organized college clubs. Student activities are limited at this all-commuter college. There are informal, student-initiated activities such as cookouts, going to movies or playing soccer.

The campus is quiet, but the college sees this as a plus. The campus website comments: "Students treasure the abundant peace and extraordinary beauty of Holy Apostles' hillside campus above the Connecticut River because moments of quiet and beauty are often times when you learn the most about God and yourself."

This perspective resonated with the mother of a daughter who began her freshman year at Holy Apostles in August 2007. She said, "The atmosphere on campus is comfortable and peaceful. Everyone, whether they know you or not, is kind and thoughtful. This is truly a Catholic institution that is thriving in spite of its size."

Residential Life

There are no residential facilities for lay students. Some share local apartments, but most commute from their homes. Here, too, the college views its lack of facilities as a positive point, citing how residential life can easily distract students from their studies. Residential life, they also note, is costly for the college—and the student—because it requires health services, resident advisors, campus social activities and personnel to supervise them, and a security force.

Further, they say, commuter students living at home "can bring the Truth you have learned back to your community and start sharing it and living it immediately."

While students may come from several nearby communities, health services are available at two hospitals, Middlesex Hospital and Connecticut Valley Hospital, each located five minutes away in Middletown.

The Community

Cromwell is a town of 13,500 people which is 15 minutes from the state capital of Hartford and about one-half-hour from New Haven. The quiet town also is a safe one, with virtually no violent crime and a crime rate only about 40 percent of the national crime index.

Hartford, a long-time center of the insurance industry, has a population of 125,000. It has a number of attractions including the Mark Twain House and the Hartford Civic Center, which hosts cultural and sports events.

The north-south Interstate 91 serves Cromwell, while the east-west Interstate 84 and Interstate 91 meet in downtown Hartford. Amtrak services Hartford, and the city's Bradley International Airport provides non-stop service to several major cities, including Los Angeles, on national carriers.

The Bottom Line

One representative of Holy Apostles College said they like to promote their institution as being "really Catholic, really close and really affordable." Add to that, "really supportive of the Catholic intellectual tradition," and you have a rather impressive mix.

The college, long dedicated to training seminarians, is embarking on expanding its very small lay presence. It does not have residential facilities, and social activities on campus are limited. But the college sees all this as major selling points in presenting an environment that sticks to the essentials—faith formation and liberal arts education without frills.

At this point, the college is unlikely to draw many students from around the country. It is, however, an attractive option for students living in central Connecticut and perhaps the rest of the state as well. If fidelity to mission is any indicator, Holy Apostles College & Seminary has a bright future.

John Paul the Great Catholic University

San Diego, California

www.jpcatholic.com

Overview

John Paul the Great Catholic University may be situated in San Diego, California, but the small, specialized university can trace its intellectual heritage to Franciscan University of Steubenville. It was there in 2000 that a visiting Dr. Derry Connolly had the inspiration to develop a college in his hometown.

Connolly, an administrator at the University of California, San Diego, decided that he wanted to replicate the Steubenville religious fervor on a new campus in the nation's eighth largest city. With his background in technology and business, he also wanted to combine evangelization with entrepreneurship, especially as it relates to what is known as New Media.

In the fall of 2006, the first class enrolled in two programs: entertainment media and entrepreneurial business. Eventually, this curriculum will expand to six other emphases: entrepreneurial journalism, business of entertainment, entrepreneurial publishing, digital media, computer engineering and computer science.

The first-year class consisted of 30 students, and 63 were enrolled in September 2007. All except one of the 2006–07 students was Catholic, and the lone exception attended Catholic schools and apparently fit in well, according to a campus official.

The current campus is one large, industrial building located in northern San Diego

Michaela Lawless
2004

about one mile from student apartments and one mile from a parish church. During its first year of operation one classroom was used, but expansion within the building will occur during the 2007–08 academic year. Long-range plans anticipate a campus with up to 1,600 students.

Although the institution is licensed by the state of California, accreditation by the Western Association of Schools and Colleges could take six years. It is questionable whether accreditation will be granted before the first class is graduated, but this is the standard challenge of all new colleges, regardless of their quality. Accreditation, once granted, is retroactive.

President Connolly told us, "Parents could be understandably nervous about letting their children go to a new college. I tell them to pray about it. In the six months we've been open [March 2007 interview], I have had no calls from parents who have any regrets about their decision."

The university has two "core commitments": spiritual and intellectual. The latter applies to the unique curriculum while the former is a straightforward dedication to Catholicism. The university describes this commitment as: "The spiritual development of all students, faculty and staff, and striving to put into action, in our lives and in the lives of those we touch, the teachings of Jesus Christ, being unapologetic for and uncompromising with His Word."

Although the university has a specialized curriculum—business and media majors—it works to provide a Catholic education through requiring one course every semester on some aspect of Catholic philosophy, theology, history, ethics or culture.

Governance

John Paul the Great has the consent of Bishop Robert Brom of the Diocese of San Diego but is independent of the diocese. It is governed by an 11-member board of trustees. The chair of the board is a permanent deacon and banker. The other members include one priest and several engaged in senior positions at area businesses. Dr. Connolly, the president and one of the five founders of the university, also is a member.

Public Identity

According to the university, "John Paul the Great Catholic University will intentionally seek to avoid causing controversy and confusion among its students in matters of faith. JP Catholic seeks to shape and form solid Catholic leaders and innovators poised to put into action the teachings of Jesus Christ, and not to become agitators for change on matters of doctrine."

President Connolly adds, "The most important part of our university is the Catholic dimension. The only type of student who would want to be here is someone for whom faith is important." One faculty member added, "If our students don't know the Lord or the Faith, we haven't succeeded."

Bishop Brom celebrated the first Mass in the small campus chapel in September 2006, and an Opening Mass was held shortly after in the neighboring Good Shepherd Catholic Church. Such a beginning was appropriate for what one student said was "a Catholic identity that drives everything that we do here."

Speakers on campus have included Steve McEveety, producer of *The Passion of the Christ*; representatives of Sony Online Entertainment; Act One, a Christian acting group; the Goretti Group, dealing with chastity; and freelance scriptwriters. Outside speakers are vetted for their orthodoxy.

The patron of the university is the 17th-century Italian St. Joseph of Cupertino. The Franciscan priest is also the patron of students and test takers.

Spiritual Life

Mass is offered every Friday in the campus chapel. The class schedule is set up so that students who wish can attend daily Mass at Good Shepherd parish. The campus chaplain, appointed by the bishop, hears confessions every Thursday and by appointment. Adoration also takes place every afternoon on campus. Students attend Sunday Mass at Good Shepherd or elsewhere.

Students have become involved in Good Shepherd and other parishes, and this activity includes teaching CCD classes, pro-life work, helping with homeless people and attending Prayer and Worship services.

Classes begin and end with prayer, reinforcing what the theology professor told us, "Everything the university does, every course and field, is permeated with themes from theology and philosophy."

Catholicism in the Classroom

John Paul the Great is emphatic in its fidelity to the Magisterium. "All teaching faculty," the university reports, "will commit to harmony with Catholic Church teachings (the pope and bishops) in speech and action. Faculty, staff, students or volunteers who knowingly in public speech or actions take positions against the Catholic Church compromise their relationship with JP Catholic. JP Catholic will expect all trustees, faculty and staff to celebrate the positive spiritual and entrepreneurial components of its mission and eschew cutting down what the institution is striving to build."

The *mandatum* is required for all faculty members who teach theology. Currently, the only theology professor describes himself as a "biblical Thomist." Overall, there are three full-time faculty and eight adjunct professors. All professors must maintain some part-time work in their field, whether it is in business or media.

The business math course, taught by Alan Lane, is started by prayer and—when applicable—raises Catholic themes such as tithing and the need to place the acquisition of money in its proper perspective. Business morality themes are addressed in theology.

Tom Dunn, adjunct professor of digital media production, said to us, "From day one, we show students the scripture passages that call us to be perfect, that they should not settle for something less. No matter what they may end up being called to do, they must do it in a way that is truthful and faithful to Christ."

Although John Paul the Great is not a liberal arts institution *per se*, it has a 57-credit core curriculum. This includes four Catholic religious studies courses as well as four philosophy courses such as "Catholic Social Teaching" and others that have a Catholic approach.

The university assumes that most students will be called to work in business, entertainment and the new digital media. Although there is a certain evangelization component present, one student reported, "It doesn't mean that everything we end up doing is openly 'religious,' but our faith will be part of what we do."

In the third and fourth years, students will participate in teams to develop a Senior Business Plan. This project will allow students to bring their entrepreneurial skills and values together to create a blueprint for a company. The university expects that half of the students will use these plans to launch their own businesses after graduation.

In the summer of 2007, high school students interested in exploring whether John Paul the Great is right for them were able to participate in four different week-long programs: "Faith, Story & Film," "Faith, Art & Film," "Faith & Film Criticism," and "Faith and Business."

Student Organizations

The fledgling college is just beginning to develop student organizations. In addition to the local parish-centered activities, there are informal events such as a monthly Open Mike or variety program. There is a writing group. And the university is working to set up some intramural sports, including volleyball.

Residential Life

Students live in the Legacy Apartment Homes complex spread through four different buildings. Men and women are kept in separate parts of the complex, and no visitation between men and women is permitted. Two married couples who live in the apartments serve as residential directors who work with seven residential associates.

The apartments form a typical complex and also house people who are not part of the university. These residential units are near the university's building, and they usually are reached by way of a nine-minute bus ride. JP Catholic students use public buses extensively; cars are discouraged on campus.

Related to residential life, the university encourages chastity through teaching scripture and St. Francis de Sales's work on chastity. The university has weekly get-togethers where participants talk about spiritual life, including chastity. The Rosary is recited nightly in the student residences.

The Community

Sunny San Diego is one of the most attractive American cities. With a population of about 1.3 million, it presents a broad array of economic, social and cultural opportunities. The diversified economy includes naval, military and port facilities; tourism; biotechnology; marine science; and many start-up businesses, particularly in the area of technology.

Among the cultural offerings are the San Diego Museum of Art, the San Diego Zoo and a wide range of professional sports teams, including those in baseball, football and basketball. San Diego is one of the safest large cities in the nation.

The city, located near the Mexican border, is a major transportation hub. The San Diego International Airport handles 18 commercial carriers. Amtrak and other rail and public bus systems are available. Among the road systems that traverse the area is Interstate 5, which runs from Mexico to Canada.

The Bottom Line

John Paul the Great Catholic University is part of the new breed of small Catholic colleges born from the crisis in higher education of the past generation. Its founders have developed a formidable vision: Create a traditionally orthodox institution that prepares students for 21st-century careers in entrepreneurial business and media technology.

As the college moves into its second year of matching evangelization with vocation, they face the usual early challenges. But they are approaching them with faith as well as with the start-up enthusiasm they seek to impart to their students. The late pope's admonishment to "Be Not Afraid" might be their watchword.

JP Catholic is seeking to establish a unique niche among Catholic colleges. Their approach has attracted our attention, and students with an adventuresome streak would do well to investigate this opportunity. After all it brings together three attractive components: A strong Catholic identity; an impressive, modern curriculum; and one of the most livable and appealing cities in the country.

Our Lady Seat of Wisdom Academy

Barry's Bay, Ontario, Canada

www.seatofwisdom.org

Overview

It may seem unusual to include a small Canadian college in this guide, but the arguments to do so are compelling. First, it is another example of the establishment of a faithful liberal arts college on this continent, emphasizing that there are "born from the crisis" institutions springing up north of the border.

Second, Our Lady Seat of Wisdom Academy has developed a solid curriculum that allows Catholics to get a good three-year education before transferring to another college. It has a transfer history with Franciscan University of Steubenville and Redeemer University College, a Christian university in Ontario. Surprisingly, such benefits are delivered at a very, very modest cost.

The academy grew out of a dream of homeschooling mothers for affordable Catholic higher education in this area of Ontario, a little more than two hours north of Ottawa in the Madawaska Valley. This college was started so that area young people could receive an education without having to travel thousands of miles or spending large sums of money for higher education.

It opened as a small study center for post-secondary learning in 1999. The following year, it began offering a one-year program of courses, in which a certificate was awarded. The academy later added two- and three-year certificate programs.

QUICK FACTS

Founded: 2000
Type of institution: Micro three-year academy
Setting: Small, rural town
Undergraduate enrollment: 47 full-time, 8 part-time (2006–07 academic year)
Undergraduate cost: $7,850 Canadian (tuition, room and board for 2007–08; that is, U.S. $7,431 as of August 31, 2007)
Undergraduate majors: Five concentrations

FIVE KEY POINTS

1. An example of a solidly Catholic liberal arts institution.

2. Awaiting Canadian accreditation, but has a good transfer history with other colleges.

3. It delivers a quality product at a very low cost.

4. The institution was designed to appeal to homeschooling families.

5. The spiritual life is rich and is celebrated in a strongly Catholic community.

The vision of Our Lady Seat of Wisdom Academy is to award a four-year bachelor's degree. The academy is actively preparing for accreditation and hopes to receive it within a few years. But for now, up to three years of credits can be transferred to other colleges. Due to Canadian state control of higher education, the OLSWA is not allowed to call itself a college until is granted government accreditation.

According to the academy's former executive director, John Paul Meenan, "Our vision is to be a locally based Canadian college, not 'Steubenville North,' but at the same time, we welcome students from the United States and elsewhere." There are no limits on the number of Americans, either from the academy or the Canadian government; currently, about 10 percent are Americans. A number of faculty members are Americans.

The academy is located in a former convent on the grounds of St. Hedwig's Parish in Barry's Bay. It also uses parish space for additional classroom and dining facilities, and leases a number of local residences where students live together in small households.

For the 2007–08 academic year, the academy enrolled 65 full-time and five part-time students. They seem to grow about 15 students per year, and their ultimate goal is to have a student body of between 120 and 300. About half of the students have been home-schooled.

These students pursue various certificates. They can receive a basic certificate after one year of study, an associate certificate after two years and a certificate of Christian humanities after three years. One may receive either a general certificate or one with a concentration in any of five areas.

Governance

A nine-member lay board of directors, mostly from the area, governs the academy. They are assisted by an academic senate, which shares the vision of a liberal arts education faithful to the teachings of the Catholic Church. There also is a 16-member advisory board, which includes six priests as well as the noted Catholic novelist and artist Michael O'Brien.

The academy's executive director—it is the equivalent position of a college president—implements the mission of the academy. Until recently, the executive director was John Paul Meenan, 39, who majored in neuroscience at the University of Western Ontario and then studied at Toronto's Oratory of St. Philip Neri. His position came about as a result of a retreat he made to the Barry's Bay area in 1999. We note that he admires the views of Cardinal Newman regarding a university.

Mr. Meenan left his administrative position in July 2007, but will continue to teach at the academy. The interim executive director for the 2007–08 academic year is Dr. Christine Schintgen, who is chairman of the literature department and has a D.Phil. degree from Oxford University. A search for a permanent replacement is underway.

Mr. Meenan told us, "We are eager to and do have our diocesan bishop's support and approval." In fact, in the academy's promotional material, former Bishop Richard Smith of the Diocese of Pembroke writes, "I am delighted to have Our Lady Seat of Wisdom Academy present and operating in the Diocese of Pembroke. The devotion and fidelity of students and faculty to the Church and Her teachings is impressive and inspiring." A new bishop was named in July 2007.

Public Identity

The academy's vision statement notes, "Under the mantle of Our Lady, Seat of Wisdom, we will provide a vibrant Catholic liberal arts education that integrates faith and reason in all of its disciplines, embraces Divine Revelation and is rooted in the teachings of the Roman Catholic Church."

This commitment was reinforced in interviews with representatives of the institution. Former executive director Meenan said that the academy "seeks to provide a truly Catholic, liberal education, one which sets the mind 'free' from the shackles of ignorance, so that our students can integrate the truths of both Faith and reason in seamless harmony."

Dr. Schintgen added emphatically, "Our Catholic identity is absolutely essential and is our reason for existing. Nothing else is more important." Perhaps not surprising given this faithfulness, the Apostolic Nuncio to Canada, Archbishop Luigi Ventura, celebrated the 2006 graduation Mass and delivered the keynote speech at the graduation luncheon.

Spiritual Life

The spiritual life revolves around St. Hedwig's Parish across the street from the school building. Most of the students are reported to attend the 7:30 a.m. daily Mass there. There also are two Sunday Masses offered. Students are active in parish life, serving as readers, altar servers, members of the choir, participants in Wednesday evening adoration and twice-weekly confessions. There also is the nearby parish of St. Lawrence O'Toole. All reports underscore a very vibrant prayer life on campus.

The academy arranges a couple of retreats each year, and it has invited nuns from religious communities to direct day-long, on-campus retreats on Saturdays. There are two pilgrimages each year, which have included one in the fall to St. Mary's Church and Grotto, which is a two and one-half mile walk away in Wilno, Ontario, where the first Polish-Catholic settlers lived; and in the spring to The Martyr's Shrine in Midland, Ontario.

The academy is situated in a flourishing Catholic area of Ontario, where three towns with a strong Catholic presence are within a half-hour from Barry's Bay. "This pocket of Catholicism," according to one faculty member, "draws people from all parts of Canada."

One significant factor in this Catholic enclave is Madonna House in Combermere, about 20 minutes from Our Lady Seat of Wisdom Academy. This is a lay community (with priests) whose members take promises of poverty, chastity and obedience while carrying out an apostolate of service to those in material and spiritual need. Madonna House, which draws visitors from Canada and abroad, was founded by Catherine Doherty, a 20th-century Russian-born aristocrat who aided the poor both in the United States and Canada.

A priest from Madonna House serves as the academy's chaplain. He celebrates a Mass every other Monday at 5 p.m. at the campus. On alternate Mondays, Mass is offered by a priest of the Companions of the Cross order.

Catholicism in the Classroom

OLSWA trains students to think and learn in the Catholic intellectual tradition and to be able to transport their knowledge and credits to other colleges to successfully complete their work.

Successfully completing three years of academic work, taking 96 credits, qualifies the student for a Certificate of Christian Humanities. Students have transferred to Franciscan University of Steubenville and Ave Maria College when it was in Michigan. In 2007 four students who had attended OLSWA graduated from Redeemer University College, about 250 miles away in Ancaster, Ontario.

One instructor said, "I've never heard any student say they thought their years here were wasted, even though they may need to transfer to another school to receive a four-year degree."

In the first year, students take year-long courses in "Christian Doctrine," "Church History," "Introduction to Philosophy," "Freshman Writing," Latin and either chorus or "Liturgy for the Laity."

In the second year, courses include two more in Scripture and two more in philosophy, including "Thomistic Thought." Among other courses is intermediate Latin. Students can take electives and concentrate in five areas: liberal arts, literature, history, philosophy and theology.

Among the courses that seem to be popular are "Thomistic Thought" and "Magisterial Thought." In the course on the Magisterium, students read key Church documents.

All nine full-time faculty members are Catholics, and none is a dissenter. One faculty member said, "We have small classes, and students have so many opportunities to learn from their professors by asking questions, speaking with them after class, at lunch, etc."

Michael O'Brien, the novelist and artist whose living room was the venue of the academy's first organizational meeting, has written of the faculty's commitment on his website. He said, "One of the significant aspects of it [OLSWA] is the spiritual principle of sacrifice. Our full-time professors, as well as associate and adjunct professors, all receive a pittance of a salary. Most have taught here for several years at about 25 percent the salary a professor would receive at any other college or university."

Residential Life

Most students live in seven single-sex residence houses. Female students reside at the Edith Stein, Little Flower, Rose and Siena houses. Males are in the St. Francis and Ignatius houses. The seventh house, which is for women, is not yet named. Each household has six to eight students along with one residence assistant, who is an older student. Meals, formerly provided in the school dining room, moved to St. Hedwig's parish in the fall of 2007.

Chastity is encouraged through these households, as is a "moderate" dress code and an encouragement that students hold off on dating during the first year of school.

There also are women's nights and men's nights, where students gather with others of their gender to discuss topics of interest and also to enjoy each other's company. The idea, we are told, is for them to grow and mature in their femininity and masculinity in healthy ways.

All students have chores assigned on a weekly basis. These include such duties as helping with the dinner dishes, sweeping the floors of the classrooms and shoveling snow. Students spend approximately three or four hours a week in this service.

Student Activities

There are few student organizations at this small academy. One is the Don Bosco Drama Club, which has produced several plays including *A Man for All Seasons*, about the life of Saint Thomas More. They hope to establish a pro-life club, which would complement their participation in the annual Canadian March for Life in Ottawa each May.

Social activities are mostly student initiated. They include things like going to sports events such as a hockey game, swimming, canoeing, hiking, movies or planning a party at one of the households. One instructor said, "Because we are so small, we are like a family," and many of the activities reflect that.

The Community

Barry's Bay is known as the "Polish Capital of Canada." Kashubian people from north-central Poland founded the town in the mid-19th century, and their descendents and other ethnic Catholics make up a majority of the 1,200 residents.

The area is lovely, scenic and clean. The main industries are lumber and tourism, but agriculture also plays an important role. Among local points of interest are the Algonquin Provincial Park, which offers many outdoor activities, and a park dedicated to Janusz Zurakowski, a Canadian aviator and hero.

St. Francis Memorial Hospital is located in the town. There are no significant airports nearby; Americans flying to Barry's Bay are likely to use Ottawa International Airport, a two and one-half-hour drive away, or Toronto Pearson International Airport—Canada's most important airport—four hours away. Route 17, known as the Trans-Canada Highway, is located not far from the town.

The Bottom Line

We are pleased to recommend Our Lady Seat of Wisdom Academy as an option for faithful Catholics. This small institution, committed to its motto of *Veritas vos Liberabit* ("The Truth will set you free"), provides a wonderful curriculum at a breathtakingly low cost.

This academy can help students get acclimated to college life, strengthen their faith formation and then move on to another solid Catholic college to finish their studies. The opportunity to grow in such an intellectual and spiritual environment is enhanced by the beauty of studying in this rich Ontario valley. This is an educational institution that should not be overlooked.

Southern Catholic College

Dawsonville, Georgia

www.southerncatholic.org

Overview

The city of Atlanta, the long-time symbol of the New South and one of the largest cities in the region, has been a Protestant bastion. But in recent years, the number of Catholics in that metropolitan area has increased along with the overall growth in population. In fact, the Catholic population within the confines of the Archdiocese of Atlanta more than doubled from 1990 to 2004.

Thomas Clements, a Catholic business-man, told us, "In the last 20 years, 40 new Catholic churches have been built in the Atlanta archdiocese. In the last 10 years, five new Catholic high schools have opened." But there was no Catholic college in the state of Georgia.

As a result, he and several like-minded people decided there was a need for a Catholic college in the Atlanta archdiocese. Southern Catholic College was launched in 2000 and opened its doors in September 2005 with its inaugural class of 72 students. Clements said, "We are working to build this college at no cost to the archdiocese in order to provide a Catholic higher education for our growing Catholic population."

The college is located one hour north of Atlanta on a 100-acre campus outside the small town of Dawsonville on the site of the former Gold Creek Country Club. The attractive campus, with includes a lake, waterfall and residential villas, attracted students from 20 states in its second year as the student body increased by 60 percent. Plans call for

QUICK FACTS

Founded: 2000 (first students in 2005)
Type of institution: Small liberal arts college
Setting: Rural
Undergraduate enrollment: 124 (2006–07 academic year)
Total undergraduate cost: $24,125 (tuition, room and board for 2007–08)
Undergraduate majors: Seven

FIVE KEY POINTS

1. The college is fully supportive of the Magisterium and *Ex corde Ecclesiae.*

2. There is an extensive core curriculum that reflects the Catholic intellectual tradition.

3. It seeks to support Catholic life in its archdiocese and region.

4. The new chaplain is a former archdiocesan director of vocations.

5. The attractive campus is located at a former golf resort outside of a small town.

the student body to reach 500 over the mid-term and to eventually rise to 3,000, drawing young men and women from throughout the nation.

Perhaps the two factors that have most accounted for its growth are a firm commitment to Catholic teachings and a strong core curriculum. The college administration is strongly supportive of *Ex corde Ecclesiae* and enjoys a warm relationship with the archdiocese.

The core curriculum reflects a traditional liberal arts program in the Catholic intellectual tradition. Students need at least 65 credits, more than half of the overall undergraduate program, in specified courses in six disciplines. These include six to 12 credits in a foreign language.

According to the college, the integrated core curriculum "offers an internally coherent program of required courses designed to help students soar on 'the two wings on which the human spirit rises to the contemplation of Truth, namely faith and reason'" (this refers to Pope John Paul II's encyclical *Fides et Ratio*).

There are seven majors: business, English, history, integrated sciences, philosophy, psychology and sacred theology. To date, the most popular majors have been business, sacred theology and psychology. The college also has a cooperative elementary education program with Brenau University, located about 30 miles away in Gainesville, Georgia.

Fifty-six percent of the college's students last year came from public schools, 32 percent from private schools and 12 percent were homeschooled. The college received pre-accreditation from the American Academy for Liberal Education in May 2007, and full accreditation will not occur until the first class graduates in 2009. The college also plans to seek accreditation from its regional agency, the Southern Association of Colleges and Schools.

Public Identity

Clements told us that when he was working on the bylaws of the college he "wanted it to be as clear as possible that Catholicity is to be the overriding priority." The result was the creation of a five-member board of fellows, whose only role is to evaluate and uphold the Catholic identity of the college.

Every two years, the board reviews the Catholicity of the campus—its curriculum, activities, policies and external manifestations of faith. The board also reviews the appointment of the college president and chaplain. It has purview over the core curriculum, which is considered such an important part of the Catholic identity, according to Clements, that it cannot be changed by the faculty on their own. Among the five members of the board of fellows is retired Atlanta Archbishop John Donoghue.

The college is solidly committed to the Magisterium and stresses that it "consults with the Archbishop of Atlanta regarding the orthodoxy of the Catholic doctrine taught at the College." The college has been embraced by Archbishop Wilton Gregory and his predecessor, Archbishop Donoghue.

Archbishop Gregory has celebrated opening Masses each year. He and Archbishop Donoghue concelebrated the dedication Mass for the chapel in November 2005.

The college has not had many speakers, we are told, but those who have come are faithful to Catholic principles. Among the speakers have been Thomas Woods, author of a well-received 2005 book, *How the Catholic Church*

Built Western Civilization, and Joseph Pearce, a biographer of G. K. Chesterton and Hilaire Belloc.

Governance

A predominantly lay board of trustees governs the college. The 20-member board includes 18 people from Georgia, most of them business leaders. The two religious members are the vicar general of the Archdiocese of Atlanta, Monsignor Luis Zarama, and Father Dennis Dease, president of the University of St. Thomas in St. Paul, Minnesota.

Dr. Jeremiah Ashcroft is the first president and has served since 2001. He previously was president of East Georgia College. Dr. Ashcroft is an *ex officio* member of the board of trustees.

The governance is bolstered by the existence of the board of fellows that, in addition to the duties mentioned above, has veto power over appointments if Catholic identity is at stake.

Spiritual Life

The first building erected on campus was the 120-seat chapel, which has not been named. There is a daily noon Mass Monday through Friday and a 10 a.m. Mass on Saturday and Sunday. According to one professor, "Masses are traditional, upholding the standards of devotional liturgies." It was reported that between 25 and 40 students and about half the faculty attend Mass daily. No classes are held during Mass times so students can attend.

Confessions are held four times weekly and by appointment. Adoration of the Blessed Sacrament is held every Monday evening, and recitation of the Rosary takes place on Thursday evening. A number of students also get involved in youth ministry work at local parishes, we are told, including Christ Redeemer Catholic Church, which is located 10 miles away in Dawsonville.

Archbishop Gregory appointed Father Brian Higgins college chaplain in June 2007. He previously was archdiocesan director of vocations. One faculty member said, "Many of our students are from the local area, and his work at Southern Catholic will be very helpful to those students who want to remain and increase their involvements with local parishes."

One student group is Apostolic Works, which undertakes service projects, supports pro-life activities and engages in Bible study. Students have attended the March for Life both in Washington, D.C., and Atlanta. Since 80 percent of the student body is Catholic, this is a group that should have broad appeal.

Catholicism in the Classroom

"A college is primarily defined by its academic dimension," one Southern Catholic professor told us, "and Southern Catholic is squarely rooted in a Catholic liberal arts tradition. Our core curriculum is based upon the Catholic principle and tradition of faith and reason working together."

The theology requirement is satisfied by taking three courses, "Introduction to Catholicism and Sacred Theology," "Introduction to Sacred Scripture" and "History of the Catholic Church and Thought." All theology courses are taught from within the Magisterium. Theology professors have the *mandatum*; at the moment, there is only one full-time theology professor and two adjunct professors who are priests of the Archdiocese of Atlanta.

There are three required philosophy courses, including "Philosophy of God and Creature." Among the impressive elective philosophy courses is one on "Love and Responsibility," an issue of particular importance to college-age students.

Among other requirements are four history and political science courses. Another professor told us of these courses: "They have a focus upon the history of ideas, on the role of religion in general and on the role of the Church in particular.

"In this past year [2006–07 academic year], many writings on Pope Benedict XVI on moral and religious foundations of political life were included. We also offer courses on such topics as 'History of the Papacy.'"

From our interviews, it was clear that a Catholic understanding of the human person permeated the core curriculum. In fact, one of the required philosophy courses is "Understanding the Human Person," which is undergirded by the Catholic view of the dignity of all people.

In the area of natural sciences, there is a required course on the principles of scientific investigation. According to one professor, "Students are made aware of the type of knowledge science discovers and the limits of it. We try to show that scientific knowledge is one manifestation of reason, but that objective knowledge in the realm of morals is accessible through natural reason."

Even in the more specialized areas, such as the business curriculum, students are required to take a course on values, in this case "Business Leadership, Values, and Society." Here, we are told, ethics and the question of treatment of humans in the for-profit arena are raised. A one-credit course in "Leadership Studies" is part of the core curriculum.

About 75 percent of the full-time faculty and all in the humanities area are Catholic. All interviewees spoke well of the faculty, but two names consistently emerged as exemplary teachers: Dr. Kelly Bowring in theology and dean of spiritual mission, and Dr. Herbert Hartmann in philosophy—formerly of Thomas Aquinas College.

As part of the college's academic support program, there is a peer tutor program.

Student Activities

Besides Apostolic Works, there are 13 other student groups, covering such areas as art, dance, debate, drama, and liturgical music and choir. There also is a student newspaper and club athletic teams in cross country, golf, soccer and tennis.

Since the college is still new and has had only two years of students, social traditions are still developing. Among the recent student-driven activities has been the screening of classical movies. Students are able to mingle at the Campus Center and the Campus Coffee House. A 27-hole golf course abuts the campus.

Residential Life

The campus is situated on a former golf resort, and students live in nine villas that once formed part of it. Students are grouped three to each room with its own bathroom, and there generally are four rooms per floor. These residential facilities are near capacity and there are already plans to expand them.

Each villa is restricted to a single sex, and there is no visitation by a member of the opposite sex at any time. A resident assistant is assigned to each villa. Chastity is encouraged by the college rules, and faculty members talk

called during the annual Moonshine Festival, which has been held in Dawsonville every fall for the past 40 years.

Within the county is Amicalola Falls State Park, which features a 729-foot waterfall, the tallest of its kind in the eastern United States. Hiking opportunities exist along the Appalachian Trail, the 2,175-mile challenge that begins (or ends) eight miles from the falls and extends to central Maine. Boating is available at Lake Lanier.

Georgia Route 400 is the main artery from Dawsonville to the state capital of Atlanta, about 60 miles away. Atlanta has a population of 483,000 and is the hub of a 5.5 million-person metropolitan area, which has nearly tripled since 1970.

Atlanta has been an historic city, playing an important role in the Civil War as well as the civil rights struggle, and there are a number of reminders of this heritage. The 1996 Summer Olympics was held in Atlanta, and the remaining Centennial Olympic Park is an important part of the downtown.

Among the many cultural and entertainment opportunities in Atlanta are four major-league sports franchises: baseball (Braves), football (Falcons), basketball (Hawks) and hockey (Thrashers). Southern Catholic has sponsored a number of trips for students to Atlanta, including to sporting events.

The Atlanta region is served by Hartsfield-Jackson International Airport, which served more passengers than any other airport in the world each year between 1998 and 2006. Amtrak also services the city, and there is a vast network of highways that makes the city accessible from every direction.

about it in lectures. No major problems have surfaced in the residential units.

Students have access to the Neighborhood Health Care Center, which is 10 miles from campus. Chestatee Regional Hospital is located in Dahlonega, 14 miles away, and the larger Northside Hospital-Forysth is in Cumming, 25 miles south of the college.

The Community

Nearby Dawsonville had only 619 people in the 2000 census. It is the county seat of Dawson County, which has about 21,000 residents. The area has a NASCAR heritage, and it is re-

The Bottom Line

Southern Catholic College is another example of the crop of small liberal arts colleges created to meet the needs of Catholic students in recent years. Although it initially will appeal to those in the Atlanta area and nearby, its mission is likely to attract students from throughout the South, if not the nation.

The formula here is simple and yet rather uncommon among many Catholic colleges today: Be faithful to the Church and its teachings, and immerse young men and women in the great Catholic intellectual tradition. This is a winning formula, and there is every reason to believe it will prosper in the years ahead.

Southern Catholic deserves a look for those students who seek this traditional education in a region that is experiencing dynamic growth and change.

Wyoming Catholic College

Lander, Wyoming

www.wyomingcatholiccollege.com

Overview

There may be no more beautiful place for faithful Catholics to pursue an undergraduate education than the brand-new Wyoming Catholic College in the Rocky Mountains. Situated by the Wind River Mountain Range and the Popo Agie River, the college will be a delight for outdoor enthusiasts. It's such an impressive site that the 42-year-old National Outdoor Leadership School is located nearby.

But there is more here than an idyllic setting. When it opened its doors to the first class in September 2007, Wyoming Catholic embraced a Great Books and classical curriculum strongly permeated by orthodox Catholicism. It aspires to provide the quality of education evident at Thomas Aquinas College in California.

To do so, the college is emphasizing seven key objectives: Catholic community, spiritual formation, liberal arts education, integrated curriculum, great and good books, immersion in the outdoors and excellent teaching.

One administrator told us, "The Catholic identity is the main reason we are here. John Paul II in *Ex corde Ecclesiae* says that the purpose of Catholic education is to serve the Truth, and to bring students to the Truth."

"Since the vast majority of schools are no longer even attempting to do that," he added, "and since it is not a mere question of 'culture' but of salvation and happiness, we feel justified in founding a college dedicated above all

QUICK FACTS

Founded: 2005 (first students in 2007)
Type of institution: Micro liberal arts college
Setting: Rural
Undergraduate enrollment: 35 (2007–08 academic year)
Total undergraduate cost: $19,500 (tuition, room and board for 2007–08)
Undergraduate majors: One

FIVE KEY POINTS

1. Strongly orthodox Catholic.
2. Emphasizes a Great Books and classical liberal education.
3. Located in a beautiful setting in the Rocky Mountains.
4. Seeks to capitalize on wilderness environment.
5. As with all new colleges, accreditation takes time.

---

to joyful and wholehearted pursuit and passing on of natural and supernatural truth."

This mission in the wilderness is located in Lander, which has a population of 7,000 people in west-central Wyoming. The area, as perhaps befits its western image, is sparsely settled; the nearest large city is Billings, Montana, about 200 miles north. Denver is the closest major metropolitan area, and it is a five- to six-hour drive.

The college's initial location is Holy Rosary Church, which provided religious, classroom and dining facilities. The six-credit equestrian program is offered at Central Wyoming College, a half-hour away.

A 14-square mile parcel of land has been acquired nearby which will eventually serve as the permanent campus. A breathtaking rendering of the future campus is shown on the WCC website. At the entrance will be the chapel followed by academic, recreational and residential precincts.

The first-year class has 35 students, 16 males and 19 females housed in separate apartment facilities. They come from 23 states ranging from Vermont and Georgia to California and Washington. The college expects to eventually enroll 400 students.

These students will study a prescribed four-year program. Eight Catholic theology and five philosophy courses are required. Many of the other courses have Catholic overtones. Graduates will all receive the same Bachelor of Arts degree.

All new colleges need to go through an accrediting process, which takes several years. Wyoming Catholic is applying for accreditation from The American Association for Liberal Education. Among colleges pre-accredited or accredited by the AALE are Ave Maria University, Magdalen College, Thomas Aquinas College, The Thomas More College of Liberal Arts and the University of Dallas. The college is also exploring accreditation with the North Central Association Commission on Accreditation and School Improvement.

Governance

Wyoming Catholic is a lay-run, independent college with a strong connection to the local bishop who will always be chairman of the six-member board. Bishop David Ricken of the Diocese of Cheyenne, Wyoming, helped start the college and bestowed his Apostolic Blessing in 2005.

Also on the board is Father Robert Cook, the college president, who has been a practicing attorney, pro-life advocate and monk. Among the members of the academic advisory board is Father James Schall, S.J., a noted scholar and professor at Georgetown University.

Public Identity

Everyone associated with building the college is a strong Catholic, committed to vigorously promoting its religious identity. Father Cook told us, "We will encourage full participation in the liturgical celebration of Mass, Rosary and Adoration by all students all the time. We intend to do everything we can so that upon graduation, the students will leave stronger in the faith than when they came."

The first year of the college was launched with a Convocation Mass concelebrated by Bishop Ricken on September 3, 2007. Classes began the following day, and former U.S. Secretary of Education William Bennett visited the campus on September 5.

In general, there will be four outside speakers per academic year, making their presentations on Catholic feast days: All Saints; Immaculate Conception; Our Lady, Seat of Wisdom—the patroness' feast day (February 4); and Annunciation. All speakers will be faithful to Catholic teachings.

The speakers for this 2007–08 Guest Lecture Series have been announced. The series will begin with Father Frederick Miller of Mount St. Mary's Seminary, who will speak on *"Sedes Sapientiae*: Our Lady, Seat of Wisdom," and end with Dr. Dominic Aquila of the University of St. Thomas, who will talk about "What Music Can Mean to Our Living: The Rise and Fall of Classical Music in American Radio."

Bishop Ricken sees the college fitting in with the missionary role of the diocese, which is only 10 percent Catholic. He told us, "We hope that some of the graduates of Wyoming Catholic College, with good formation there, will consider staying in Wyoming and become trained catechists and teachers for our diocese."

Spiritual Life

The religious life for the foreseeable future will take place at the Holy Rosary Church. Daily Mass attendance is encouraged, for, as theology professor Peter Kwasniewski said, "the Mass is the center of all that we are and will be."

The parish's pastor, Father Randall Oswald, also serves as chaplain of the college. A full range of religious activities will be offered. In addition, students will be taught about prayer through the study of *Lectio Divina*, St. John of the Cross and Teresa of Avila.

Catholicism in the Classroom

All faculty members must agree not to undermine Church teaching or the pope's authority. Catholics will profess their faith and recite an Oath of Fidelity. The five-paragraph oath, drafted by the Vatican's Sacred Congregation for the Doctrine of the Faith, includes this statement: "I shall follow and foster the common discipline of the whole church and shall look after the observance of all ecclesiastical laws, especially those which are contained in the Code of Canon Law."

All faculty members are reported to be supportive of WCC's spiritual vision. Two of them are non-Catholics, but one has already announced she will enter the Church. Two-thirds of the faculty will be Catholics.

Theology professors will have the *mandatum*. And, according to Father Cook, all professors "have been advised and will teach in such a way that the teachings of the Magisterium will permeate their teaching, regardless of subject."

In addition to the large complement of theology and philosophy courses, students will take eight courses in humanities; eight in trivium or reading, writing and speaking; four in Latin; four in art history; three each in science and mathematics; and two in music and in horsemanship.

The goal of this study is a classical education. According to Father Cook, "We want our students to graduate being able to find joy in learning, able to learn, think critically and clearly in speech and writing, being good people that will have joy in life with these skills being led by our Lord, and doing it well. We want a fully educated human being."

Student Activities

Student activities will develop with the college. Significant emphasis will be placed on outdoor activities, taking advantage of a nearby wilderness area, state park and national forest. Horseback riding opportunities and programs with the National Outdoor Leadership School will be available.

The college also is going to have two student religious musical groups, a liturgical choir and the WCC Chorale. Classic movie nights and traditional dances also are envisioned. Other informal social activities are expected.

Residential Life

Until the permanent campus is built, students will reside in gender-separated apartments.

Opposite-sex visitation will be prohibited, as will drugs and alcohol. The college will have a strict technology policy: No cell phones, Internet or television will be allowed in the residences. Internet access will be provided in certain areas.

The Community

Lander is a small town that might be challenging for students used to the hubbub of urban areas. The obvious appeal is to young people who have a passion for outdoor activities, including hiking, fishing and horseback riding.

The crime rate is below the national average and reflects property, rather than violent, crime. One statistic that is well above the norm is snowfall; Wyoming winters are severe but they do provide for an abundance of winter sports, including skiing. A notable ski resort is Jackson Hole, which along with the Grand Teton and Yellowstone National Parks, is less than 200 miles from Lander.

The town has an 81-bed Lander Valley Medical Center that is supplemented by the Riverton Memorial Hospital, about a half-hour away.

Riverton, only slightly larger than Lander, also has a regional airport with two daily flights into and out from Denver International Airport. The Denver airport is one of the largest and busiest in the world and will likely provide the best access to out-of-state students traveling to campus. For road travelers, the east-west Interstate 80 is not far from Lander.

The Bottom Line

The motto of the fledgling Wyoming Catholic College is "Wisdom in God's Country." This college, which seeks to provide a classical Catholic education under the wide-open skies of the West, is likely to appeal to students seeking a different kind of undergraduate experience.

One faculty member there perhaps best characterized to us the issue to be posed to high-school college seekers. She said, "I would say that this is an opportunity to be a pioneer, a once-in-a-lifetime opportunity. If I were 18 years old now, I would be very interested."

She continued, "The opportunity to get in on the ground floor of an institution is really something to be seized upon. The students who come now and in the next few years are going to be the co-creators, actively involved in something that is going to make a significant contribution to Catholic colleges in America."

Fighting the Tide

Aquinas College

Nashville, Tennessee

www.aquinas-tn.edu

Overview

Nashville lives large in the American psyche as "Music City," the long-time center of country and, more recently, Christian music. But this growing capital city in north central Tennessee harbors a number of other institutions that also impact the region, if not the nation.

One such institution, a small and emerging gem in west Nashville five miles from downtown, is the 92-acre Aquinas College. Founded by the Dominican Sisters of the Congregation of Saint Cecilia, it is an oasis of Catholic liberal arts education in an area with a miniscule three percent Catholic population. Indeed, Nashville's strong Protestant heritage has also earned it "The Buckle of the Bible Belt" title.

The sisters, popularly known as the Nashville Dominicans, came to the city in 1860 at the invitation of Bishop James Whalen, who asked them to educate girls in the arts and music. St. Cecilia Academy grew into a teacher preparatory school with a relationship with The Catholic University of America in the early 20th century.

By 1961 it became a junior college and then a four-year college 33 years later. The sisters also operate a coed elementary-middle school and a girls' high school on the campus grounds, whose focal point is a large mansion, the White House, which houses administrative offices.

The order, which has a special charism of education, operates 32 schools (with one more

on the way) in 17 dioceses. Eight of these schools are in the Diocese of Nashville, where the Motherhouse is located. Aquinas College is the only college of the 147-year-old order.

The sisters belong to one of the few orders of women religious enjoying phenomenal growth. Noted for their love of traditional religious life, their contemplative focus prepares them for this active education apostolate. They also are known for their Catholic faithfulness and commitment to the Magisterium.

Under the presidential leadership of Sister Thomas Aquinas, O.P., who took her religious name from her alma mater of Thomas Aquinas College (California), Aquinas College has promoted its Catholic identity, strengthened its curriculum and expanded its academic program.

The college is on the move: enrollment doubled between 2001 and 2006, and further expansion is anticipated when residential facilities are built. Currently, all students are commuters.

What is particularly impressive is that only 20 percent of the student body is Catholic, but that has not deterred the president in pursuing her vision of making *Ex corde Ecclesiae* a touchstone for the college. In a 2002 Thomas Aquinas College newsletter she is quoted: "We want to do the right thing, rather than follow some path of least resistance."

Although Catholics are a minority among students and comprise only 50 percent of the faculty, one college official told us "there is no non-Catholic faculty member in the philosophy, literature, theology or department departments. All non-Catholic faculty are at least Christian."

As a junior college, Aquinas provided training in criminal justice and dental hygiene through associate degree programs. The first bachelor's programs were in teacher education and nursing. Today, the college is moving into liberal arts fields, adding theology and English majors in the fall of 2006. More are anticipated, and this comes at a time when many colleges are migrating from the liberal arts and into more career-oriented programs.

In addition to these majors, the college for some time has also offered undergraduate degrees in business and interdisciplinary studies—as well as continuing its work in teacher preparation and nursing. Minors are available in English, history, philosophy, psychology and theology. Associate degree programs are offered in nursing and liberal arts.

Aquinas also appeals to older, working students through its PRIMETIME program, which is available on its main Dominican campus and two smaller campuses devoted exclusively to this program. PRIMETIME degrees are available in business administration and management information systems.

Nearly 80 percent of the student body is female, which makes it distinct from other colleges in this guide. Perhaps this figure reflects the historical commitment that the college has made to nursing and K–12 education, two careers long favored by women over men.

Aquinas is fully accredited by its regional body, the Southern Association of Colleges and Schools. It received its initial accreditation in 1971.

Governance

The Dominican Sisters of the Congregation of Saint Cecilia owns and governs the college.

Sister Thomas Aquinas has been president since 2002. In addition to being a supporter of *Ex corde Ecclesiae*, she is interested in strengthening the curriculum in the Catholic intellectual tradition.

In August 2007, the college announced that Sister Thomas Aquinas would be on an academic sabbatical during 2007–08. In her absence, Sister Mary Peter Muehlenkamp, O.P., a lawyer who has taught in Catholic elementary schools, is serving as president pro tem.

Public Identity

The various statements issued by the college emphasize its Catholic identity and, impressively, emphasize routes to salvation.

In its mission statement, for example, it is noted: "Faculty and staff seek to make students aware that a relationship exists between human culture and the message of salvation. Thus, the mission of Aquinas College is to bring this message of salvation to bear on ethical, social, political, religious and cultural issues."

This theme is reinforced in discussing various programs and even the goals of the library, which provides "services that illuminate the importance of the message of salvation for moral development, intellectual achievement and personal growth." Such explicit, across-the-board commentary on the link between education and salvation is rare and welcome.

By all accounts, Sister Thomas Aquinas has revitalized the institution and its Catholic mission. In addition to the academic developments, she was responsible for obtaining a full-time Catholic chaplain. Also, there is an active faculty development program where Catholic teachings are discussed monthly.

We expect these initiatives to continue under Sister Mary Peter. She has said, "Many exciting changes have happened in recent years, and many more are in our plans."

The presence of the Dominican sisters underscores the college's Catholic identity as does its modest speakers programs, which include a semi-annual Aquinas Lecture and a Dominican Campus Lecture series. There also is a campus Holy Spirit Mass in the fall and a St. Thomas Aquinas Mass in the spring.

Among former students at Aquinas College is Bishop David Choby of the Diocese of Nashville. He attended the-then junior college in the mid-1960s before moving on to the seminary. He also has taught moral theology at the college and is a strong supporter of the congregation and the college.

Spiritual Life

The 50-seat St. Jude's Chapel is the center of the campus' spiritual life. With the addition of a reported "top notch" full-time chaplain, more activities have resulted. There is now a daily Mass which is "traditional in every instance" and varies from vernacular Masses to some with Latin portions.

The chapel is open 13-and-a-half-hours a day, allowing for a variety of spiritual programs, including twice weekly confessions and twice yearly penance services; weekly Rosary and an annual living Rosary; weekly Adoration; and Lenten Stations of the Cross. We were told that the sisters and faculty encourage students to visit the chapel. There are plans to build a larger chapel.

The campus ministry is involved in various pro-life and social justice activities. Students pray at abortion clinics and a Cemetery of the Innocent, where crosses representing aborted children have been erected.

Among the other student organizations is the Frassati Society, which promotes the Beatitudes; Blessed Pier Giorgio Frassati was an early 20th-century Dominican tertiary who exemplified the Beatitudes. There also is a weekly student discussion group that is similar to the popular "Theology on Tap" programs around the country.

In October 2006, the college hosted a "Teens with Christ" weekend retreat for eighth-through-10th graders. It was a project of the Dominican Sisters and the diocese; Bishop Choby celebrated both Masses of the retreat and participants heard talks on chastity, vocations and other topics.

Catholicism in the Classroom

The Dominican Sisters state that their mission in Catholic education is "to provide students with the freedom of a liberal arts education so that with the development of skills and a strong academic foundation they may fulfill their God-given vocation."

The college tries to integrate the teachings of the Church into all of its programs. According to one administrator, "The school is working to do a better job emphasizing what theology and philosophy have to say about other disciplines."

In the business program, for example, support for a free-market economy is complemented by a desire for "Christian moral constraints." Students in the popular nursing program are taught about the Church's teach-

ings in this important area. As the director of the associate degree in nursing program told us, "We give students the tools to help their patients make the right moral decisions."

The nursing department has had guest speakers who reinforce the moral nature of the curriculum. Among these have been Brother Ignatius Perkins, O.P., a dean and nursing professor at Spalding University, and Sister Renee Mirkes, head of the moral and ethics department at Pope Paul VI Institute in Omaha, Nebraska.

All of the theology faculty, we are told, have received the *mandatum*—in fact, they all "jumped at the opportunity," according to one college official. Moral theology courses are reported to be especially good.

Eight sisters teach at Aquinas. They and their lay counterparts, Catholic and non-Catholic, "not only don't contradict the Magisterium but students are led to see that the teachings of the Church touch on all parts of their lives," according to one Aquinas administrator.

While graduation requirements vary slightly from discipline to discipline, the Bachelor of Arts curriculum is indicative. Here students take slightly more than half of their total credit hours, 65, in a core that runs the gamut of the traditional liberal arts curriculum. Three specific philosophy courses are required and students can select from a range of theology courses to satisfy a two-course requirement. Two foreign language courses and one computer course also are mandated.

The college makes an effort to ease the challenge of the first year for students through its Aquinas College Cares about Every Student's Success (ACCESS) program. It is a required program of mentoring, tutoring and advising for them and for other new students.

Student Activities

There is a Student Activities Board that sponsors speakers and other events. There are about 10 organizations that include the Frassati Society, the Salvation Army Angel Tree program, groups for student nurses and prospective teachers, Aquinas Singers, a business fraternity and a classics club.

Among campus events scheduled for fall 2007 is a dramatic presentation, *Therese, the Story of a Soul: A One-Person Play on the Life of St. Therese of Lisieux*, at the St. Cecilia Theatre.

The college, which once successfully competed on an intercollegiate basis as part of the National Junior College Athletic Association, currently does not field athletic teams.

One faculty member, strongly supportive of the college, told us that social interactions were limited. She said, "This is a commuter college with few opportunities for students to 'hang out' and develop friendships with each other."

Residential Life

Some of the dynamics of the college might change when residential facilities are built. It is our understanding that the building of the first residence hall by fall 2009 is at the top of the college's strategic plan. According to Sister Thomas Aquinas, such expansion will allow the college to attract Catholics from other parts of the country.

Students have access to St. Thomas Hospital, which is next to the college. The Daughters of Charity started the facility in 1898, and it is now a comprehensive, 541-bed hospital.

The Community

Nashville is one of the most vibrant cities of the upper South. Its population recently exceeded the 600,000 mark and is growing fast. In addition to historical ties to the country music industry, Nashville has a big health care sector, including serving as the home of the behemoth Hospital Corporation of America.

The city offers many cultural, social and entertainment opportunities. There is, of course, the venerable Grand Ole Opry, with its Saturday night performances, but there also are National Football League (Tennessee Titans) and National Hockey League (Nashville Predators) teams to follow.

Nashville is a transportation hub, which includes the Nashville International Airport, a hub for Southwest Airlines and host to other major carriers. Three major national highways, Interstates 24, 40 and 65, serve the city.

The Bottom Line

Aquinas College is a small college with a proud local tradition, particularly in areas such as nursing and teaching. With several promising initiatives underway, it is poised to expand its curriculum and attract students from beyond the Nashville area.

The fact that the city and state are so overwhelmingly Protestant does not deter the college from living its Catholic identity.

Even with a student body of only 20 percent Catholics, Aquinas College embraces *Ex corde Ecclesiae*, making it a cause for celebration in a changing South.

This is a college worth considering both for students in Tennessee and increasingly for those around the nation who are looking for the careful attention and dynamic spirit that the Dominican sisters provide to faithful education.

Belmont Abbey College

Belmont, North Carolina

www.belmontabbeycollege.edu

Overview

Benedictine monks migrated from Pennsylvania to Gaston County in south central North Carolina in 1876 and began an education ministry that eventually became Belmont Abbey College in 1913. It first granted bachelor's degrees in 1952 and became coed 20 years later.

For most of its existence, the college was a base for quiet evangelization in the midst of the Protestant Bible Belt. Today, it is moving outward a bit more aggressively as the college grows in size and appeals to more students outside the region.

The locale is compelling and offers an opportunity for Belmont Abbey to attract broader interest in a rapidly growing area. Situated in the small town of Belmont, with a population of about 8,700 people, it is only 10 miles west of Charlotte, North Carolina's largest city; the impressive urban skyline is very prominent from the campus.

Charlotte's population has nearly doubled since 1980, and it is today a major banking center and the epicenter of the booming NASCAR motor sport industry. Belmont Abbey has taken advantage of its location by, among other things, establishing a unique undergraduate concentration in motor sports management.

But what distinguishes the college is a revitalized commitment to its Catholic and Benedictine roots, as evidenced by a national advertising campaign called "Got Monks?", which began in October 2006. This has been

QUICK FACTS

Founded: 1876
Type of institution: Small liberal arts college
Setting: Suburban
Undergraduate enrollment: 1,100 (2006–07 academic year)
Undergraduate cost: $28,505 (tuition, room and board for 2007–08)
Undergraduate majors: 20

FIVE KEY POINTS

1. The Benedictine abbey influences the college.

2. Recent initiatives have strengthened the college's Catholic identity.

3. There is an effort to create a Catholic outreach into the local community.

4. An Honors Institute and program allows students a broader Great Books exposure.

5. There is a core curriculum, but it could be enhanced, including in theology.

only one of the initiatives launched by Dr. William Thierfelder, who became college president in 2004.

Dr. Thierfelder, a sports psychologist and former college All-American high jumper and Olympian, has established his priorities as strengthening the college's Catholic identity, emphasizing its academic credentials and promoting athletic opportunities.

Some of these enhancements are embodied in one of the more impressive strategic plans that we have seen in our research on Catholic colleges. It has three components: Catholic and Benedictine goals, liberal arts programs, and efforts to improve overall "excellence and virtue."

Progress has been considerable on the plan, which was launched in 2005. One result of their advertising campaign and the overall strengthening of the college was a 15 percent increase in enrollment among traditional-aged (18- to 22-year-old) students in 2006–07 over the previous year.

Although 43 percent of traditional students are from North Carolina, during this past academic year students came from 34 states and 26 countries as the college expands its appeal to a broader base.

Students become acclimated to Benedictine values through a First Year Symposium and end their work with a capstone Great Books course four years later. They can undertake a more extensive Great Books program through the new Honors Institute, which provides for broader intellectual opportunities as well as a stipend.

There are 20 majors offered, most of which are common programs. About 50 percent of students major in business and accounting and another 30 percent major in education. Among the less common are environmental science, sports management and the motor

sports management program that includes four courses in management and marketing as well as an internship. There is a theology major.

Homeschooled students are welcomed. Part of that support comes from President Thierfelder whose children are homeschooled and who has spoken to homeschooling groups.

Although about 65 percent of the students are "traditional," the college also provides evening and weekend classes in its Adult Degree Program; this is a rapidly growing group, which included 380 students in the 2006–07 academic year. These non-traditional students, similar to the traditional ones, are most concentrated in business and education majors. The college does not have a graduate program.

One other aspect of Belmont Abbey is the arsenal of scholarship programs. Ninety percent of students receive merit-based aid. Among this assistance are stipends for honors students, the Felix Hintemayer Scholarship for student leadership, Benedictine Hospitality Award and the Sport at the Service of the Spirit Scholarship.

Governance

Belmont Abbey College is run by the Southern Benedictine Society, which consists of two separately incorporated entities, Belmont Abbey monastery and the college. The Abbey is the largest donor to the college, which ensures Benedictine influence.

Abbot Placid Solari, O.S.B., who has been abbot since 1999, is a former president and dean of the college. He is currently chancellor of the college and interviews all college hires. The abbot, who is a theologian with a degree in patristics, is reported to be "strongly orthodox."

The abbot also is a member of the college board of trustees, which is largely a lay board including many Charlotte area businesspeople. Of the 38-member board, five are monks, one is a member of the nearby Sisters of Mercy and one is the chancellor of the Diocese of Charlotte. Two members are non-Catholics.

Dr. Thierfelder, a lifelong devout Catholic, was a sports psychologist and president of York Barbell Company before assuming the presidency of the college three years ago. He and his wife are Benedictine oblates, lay followers of the Rule of St. Benedict.

Public Identity

At the heart of Belmont Abbey College is its Benedictine identity, sustained by 20 monks at the Abbey. There is an atmosphere steeped in the Rule of St. Benedict and the values that it reflects. According to Abbot Solari in a Spring 2007 interview in the college's alumni magazine, *Crossroads*, the Benedictine heritage "ensures that the educational approach established and maintained here reflects the Catholic intellectual tradition."

This commitment is reflected in various college documents, including the mission and vision statements. The vision statement, for example, states: "Belmont Abbey finds its center in Jesus Christ. By [H]is light, we grasp the true image and likeness of God which every human person is called to live out."

The college embraced *Ex corde Ecclesiae* when it was issued in 1990, according to one theology faculty member. And at a March 2007 faculty retreat, there was a discussion of the document and how Catholic teachings on the relationship between faith and reason apply to colleges.

A college staff member told us that such objectives were diligently followed in a "quiet, Benedictine way but now we are moving outward." By all accounts, President Thierfelder has had a big impact in helping reshape the college into a more visibly Catholic institution that is increasingly drawing national attention.

This is reflected in the "Got Monks" campaign, which also appears to be helpful in ongoing recruiting for vocations. Three of the five priests ordained in the Diocese of Charlotte in June 2007 were Belmont Abbey College alumni.

There are a number of ways in which the Catholic presence on campus is being strengthened. One is through several new, full-tuition scholarships aimed at attracting Catholic students.

Another is faculty hiring, a matter of some importance since Catholics number just "over 50 percent" of the faculty, according to one senior staff member. The same staff member told us, "In the last three years, almost all of the faculty hires have been Catholics. In addition to the president, all the vice presidents are Catholic. All the job postings stress the Catholic mission."

Recent hires include Dr. Anne Carson Daly as vice president for academic affairs and dean of the faculty. She is an English literature professor with an expertise in J. R. R. Tolkien and C. S. Lewis.

Among other recent developments is the construction of a new, larger Eucharistic Adoration Chapel, for which ground was broken on August 22, 2006, Feast of the Queenship of Mary. Bishop Peter Jugis of the Diocese of Charlotte participated. The new chapel will allow for perpetual adoration.

Also in 2006 was the opening of The Catholic Shoppe, a Catholic book and supply cen-

ter that offers study courses and vespers for students and the community. Future plans for the shop include story hours for children and prayer time. In April 2007 a three-day Catholic Family Expo was held on campus in conjunction with the Diocese of Charlotte.

In summer 2007, it was announced that *Envoy* magazine, a Catholic evangelical publication, will be housed at the college and will expand to include an Envoy Institute. This institute will focus on the spiritual needs of youth and should help with the faith formation of Belmont Abbey students.

As part of its commitment to pro-life Catholic principles, the college announced in 2007 that it will work with an existing Charlotte Catholic maternity home to develop a Room at the Inn facility for pregnant and unwed mothers. It will provide educational opportunities, support and health care.

These new programs supplement others, in particular the Bradley Institute for the

Study of Christian Culture, which was established in 1996 in honor of former college president Father John Bradley, O.S.B. Dr. Robert Preston, another former college president, is director of the institute and was a student of Father Bradley's.

According to the college, the institute "supports the mission of the college by fostering an understanding of the Catholic Intellectual Heritage and by advancing the truth of Christian thought and an appreciation of their unique impact upon the development of Western culture." In December 2006 the Vatican designated the institute as a Seat of Catholic Culture.

The institute has monthly speakers and attracts students and others from the Belmont area. Among upcoming speakers in fall 2007 will be Father Joseph Koterski, S.J., of Fordham University, who will speak on "The Importance of Natural Law in Catholic Moral Theology."

One recent speaker in another lecture series was Catholic writer John Allen, author of a 2005 book on Pope Benedict XVI, who spoke on "Understanding the Megatrends Affecting the Catholic Church" in April 2007. Overall, the speakers program includes business leaders or religious commentators.

Interestingly, Belmont Abbey does not have outside speakers at their commencement ceremony. Rather, as Ken Davison, the vice president of college relations, told us, "the Baccalaureate Mass is the focus and highlight of commencement. The homilist, therefore, is the 'speaker' and is so honored. Since it's a Mass, the homilist must be a priest or bishop and approved by the abbot. There are no problems with dissidents." The 2007 homilist was Archbishop Wilton Gregory of the Archdiocese of Atlanta and a former president of the U.S. Conference of Catholic Bishops.

As a physical example of the college's public identity there is a lovely Lourdes Grotto, which was dedicated in 1891 and has been given special status as a Pilgrimage Shrine. In addition to ongoing visits, there is a program of prayer each May. The grotto complements the impressive Abbey Basilica and the monastery, both of which are close by on campus.

Spiritual Life

The spiritual life at Belmont Abbey is centered at the basilica, which is officially known as Abbey Basilica of Mary Holy of Christians. The beautiful 19th-century Gothic structure served as a cathedral for 67 years and is now on the National Register of Historic Places. It seats about 300.

There are three Masses per weekend at the basilica, one on Saturday morning and two on Sunday, including a 7 p.m. student Mass, which draws about 200. Daily Mass is at 5 p.m. Students also can participate in the Divine Office prayers of lauds, midday and vespers throughout the week, and about 10 to 12 students participate daily with the monks.

The Mass is said in the vernacular. On Sunday, there is organ music but weekday Masses have *a capella* singing. The Divine Office is recited in *recto tono* chant. Priests and monks are active in campus ministry.

Confessions are held six days a week. One staff member said of the chaplain during the 2006–07 academic year, "He challenges students, he 'gets in your face' about going to confession; students respond well." The adoration chapel is always open and there is an exposition of the Blessed Sacrament 16 hours a day. There also are days of recollection and "fasting opportunities."

Students must perform 10 hours of community service each semester, and this program falls under campus ministry. Among the options available are working with maternity homes such as Room at the Inn or crisis pregnancy centers; helping needy and homeless people in the area; teaching religion to young people through the Queen of Apostles program; and mentoring and coaching at local schools.

One professor said, "The campus ministry emphasizes the life issues as taught by the Catholic Church—not just abortion but on issues such as war." Some students have engaged in war protests. There also is a contingent that participates in the annual March for Life in Washington, D.C. In 2007, two buses of students, faculty and staff made the 400-mile trip. President Thierfelder was among them.

Other campus ministry projects include Homelessness Awareness Week and a Habitat for Humanity program. Students also participate in alternative spring break programs that have included trips to the Dominican Republic, Honduras and the U.S.-Mexican border.

Some of the campus ministry programs appeal to non-Catholic students but, according to one faculty member, "Because the school is in the Bible Belt, it has no specific ministry to non-Catholics recognizing that the area offers an array of opportunities for Protestant students."

Catholicism in the Classroom

Belmont Abbey is proud of its core curriculum, emphasizing that it reflects the Catholic and Benedictine tradition. "But," one faculty interviewee said, "since up to 45 percent of the student body is not Catholic, the courses are not labeled Catholic—though they operate from a baseline Catholic perspective."

What this means is that of the required 120 credit hours, 59 are in the core curriculum. There are 12 credits in "Foundational Skills," including writing, critical thinking and mathematics. An additional 41 credits are required in seven broad disciplines in the traditional liberal arts. Within these categories there is considerable choice.

In philosophy, students need to take a survey ethics course ("Philosophy 250") and can choose either ancient and medieval philosophy or modern and contemporary philosophy. There is, thus, a six-credit philosophy requirement.

There are six credits required in theology, which are comprised of one course in early and medieval Christian thought and one in Reformation and modern Christian thought.

Theology faculty members have received or applied for the *mandatum*. But, one faculty member said, "The college provides a learning experience that gives students an introduction into an ethical and moral view of the world shaped by a Catholic philosophy that avoids the left and right extremes."

Given the influence of Abbot Placid, the leadership of President Thierfelder and the launching of a number of strong Catholic initiatives, it could reasonably be expected that the Catholic content of the curriculum will be enhanced in the near future. Such strengthening is at least implicit in the current strategic plan.

For most students, Belmont Abbey provides a small environment to develop marketable skills. About 50 percent of students major in business-related concentrations, which is not surprising given the array of offerings. These include business management, international business, sports management and motor sports management. There also is a Centre for Global Commerce.

In the fall 2007 semester, a new Honors Institute began with an emphasis on Great Books; the college expects it to consist of about 18 students. This competitive, 15-course program replaces a less-defined honors program that had only nine courses. Honors Institute students will have the opportunity to interact with faculty and others in informal settings and will be eligible for grants, including full tuition remission.

Scholarships, including those that attract Catholic students, are an impressive part of the current Belmont Abbey outreach program. The Felix Hintemayer Scholarship, named after a former prior and vicar general of the Benedictine order, encourages student leadership.

There also is the Sport at the Service of the Spirit Scholarship, an initiative of Dr. Thierfelder, and a Benedictine Hospitality Award, which was competitively offered for students applying during the month of May 2007. This latter award, up to $10,000, was to be given to a student reflecting the spirit embodied by the Rule of St. Benedict.

Finally, there is a modest study-abroad program. The college does not operate or participate in an overseas campus but allows students to take part in several overseas programs offered by the School for Field Studies.

Student Activities

Students have access to about 30 recognized student groups, which run the gamut from quilting and chess clubs to Crusaders for Life and the Student Government Association. There is a monthly student-run newspaper, the *Crusader*, and a literary magazine, *Agora*. Four sororities and three fraternities also are available. There are no clubs that are at variance with Catholic teachings.

Some students take advantage of religious-oriented groups known as households. Presently, there are four such households: Brothers in Christ Sons of Mary Household, Faithful Daughters Household, Our Lady of Good Counsel Household and One Body in Christ Co-Educational Household.

One especially prominent campus organization is the Abbey Players, which can trace its history back to 1883. Recent Abbey Players productions have included *Good*, a play about an academic who falls prey to Nazism, and *Copenhagen*, a discussion between Danish physicist Niels Bohr and German physicist Werner Heisenberg about the nature of atomic weapons. Student performers can minor in theatre arts and are eligible for the John Oetgen, O.S.B., Excellence in Theatre Scholarship.

For others, there is an active intramural sports program that includes the typical sports as well as offerings such as wiffle ball and billiards. Students also are able to use the facilities of the R. L. Stowe, Jr., Family YMCA in Belmont, which is about five minutes from the campus.

BAC fields seven men's and seven women's sports team that compete in NCAA Division II through the new Conference Carolinas. President Thierfelder, who has had a long career in sports, is working to upgrade the program. As part of that process, in July 2007 the college hired a veteran athletic director from Cal State-Northridge, promoted the assistant men's basketball coach to the top spot and signed a women's professional basketball assistant coach to coach the women's basketball team.

Residential Life

Campus housing accommodates about 625 students in three residence halls with single-sex suites and apartments. Overnight opposite-sex visitation in rooms is prohibited, but we understand it is not closely policed. There is no curfew. Chastity is encouraged both through policy and by resident staff.

To address student drinking, the Student Life office has launched a quarterly Alcohol Education Seminar. Students who run afoul of alcohol rules are required to attend the seminar in lieu of being assessed a fine. In 2005, there were 47 campus liquor law violations that rose to the level of disciplinary action.

The campus is relatively safe. In the three years of 2003, 2004 and 2005, there were 26 criminal offenses, 20 of which were burglaries. The town of Belmont, however, has a crime rate that is about 20 percent above the national index average.

Students have access to a health center where routine medical issues are addressed by a nurse practitioner and others. The 435-bed Gaston Memorial Hospital is located in Gastonia, about 15 miles west of the campus. And, of course, Charlotte offers a variety of medical facilities.

The Community

Belmont is a small town that is about 15 minutes from Charlotte, a major urban center. Charlotte, which has a population of 664,000, is the home of the nation's second and fourth largest banks, Bank of America and Wachovia. NASCAR, now a major sports entertainment industry, looms large in the area's economy.

Evangelist Billy Graham was born in Charlotte 88 years ago—when the population of Charlotte and its county, Mecklenburg, was only about 12,000—and evangelical and Protestant influences in this southeast section of North Carolina remain strong.

But with its rapid growth and prosperity, the Charlotte area is now a diverse mix and offers what you would expect of the nation's 20th largest city. Belmont Abbey students are able to take advantage of the many social, cultural and sports opportunities.

The Charlotte Douglas International Airport is about 10 minutes from Belmont. It is a major hub for U.S. Airways and hosts many major carriers. The area also is easily accessible by road through Interstates 85 and 77.

The Bottom Line

Belmont Abbey is on the move. After providing a liberal arts education to students, often Protestants, in the region for more than a century, the college is repositioning itself. With impressive marketing skills and the Catholic commitment of a new president, Belmont Abbey has embarked on a campaign to make itself a national institution with a stronger Catholic presence.

Some of the enhancements are subtle, such as broadening its outreach to the community, while others are more substantial as evidenced by a broader array of targeted scholarships and a revitalized core-curriculum Honors Institute. The college also has been nimble in taking advantage of regional partnerships, including one that supports a motor sports management program.

Undergirding its expansion and new strategic thinking has been the presence of the Benedictine monks and the Abbey. Most of the key ingredients are in place to help move this small liberal arts college to the next level of national prominence. For that reason, it is worth consideration from Catholic students wishing to ride the wave.

Benedictine College

Atchison, Kansas

www.benedictine.edu

Overview

Atchison, Kansas, has been known historically for its railroad identity (Atchison, Topeka & Santa Fe) and as the birthplace of aviator Amelia Earhart in 1897. It also has long been a center for Benedictine life, hosting separate orders of Sisters and Brothers.

St. Benedict's Abbey spawned a college for men in 1859, while the Benedictine Sisters of Mount Saint Scholastica opened a women's college in 1923. The two institutions merged to form the coed Benedictine College in 1971.

Nestled along the Missouri River in a town of 10,000 people, this college attracts students from 38 states to study the liberal arts amid a Catholic culture. The administration takes their Catholic and Benedictine identity seriously as is evidenced in their vision statement: "Benedictine College's vision is to be one of the great Catholic colleges in America."

There are 39 majors running the gamut from traditional liberal arts disciplines to athletic training to youth ministry. Three of these majors—international studies, international business and foreign languages (covering two or even three languages and study abroad)—were added in fall 2007. In addition, there are opportunities to pursue many minors and double majors. Graduate programs are restricted to business administration and school leadership.

The college drew students from 43 states, Puerto Rico and 21 other countries in the 2006–07 academic year. Undergraduate en-

QUICK FACTS

Founded: 1971 (merger)
Type of institution: Small liberal arts college
Setting: Small town
Undergraduate enrollment: 1,229 (2006–07 academic year)
Total undergraduate cost: $24,180 (tuition, room and board for 2007–08)
Undergraduate majors: 39

FIVE KEY POINTS

1. Commitment to a Catholic and Benedictine mission.

2. One of the most extensive campus ministry programs.

3. Strong religious studies and philosophy departments.

4. Its Institute for Religious Studies helps train lay ministers.

5. A welcoming and family-like environment.

rollment for fall 2007 was the highest in the college's history and represented the ninth consecutive year of enrollment growth.

Governance

Twenty-five of the 31 members of the board of trustees are lay representatives. Each of the two Benedictine orders has three members on the board.

Stephen Minnis, a lawyer and Benedictine College alumnus, has been college president since 2004. Mr. Minnis promotes the college's Catholic identity, urging on his website welcome, "Let us have Jesus in our hearts forever."

At his installation, Mr. Minnis was presented by the co-chairs of the board with symbols of the institution's four pillars: representing Catholicism was a cross; Benedictine heritage, the Medal of Saint Benedict; liberal arts, a copy of Venerable John Henry Cardinal Newman's book *The Idea of a University*; and residential life, a drawing of a new residence hall with a verse from the Acts of the Apostles.

Public Identity

"The second you step on campus," one student told us, "you realize it is a Catholic college." The college repeatedly refers to its four pillars. For example, in recruiting for assistant professors of English and sociology in early 2007, the website notes: "Candidates must support the Catholic, Benedictine, Liberal Arts and Residential mission of the College."

The college works to create a Catholic culture in its spiritual life, curriculum and student activities. The Benedictine influence remains strong, as is seen by the annual Solemnity of the Passing of St. Benedict Mass on

March 21; Bishop Robert Finn of Kansas City-St. Joseph was the principal celebrant of the 2006 Mass.

The Catholic mindset starts at the top; among other things, the president holds a morning Rosary group that now attracts students. The Benedictine monks are reported to be resurgent, a definite presence and viewed as role models. Faculty and staff attend campus Masses.

The students also make an important contribution to the Catholic environment. After grieving over the death of Pope John Paul II, 300 students held a "Pope Party" to celebrate the election of Pope Benedict XVI in April 2005. Another example is the Lenten tradition where students perform an outdoor Living Stations of the Cross.

In January 2007, Nobel Peace Prize recipient Dr. Wangari Maathai was an honored guest and speaker on campus. A 1964 graduate of forerunner Mount St. Scholastica College, Dr. Maathai has achieved fame as founder of the Green Belt deforestation program in Kenya. Although she did not raise the issue during her visit, some on campus were disturbed by her history of supporting contraceptive use to address AIDS in Africa.

Nevertheless, most speakers on campus tend to be solidly orthodox Catholics, often part of the John Paul the Great Speaker Series. These include papal biographer George Weigel; FOCUS founder Curtis Martin; Dr. Scott Hahn; Father Benedict Groeschel, C.F.R.; and Christopher West of the Theology of the Body Institute. Mother Teresa also visited the campus in 1981.

The 2007 commencement speaker was former Notre Dame football coach Lou Holtz, who was awarded an honorary degree.

Spiritual Life

President Minnis has said, "There are some who say young people don't care about their faith any more. Let them come to Benedictine College where 150 to 200 of our students attend daily Mass and almost 250 of them participate in voluntary Bible study through the FOCUS [Fellowship of Catholic University Students] program."

Indeed, all the elements of a vibrant Catholic spiritual life are present at BC. There are 10 Masses per week at St. Martin's Chapel. In addition, another 23 Masses are offered at the St. Benedict Abbey Church, the Mount St. Scholastica Chapel and St. Benedict's, the nearby parish. One student reported, "You have your options from a very conservative Mass [Abbey] to a more charismatic Mass with Praise and Worship [the youth-based campus chapel]. There is nothing irreverent and you can find one that fits your spirituality."

Mass attendance is high, especially those emphasizing charismatic worship. Students are very engaged in assisting with all aspects of the campus chapel. In addition to serving as Eucharistic ministers and lectors, there also are contingents dealing with distributing fliers (Tack Ministry), working on the website and keeping the chapel clean (Chapel Dusters).

The priests are very active, too. Perhaps this has helped boost the work of the St. Gregory the Great vocational discernment group on campus, which can claim more than 30 students who have entered religious life since 2000. Certainly the fact that there has been an average of one new Benedictine novice on campus each year for about the last eight has helped in this effort.

Priests and monks are readily accessible for consultation or spiritual direction, and opportunities for confession are available beyond the daily scheduled time. Eucharistic adoration is held on Wednesdays, and students have taken the initiative to promote one-hour participation.

The glue that holds much of the spiritual life together is a phenomenally active campus ministry. There is an athletes-in-training scriptural study program, prison ministry, social justice programs, targeted events such as Guadalupe Day and Day of the Dead, a weekly Wednesday Skip-a-Meal fasting program, Daughters of the King (Catholic fellowship among women), international mission trips and many other activities.

The FOCUS group involves about one-quarter of the undergraduates. FOCUS, which is an acronym for Fellowship of Catholic University Students, is a national Catholic evangelization program on 32 campuses. Although mostly present on secular campuses, three Catholic colleges, including Benedictine, have FOCUS chapters.

Retreats are also extensive, prompting one student to say, "The joke on campus is 'Which retreat should I go on this week?'" These retreats include those targeted for men, women and freshmen as well as an Abbey Triduum Retreat during Holy Week. Also prominent are evangelization programs and charismatic initiatives such as Rave N Worship.

One graduate student living on campus said, in summary, "There is so much spiritual activity going on at the campus, it is unbelievable." In fact, this was a typical comment of current and former students. One 2004 alumna summed up her Catholic experience there by saying, "Mass, campus ministry, FOCUS—from day one I was like a kid in a candy store!"

Catholicism in the Classroom

All those who teach theology at BC are required to receive the *mandatum*, which prompted one alumnus to tell us, "Everyone is a straight arrow." This characterization extends to both the religious studies and philosophy departments. Another student said, "All were excellent men inside the classroom as well as in their personal life."

Although many of the faculty in religious studies and philosophy received plaudits, two consistently surfaced in our research: Dr. Mark Zia, assistant professor of religious studies, and Dr. John Rziba, the philosophy chair. Among teachers in other fields is Dr. Michael King, an assistant professor of business. Dr. King, the father of five and a BC alumnus, brings Catholic and ethical examples into his teaching. Many of the faculty and their families participate in student events.

The college lost an influential and popular faculty member when Dr. Edward Sri, a debunker of the "DaVinci Code," left in 2006 to join the faculty of the graduate Augustine Institute in Denver. He taught courses on the Christian moral life and love and responsibility.

About 60 percent of the courses must come from various categories the college has designated for its educational plan. There are eight core courses all students take, including one in classical philosophy and introductory theology.

Students then have broad choices from several liberal arts fields in order to fulfill 11 "foundation" courses. They also select eight courses from numerous offerings under the heading "skills and perspectives."

To help ease them into college life, first-year students participate in a two-day advis-

ing program in the spring or summer before beginning their studies. The program is called Student Orientation, Advising, and Registration (SOAR).

The religious studies major accounts for nearly 10 percent of the student body. But students can choose from most traditional majors—there are 39 overall, a large number for such a small college.

These pursuits are enriched by various exchange activities and a formal study-abroad program centered in Florence, Italy. Here, too, the college emphasizes its four pillars.

Since 1990 an Institute for Religious Studies has worked with the Archdiocese of Kansas City, Kansas, to provide lay ministry training. Courses are offered in 10 Kansas cities and participants can pursue three separate certificates.

Student Life

Students can join 33 clubs. In addition to campus ministry activities, organizations include a Knights of Columbus council, a Ravens Respect Life pro-life group and the faith-sharing Koinonia. There is a student government association, and the five officers each hold posted office hours four or five days a week.

Benedictine students have participated in every March for Life in Washington, D.C., since it was begun in 1974. In 2007, the Benedictine contingent reached a record number of 98. The campus is located 1,100 miles from the nation's capital, making it an 18-hour bus trip.

There are no questionable clubs on campus. An effort to launch a general anti-discrimination group called Spectrum languished. The student newspaper, the *Circuit*, occasionally prints pro-abortion letters but these are anomalies.

The Ravens participate in 11 intercollegiate sports, perhaps the most popular being men's football. The team, which competes in the Heart of America Athletic Conference and is a member of the National Association of Intercollegiate Athletics (N.A.I.A.), has a 77 percent winning record over the past 13 years, the best among 11 colleges in the region. They play in a 3,000-seat stadium.

Notable is the commitment of Larry Wilcox, who is entering his 29th year as head football coach in fall 2007. Wilcox, who graduated from BC in 1972, donated his salary in 2004 to the building fund for the Amino Center, a sports training facility.

Residential Life

Benedictine has seven residence halls—three for women, three for men and one that is coed. The coed Ferrell Hall, a former 19th-century monastery building, is separated by floor. There is a visitation policy for the single-sex halls, and the residential staff monitors it very carefully and penalizes transgressors with community service.

To assist in the process, chastity talks are given at the beginning of the year and there are groups that support men and women to lead chaste lives. The seven resident directors, one for each dormitory, are trained in Catholic classics, including the Order of St.

Benedict and *Ex corde Ecclesiae*. The residence halls can accommodate about 70 percent of the undergraduates.

Students report that sometimes there are tensions between athletes and other students. There also are some drinking problems with students attending off-campus parties. To address alcohol issues, the residential life team has weekly root beer keg parties and sponsors other activities. The Student Government Association recently passed a resolution looking to call attention to alcohol and drinking issues.

All students have access to a part-time health center whose nurse tends to routine health matters. A 96-bed community Atchison Hospital is located near the campus. More sophisticated medical care is available in Kansas City, which is about one hour from the town. There also is a counseling center staffed by two professionals.

The Community

Atchison is small-town America. Its charming Victorian houses and trolley tours highlight a low-key lifestyle. A major annual event is the Amelia Earhart Festival, which draws a big regional crowd in July. Crime is significantly below the national average, and violent crime is very rare.

Students have become involved in the community through the Hunger Coalition. Among its activities is the Skip-a-Meal program that allows students to forego a meal that is then donated by the cafeteria and distributed by students to needy area residents. Once a month students venture to Kansas City to assist homeless people through the Uplift KC program. They also tutor in Atchison schools.

In addition to Kansas City, students can easily reach St. Joseph, Missouri, which is about 20 miles across the state border. Local road transportation is good, and the Canada-to-Mexico Interstate 59 passes through Atchison.

For those traveling some distance, the principal access to Atchison is by way of Kansas City International Airport, about one-half-hour away. Once the hub for TWA, the airport's most extensive carrier today is Southwest Airlines. Amtrak stations, through which the east-west Southwest Chief travels, are in Kansas City, Topeka and Lawrence.

The Bottom Line

While many Catholic colleges have de-emphasized their ties to religious orders, Benedictine College celebrates its Benedictine charism. And, indeed, the influence of the Benedictine Brothers is a positive one.

The college, with the leadership of a supportive lay president, emphasizes its four pillars of Catholicism, Benedictine heritage, liberal arts and residential life. This permeates an institution where faith is promoted and respected. Perhaps nowhere is this more noticeable than in what appears to us as one of the most impressive campus ministry programs in the nation.

The quality of the key departments, the spiritual vigor and the family-like environment should be enough to encourage any high school senior to give Benedictine College a serious look. Everything seems to be present here that would suggest a faithful, enjoyable and rewarding undergraduate experience.

The Catholic University of America

Washington, D.C.

www.cua.edu

Overview

With the support of Pope Leo XIII, the U.S. Catholic bishops founded The Catholic University of America as a national graduate institution in Washington, D.C., in 1887. In its unique role, the university focused primarily on teaching theology and philosophy to religious and laypeople.

The university added a number of graduate and professional schools, including the Columbus School of Law in 1897 and the National Catholic School of Social Service in 1918. In between launching those schools, the university expanded into undergraduate programs.

Although five U.S. seminaries are identified as pontifical universities, The Catholic University of America is the only broadly based U.S. university so identified. It is so designated because it offers ecclesiastical degrees, such as canon law, which are recognized worldwide within the Church. As a result, many priests from throughout the country have studied at the university.

Today, CUA joins with the Basilica of the National Shrine of the Immaculate Conception, its next-door neighbor, in forming the nucleus of a sprawling Catholic enclave of seminaries and other religious institutions in the Brookland section of Northwest Washington, D.C. The university is located about 15 minutes north of the U.S. Capitol.

The university's unique heritage and its Washington location attract students from ev-

QUICK FACTS

Founded: 1887
Type of institution: Large university
Setting: Urban
Undergraduate enrollment: 3,123 (2006–07 academic year)
Total undergraduate cost: $38,700 (tuition, room and board for 2007–08)
Total undergraduate majors: 53

FIVE KEY POINTS

1. The national Catholic university with ties to the Vatican and U.S. bishops.

2. The current president has strengthened its Catholic identity.

3. There is a strong campus ministry.

4. There are several notably strong Catholic-oriented departments, including philosophy.

5. The university has financial challenges that restrict its broader influence.

ery state and 97 other countries, even though 58 percent of them come from the Mid-Atlantic region. More than one-third of the alumni settle in the area after graduation, but the others scatter to every state and 125 countries.

Undergraduate students also are attracted to studying 53 majors in seven of the 12 schools. Most of the majors are fairly typical, but there also are some innovative ones such as international economics and finance and environmental chemistry. There also are four interdisciplinary programs: early Christian literature, Irish studies, medieval and Byzantine studies, and early Christian studies.

As part of its outreach to older and non-traditional students, the university offers three undergraduate programs—management, information technology and interdisciplinary studies—in its Metropolitan College.

Graduation requirements vary according to the school to which the student is admitted. Arts and Sciences students are required to take 24 courses distributed among eight traditional liberal arts fields. Each student in that school is required to take four courses in theology and religious studies and four courses in philosophy, but there is a certain amount of choice.

For those interested in a pursuing an honors core curriculum, there is a 20-course liberal arts program which consists of courses in five sequences: An Aristotelian Studium; The Christian Tradition; Critical Exploration of Social Reality; The Environment, Energy and Policy; and Media, Technology and Culture. Three sequences need to be completed to receive an honors degree.

Governance

The governance of the university is placed in the hands of a 50-member board of trustees, 48 of whom are elected and two—the chancellor (the archbishop of Washington, D.C.) and the president—are members by virtue of their position.

The elected board members are equally divided between clerics and lay people. U.S. archbishops and bishops must constitute at least 18 members. All seven U.S. cardinals currently heading archdioceses are members.

The Catholic hierarchy supports the university in various ways, including through the annual American Cardinals Dinner, which was established in 1989. The dinners have raised $22 million since 1989, including $1.2 million for university scholarship funds at the most recent one in April 2007. There is also an annual nationwide parish church collection taken for the university on one Sunday every September.

The chief executive officer is Father David O'Connell, C.M., who was named the university's 14th president in 1998 at the age of 42. Father O'Connell, who has helped steer the university toward a stronger Catholic identity, is a firm supporter of *Ex corde Ecclesiae*.

Public Identity

"Catholic University, for many years, beginning in the late 1960s, had developed the reputation of being the home of dissent in the Catholic Church. With all due regard for legitimate academic freedom, which I certainly support, the institution lost a bit of its credibility as the Church's university for many years," Father O'Connell said in an interview with the university's alumni magazine in 2006.

One of the most challenging issues that it faced was the public notoriety of having on its theology faculty Charles Curran, a Catholic priest known for his strong dissent on positions of Catholic moral teachings, including *Humanae Vitae*. He was finally relieved of his position in 1986 by the Vatican's Congregation for the Doctrine of the Faith, which was led by Joseph Cardinal Ratzinger (now Pope Benedict XVI).

There were other examples of lax leadership, but that changed with the appointment of Father O'Connell. One faculty member in the business and economics department told us, "CUA has come a long way in terms of strengthening its Catholic identity in the last 20 years, especially the last five to 10 years under [President] O'Connell. There is a strong Catholic mission and identity."

From that same 2006 magazine interview, Father O'Connell said, "I felt that in order for the university to succeed, it needed to reclaim its credibility, it needed to be the place where the Church did its thinking. It needed to be the place where both students and the general public at large, especially the Catholic faithful, could turn to ask questions, to seek an understanding of what the Church teaches and why, and to find support for and not opposition to the Church and its teaching."

Ways in which the university's Catholic identity has been enhanced include an emphasis on strengthening the campus ministry—which by all accounts has been effective with a new Franciscan influence—and by hiring professors and staff members who reflect Catholic identity.

One professor added, "I think a good barometer for judging such things [Catholic identity] is vocations—how many graduates embrace vocations to the priesthood, religious life, missions, etc. There has been a huge improvement in this area in the last 12

to 13 years in particular. At every graduation they announce the names of graduating students who are moving on to the priesthood or religious life."

In other areas, too, Father O'Connell has exerted leadership. Students from the drama department had proposed a performance of *The Vagina Monologues* but were told by Father O'Connell that the university would not sponsor it and that the *Monologues* were inappropriate for a Catholic institution.

There also has been much discussion about hosting Catholic speakers who are at variance with Catholic teachings. Perhaps the most controversial example took place in 2004 when the Media Studies Department was co-sponsoring a film festival that was to include an appearance by actor and writer Stanley Tucci, a pro-abortion and Planned Parenthood advocate. Father O'Connell disinvited him.

This event followed by a few weeks a statement that Father O'Connell sent to the university's academic leadership in which he wrote, "I cannot approve pro-abortion/pro-choice speakers on campus. This is not part of any vast right-wing conspiracy or an assault on academic freedom. It is simply what we are, as a Catholic institution, obliged to follow as an expression of our Catholic identity and mission."

This does not mean the system is flawless. In 2006, Pennsylvania Democratic senatorial candidate Robert Casey, Jr., was invited to speak at the law school in the midst of his general election campaign against then-Senator Rick Santorum, a staunch pro-life legislator. Casey, who was subsequently elected, had expressed support for emergency contraception and federal funding for contraceptives.

But this was a rare occurrence at a university that attracts many speakers. Nearly all speakers have views that are fully consistent with Church teachings. The 2007 commencement speakers were then-White House press secretary Tony Snow, a convert to Catholicism, and former U.S. ambassador to the Vatican Jim Nicholson.

Finally, in December 2006, CUA issued a new mission statement. It reads, in part, "As the national university of the Catholic Church in the United States, founded and sponsored by the bishops of the country and with the approval of the Holy See, The Catholic University of America is committed to being a comprehensive Catholic and American institution of higher learning, faithful to the teachings of Jesus Christ as handed on by the Church." This is clearly a different Catholic University from a generation ago.

Spiritual Life

CUA's campus ministry, under the leadership of the Conventual Franciscan Friars, offers many opportunities for the sacraments and spiritual development. Daily Masses are offered at St. Paul's Chapel in Caldwell Hall as well as at the Mary, Mirror of Justice Chapel in the law school. There are two Masses on Sunday at St. Vincent's, including a very popular one with "lively" music—guitar, violin and flute—at 9 p.m., which draws an overflowing crowd of about 300; the chapel seats 225.

Also popular among students is the 4 p.m. Sunday Mass in the Crypt Church of the neighboring Basilica of the National Shrine of the Immaculate Conception. There are six daily Masses and seven Sunday Masses at this magnificent structure, which is the nation's largest Catholic church. There are opportunities, too, for confessions, participating in pilgrimages and other activities at the Basilica.

The university holds four special Masses during the academic year at the Basilica. These are the Freshman Orientation Mass, the Mass of the Holy Spirit, the Mass in Honor of St. Thomas Aquinas and the Baccalaureate Mass. The University Commemoration of the Faithful Departed is held on campus at St. Paul's Chapel on November 2.

In fact, because of the concentration of Catholic religious houses and seminaries surrounding CUA, there is a large number of opportunities for worship. Among these are St. Anselm's Abbey, the Dominican House of Study, Capuchin College, the Franciscan Monastery, the Poor Clares Sisters and the Discalced Carmelite Friars communities.

Back on the university campus, there are weekly established and informal opportunities for confession. One faculty member said, "I've noticed since the arrival of the new Franciscan priests heading campus ministry, there are priests and brothers visiting dorm rooms to bless them and, especially, to hear confessions."

Eucharistic adoration is promoted on campus. The Wednesday night Praise and Worship adoration is reported to be overflowing. On Thursday evening, there is Solemn Adoration with singing in Latin. Adoration is offered more frequently during Advent and Lent. There also is an online Prayernet site.

There are class-based and student-run retreats. The freshman retreat is the most popular—we understand that students need to be turned away because the retreat site that is currently in use at the Melwood Retreat Center in Nanjemoy, Maryland, can only accommodate 200 people. The university erects a big tent, and male students sleep outside so more students can attend. The retreats for the other three classes generally are less popular.

Another retreat opportunity is the "Going Deeper" retreat series, in which a priest is invited in to lead the participants. There also are retreats for some of the small faith-based groups such as those in the music ministry, men's group and women's group.

In the 2006–07 academic year, a campus RENEW program was added and was judged to be very successful, involving more than 200 students in small groups who met weekly to grow in faith and community. There were 16 groups in the fall, and four more were added in the spring semester.

Campus ministry coordinates all community service for the university. Anyone who wishes to volunteer in a community service outreach is welcome, regardless of faith practice, but the campus ministry emphasizes that service is an outgrowth of faith. Also, we understand that there is generally a strong Catholic outreach to students of other faiths.

Among many such outreach opportunities are tutoring with the Academy of Hope and Little Lights Urban Ministries, mentoring with Project Ujima, helping with children at St. Ann's Infant and Maternity Home and assisting with the So Others May Eat (SOME) food program for needy and homeless people. There also is an active pro-life group.

As with several other Catholic universities, particularly the larger ones, the Catholic University campus ministry sponsors foreign mission trips during spring break and the summer. First initiated in 2001, students have gone to Guatemala, Jamaica, Panama and Belize, and also have worked with Habitat for Humanity at Kauai, Hawaii. In the 2007–08 academic year, trips are planned to Belize and Honduras.

One faculty member said that campus ministry lacks an intellectual dimension and could sponsor more lectures and public apologetics. But another said, "In the almost three decades that I've been here, the Franciscans who run campus ministry are the best I've seen. Everything they're doing is going in the right direction. There's really a lot of work for them to do and it's tough. I have no reason to think they could be doing a better job."

Catholicism in the Classroom

Undergraduates are required to take four courses in theology and religious studies and four courses in philosophy, and that generally translates into good news. We have been told that all the theology faculty members have the *mandatum* and that department is very good.

According to a professor who has closely observed the theology department, "I should emphasize that the tide has changed—big time! We've acquired great new, younger faculty and the 'bad apples' are really dying away." Some of the tenured theology professors she praised as "exceptional" are Dr. Joseph Capizzi and Dr. John Grabowski, who teach social ethics and moral theology, and Dr. Peter Casarella, who teaches systematic theology and patristics.

Whereas the theology courses (and faculty) are faithful to the Magisterium, the religious studies courses mirror the courses taught in religion departments or divinity schools of elite secular institutions. Religious studies courses include those on world religions and comparative religions, and we are told that some are taught by professors who do not support Catholic teachings.

Fortunately, the School of Philosophy is excellent. It is a full school and not merely a department as in many universities. One philosophy professor said, "We're all seriously committed to the Catholic academic mission of the School, to the compatible relationship between faith and reason, and to the role of philosophy in supporting and enhancing the discipline of theology."

The theology and philosophy departments are helped by the presence of the CUA University Press, which publishes nearly three dozen titles per year. In addition, a variety of magazines and scholarly journals, such as *The Catholic Historical Review, Catholic Biblical Quarterly* and *Old Testament Abstracts,* are based at the university.

Catholic University has many departments and majors in its 12 schools; they vary in their commitment to Catholic identity. The school of nursing is well regarded as a professional school and generally consistent with its Catholic identity. The architecture, engineering, English and music (The Benjamin T. Rome School of Music) departments receive high marks.

Another good department is business and economics, which tries to incorporate Catholic social teaching as much as possible, according to one faculty member, who added, "Naturally, this connection to Catholic social doctrine varies from class to class and depends primarily on the individual professor." Among those strongly recommended are two recent hires, Dr. Andrew Abela in marketing and Dr. Martha Cruz-Zuniga in economics.

In other departments, we have heard very good things about Dr. J. Steven Brown, chair of the mechanical engineering department and a long-time advocate of increasing the university's Catholic identity, and Dr. Michael Mack, who teaches Shakespeare and English Renaissance poetry in the English department. Assistant Dean Alyce Ann Bergkamp of the School of Arts and Sciences works with undergraduates and has been cited as being sensitive to their spiritual well-being.

As with any large university, several departments have surfaced in our interviews that require prudence when pursuing courses there. These include anthropology, modern languages, history and The National School of Social Service.

Catholic University also is challenged by a lack of adequate financial resources. Its $192 million endowment is 242nd in the nation and 20th among Catholic universities. This has repercussions. One faculty member said the university "is seriously underfunded and financially stretched for an institution our size." Some of the university's infrastructure and facilities need to be upgraded.

It is, however, an improvement over when Father O'Connell assumed his presidency nine years ago. His assessment: "I think that we are making real progress, but we have a lot more work to do."

Students at CUA may choose, subject to particular eligibility requirements and areas of interest, from more than 20 university-sponsored study-abroad programs. Locations include Spain, Ireland, Chile, Australia, Mexico, France and elsewhere. Students also may seek approval to study abroad through programs offered by other institutions, such as Eastern Mennonite University.

Most programs are intended for one semester during the junior year, after a major has been selected and in consultation with one's academic advisor. A special summer program in London offers internships with members of the House of Commons for students of politics.

Student Activities

Reflecting the scope of a larger university, Catholic University offers many student activities. At latest count, there are 116 student organizations, which cover a wide range of professional, social, community service and advocacy areas. Among those organizations that are Catholic-oriented are the Knights of Columbus, Pax Christi and, for the law school, the Pope John Paul II Guild of Catholic Lawyers.

The pro-life group is very active. They have been expanding their work beyond abortion and addressing lifestyle issues and chastity as part of their mission. They also are sponsoring some Theology of the Body student/reading groups.

Among the literary publications are *The Tower*, a student-run weekly newspaper, which has both print and online editions. The *CRUX* literary magazine, established four years ago, has occasionally been a critic of Father O'Connell's efforts to strengthen CUA's Catholic identity. WCUA radio station broadcasts music over the Internet.

No abortion or homosexual rights groups exist. Two groups that have stirred some controversy are the National Association for the Advancement of Colored People (NAACP) chapter—because of the parent organization's support for abortion—and the Muslim Law Students Association.

The NAACP issue goes back to 2004 when the national organization adopted a position that supported a woman's option to choose an abortion. The then-president of the NAACP,

Kweisi Mfume, visited the university shortly thereafter and criticized it for originally seeking to ban the chapter.

In addition to all these organizations, CUA has a rich array of intercollegiate, club and intramural athletic programs. The CUA Cardinals compete in the NCAA Division III (no athletic scholarships) with 10 women's and nine men's varsity sports. In 2006–07, the men's basketball team, which had a 23-6 record, won the Capital Athletic Conference title and went on to the NCAA division tournament. The football team plays a 10-game schedule and contends in the Old Dominion Athletic Conference.

Club sports exist in 12 areas, including fencing, ice hockey, ultimate Frisbee and urban dance. Intramural sports are offered in badminton, basketball, football, racquetball, soccer, softball, tennis, track and field and volleyball.

The university presents a large number of social and cultural events and speakers on many different topics. The current administration has been very good in ensuring that these programs do not conflict with Catholic teachings.

A special treat for students is the performances of the nationally recognized drama department and The Benjamin T. Rome School of Music. The Hartke Theatre—named for the long-time head of the drama department, Father Gilbert Hartke, O.P.—has produced an average of six plays each year since 1993–94.

The music school sponsors about 200 recitals a year, and students have given concerts at the Vatican, Washington's Kennedy Center for the Performing Arts and in a number of U.S. cities. The school has an affiliate, The Summer Opera Theatre Company, which gave performances of *Little Women* and *Tosca* in 2007, its 29th season; a number of theatre company students have gone on to careers in opera.

Residential Life

The university is largely a residential campus, with 2,200 students living in 18 residence halls and additional modular units grouped in five "neighborhoods" or clusters. Most residences are coed with women and men separated by floors, but there also are four single-sex residences and the number has been increasing.

Overnight opposite-sex visitation is not allowed but happens. Chastity is encouraged by official policies of the university and through campus leadership. There are 52 resident associates who are responsible for enforcement. There also is a campus ministry outreach, largely through a network of student ministers who focus on first-year students.

The university notes on its website that the residence life program, which coordinates all the residence halls, "is focused on creating residential living communities that support the university's mission, values, and Catholic identity and that promote the retention of students at all levels."

We have no indication that alcohol and drug abuse is a problem on campus. What is a problem, however, is the crime in the Brookland area that surrounds the university. Students need to exercise caution, particularly when wandering off campus.

The university has a health clinic located in the Student Health and Fitness Center. It is open weekdays for routine services as well as physical examinations, and is staffed by a physician, nurse practitioner, physician assistant and a nurse.

There are a number of urgent care clinics in the area, and Providence Hospital is very near campus. Washington, D.C., has a variety of health care facilities, including major research and teaching hospitals at Georgetown University and George Washington University.

The Community

Catholic University is located in Northeast Washington, D.C. The city is divided into quadrants, and most of the downtown and government buildings are located in the Northwest section. The university's neighborhood is known as Brookland, a residential area about 15 minutes north of the U.S. Capitol Building.

Washington, as befits a national capital, offers a wide variety of social, cultural and entertainment opportunities. Most prominent among them are the Kennedy Center for the Performing Arts, a large array of museums within the Smithsonian system (including the Air and Space Museum and the Museum of Natural History) and prominent art museums such as the National Gallery of Art and the Corcoran Gallery of Art.

Next to the university is the Pope John Paul II Cultural Center, a wonderful museum dedicated to the life of the late pope. It also features interactive activities, rotating exhibits, book signings and other events.

The Washington Redskins team of the National Football League has a rabid following among area residents. The Washington Nationals baseball team, which relocated to the city from Montreal in 2005, will be opening a new 41,000-seat stadium in April 2008. Among other professional teams is the Washington Wizards professional basketball squad.

Because of the city's role in government, there exist opportunities to observe and even intern or work in various legislative, executive and judicial offices. Students also have access to the magnificent Library of Congress, the world's largest library.

Washington is easily accessible from everywhere. Ronald Reagan Washington National Airport is across the river from the city, and Dulles International Airport is about a half-hour away. Virtually every major air carrier, domestic and foreign, flies into Washington.

Amtrak has a broad network that uses Union Station, near the Capitol Building, about 15 minutes from the Catholic University campus. The subway system, known as Metro, is extensive throughout the District of Columbia and nearby sites in Maryland and Virginia; the CUA stop is Brookland, a five-minute walk from campus. A number of major highways serve the metropolitan area, including the north-state Interstate 95, U.S. 50 and U.S. 66.

Washington has a generally pleasant climate, with mild winters and rather hot, humid summers. The city generally slows down in the summer as Congress takes a break and many government workers take vacations.

The Bottom Line

The Catholic University of America may not be the best-known Catholic university in the United States, but it has a unique status. It was established with the support of the Vatican and the U.S. bishops and is identified as a pontifical university that offers a broad range of degrees within its 12 schools.

The university underwent a period of disorientation in the 1970s and 1980s. But it is a different institution today. Largely due to the leadership of the current president, Father David O'Connell, the university has greatly strengthened its Catholic identity and commitment and continues to do so.

Catholic University is a good example of a turnaround Catholic institution, successfully "fighting the tide" in the 21st century. Given this development, the strength of many of its academic departments and its location in the nation's capital, it is a university that many faithful Catholics students and parents will want to give a careful look.

DeSales University

Center Valley, Pennsylvania

www.desales.edu

Overview

Shortly after being named to lead the new Diocese of Allentown, Pennsylvania, in 1960, Bishop Joseph McShea began to plan for a Catholic college. Allentown, located between the Philadelphia metropolitan area and former coal towns of northeast Pennsylvania, was one of the few growing cities in the state. The need for a new college in the five-county diocese seemed clear.

The responsibility for developing this vision fell to the Oblates of Saint Francis de Sales, and the Allentown College of St. Francis de Sales welcomed its first students in 1965. Graduate programs were offered in the 1980s and, reflecting its expanding role, the institution was renamed DeSales University in 2001.

The fact that the school chose to change its name from a well-known locality, Allentown, to its Catholic roots, DeSales, underscores its support for the spiritual identity that launched it two generations ago.

The campus is located on 400 acres in Center Valley, a small town only a few miles from the state's third largest city. Allentown and the neighboring city of Bethlehem present a gritty industrial appearance as reflected in Billy Joel's popular 1982 song "Allentown." The university also offers adult and graduate programs in nearby cities of Easton and Lansdale.

While taking advantage of this metropolitan location, DeSales provides an attrac-

tive campus where students from 16 states and several countries can pursue 32 undergraduate majors and prepare for the various professions. In addition to offering study in traditional areas, students can focus on e-commerce, forensics, pharmaceutical marketing and two of the university's standout disciplines, drama and the physician assistant program.

Undergraduates can choose up to 16 courses in a core program, which includes: Basic Requirements—two communications and three physical fitness courses; Cultural Literacy—six Western Civilization-related courses; Modes of Thinking—five courses covering broad liberal arts areas; and Christian Values and Theology—three courses.

Among recent graduate school developments, DeSales began an M.B.A. program with the Romanian-American University at Bucharest in September 2007.

Governance

The 35 members of the board of trustees include 10 Oblates of St. Francis de Sales, including the president, Father Bernard O'Connor, O.S.F.S. Previous presidents have been Oblates, as is the senior vice president. Father O'Connor, who assumed the presidency in 1999, has been a faculty member or administrator at DeSales for 33 years. Father John Harvey, O.S.F.S., founder of Courage, the Church's primary outreach to faithful and chaste homosexual Catholics, is a life member of the board.

Public Identity

The consensus is that not so long ago DeSales was in the middle of the road regarding its Catholic identity, but it is growing stronger.

One faculty member told us, "It has become noticeably stronger during the seven or eight years that I've been here. When I first came, there were people here who definitely did not buy into the Catholic mission of the university but, for the most part, those people have left."

The university website has a page on its Catholic identity and includes a quote and support for *Ex corde Ecclesiae*. In discussing its Faith and Reason Honors Program, the website prominently features a quote from Pope John Paul II's encyclical *Fides et Ratio*. The university also supports an annual Heritage Week that commemorates its patron, St. Francis de Sales, each January.

In addition to faculty and staff commitment, there is "a growing number of students who are 'on fire for God,'" according to one university official. Part of the resurgence is due to the continuing presence of the Salesian Fathers who reside on campus at Wills Hall and who also are scattered throughout leadership positions and university departments. Further supporting the Catholic identity are strong theology and philosophy departments.

A Salesian Center for Faith and Culture promotes the congregation's mission through research, dialogue on a number of vital issues and several university-community partnerships. Among their initiatives are the Baranzano Society, which provides a forum on bioethics; the DeSales Leadership Institute; and a monthly Bulldog Breakfast (with prayer service) for DeSales student athletes.

Most of the notable speakers who have come to campus have been part of the Rev. Thomas J. Furphy Lecture Series, which was started in 1984 to honor a late Salesian faculty member. Among its annual speakers have been the late John Cardinal O'Connor, Vatican Ambassador to the United Nations Archbishop Celestino Migliore, Supreme Court Justice Antonin Scalia, former FBI director Louis Freeh and William Bennett. Former attorney general John Ashcroft was scheduled to speak at the 24th Furphy Lecture in October 2007.

Other than this series, campus speakers have been generally low key, including recent appearances by a chastity promoter and a state legislator.

There was a bit of a surprise and furor, however, with a talk given by former *Newsweek* religion writer Kenneth Woodward in January 2007. Woodward was invited to speak during Heritage Week, presumably about the journalistic craft; St. Francis de Sales is the patron saint of journalists. But he launched a caustic attack on the Catholic Church. The *Minstrel*, the student newspaper, reported: "There were a number of times during the lecture that most everyone agreed that Woodward stepped over the line." Such an event is unusual.

DeSales sponsors a National Catholic Essay Contest, which awards three scholarships. It also provides financial assistance pools for Catholic high school students; there is a Tuition Incentive Program for those within the diocese and a Catholic Schools Grants for those outside.

Spiritual Life

While proud of its Salesian heritage, the university does not seem to reflect much of its dynamism in the campus ministry. Almost all of our interviewees noted that participation in campus religious activities is limited.

There are eight Masses per week at the Connelly Chapel or the Oblates' Wills Hall Chapel: Monday through Friday at 5 p.m., a largely faculty and staff Mass on Wednesday at 12:05 p.m. and a morning and evening Mass on Sunday. Daily Masses attract anywhere from 10 to 35 students despite being, as one reporter noted, "excellent, faithful and with nice music." Sunday morning Masses attract about 40 students and the 8 p.m. has around 180 students.

Confessions are scheduled once a week and by appointment. Currently, there is a Friday afternoon Eucharistic adoration, but it has low participation. Retreats have had to be cancelled because of lack of interest.

There appears to be little outreach or evangelization in the campus ministry. There is some social justice activity represented among the student groups, including participation in OXFAM, but, again, there is little sense of active campus ministry involvement.

Catholicism in the Classroom

All DeSales freshmen participate in Character U, which orients them to several of the Golden Counsels of St. Francis de Sales, including love, hope and forgiveness. Completion is noted on the student's transcript and some prizes are awarded. As part of this program—and to promote understanding of other cultures and develop an understanding of the HIV/AIDS crisis—a group of students undertook a two-week trip to South Africa in December 2006–January 2007.

Each year up to 15 high-achieving first-year students are invited to join the Faith and Reason Honors Program, which is administered by the Salesian Center for Faith and Culture. The four-year program includes seminars, cultural events and a senior thesis.

All students are required to take the introduction to Catholic theology course, one "intermediate theology" course and a Values

Seminar. The theology department offers 34 courses plus special topics, readings, independent study and internships.

The theology courses, according to the 2006–07 catalogue, "encourage students to reflect upon the meaning and value of the Catholic faith, and to live in a manner consistent with Catholic teaching and tradition." One of those courses must be Theology 109, "Catholic Theology: An Introduction."

The theology faculty is solid. All full-time professors are strong, orthodox Catholics who have received the bishop's approval through the *mandatum*. One campus administrator told us, "They are very good teachers and are very well liked by the students. They are very outgoing about the faith and they are very good examples for being Catholic." Other interviewees agreed.

Students can major in theology or philosophy, another discipline that is regarded as dependably Catholic. The college also offers what it identifies as the only major in marriage and family studies at any Catholic college. This unique major, sponsored by the department of philosophy and theology, draws from the works of Pope John Paul II.

DeSales generally promotes "marketable majors," and these include a highly regarded undergraduate degree in medical studies and a fifth-year master of science in physician assistant studies. Graduates of the eight-year-old physician assistant program have achieved a near-perfect passing rate on the National Certifying Examination—10 percent higher than the national average—and all of the 200-plus graduates have been employed in the growing field.

Another niche program is an interdisciplinary pharmaceutical marketing degree available through the business department. Students take courses ranging from microbiology to marketing research as part of the 16-course major requirement.

The sports management major, also in the business department, prepares students to hold positions in schools and nonprofits. This is one of only 20 such undergraduate programs endorsed by the Sport Management Program Review Council.

Among requirements for this major, students need to organize a sports event. Dr. Douglas Turco, the head of the program, told us, "Some set up a running race and the money raised was donated to New Bethany Ministries for the Homeless. There is an effort in this program to apply Catholic teaching across the curriculum."

DeSales also has one of the most extensive drama and performing arts programs at any Catholic college. More than 20 percent of undergraduates major in theatre, film or dance;

the department employs 37 faculty and staff members. One assistant professor of screenwriting, Maura Smith, has been working on a documentary on the Blessed Mother.

The university provides for limited study-abroad opportunities, especially in conjunction with the American University in Rome. It participates in programs with the local Lehigh Valley Association of Independent Colleges. It recently reestablished a two-week study tour in Peru.

Student Activities

DeSales has sanctioned 36 clubs and societies, including a pro-life club, Knights of Columbus, St. Thomas More Society and *Esti Vir*, a men's virtue and chastity group. None of the campus groups appears to have elements that are antithetical to Catholic teachings.

Students have other outlets, including writing for the biweekly, eight-page newspaper, the *Minstrel*.

The paper covers the typical campus issues and sometimes touches on religious themes. In the February 21, 2007 issue, for example, a box was included with a biblical quote for Lent and the following admonition: "Let us ponder these words while undertaking religious tasks especially during Lent, so that we may be granted eternal merit."

The campus community benefits from the modern Labuda Center, which has two theaters with a combined seating capacity of 663. One recent Act 1 performance was of Thornton Wilder's *Our Town*. Since 1992, DeSales has housed The Pennsylvania Shakespeare Festival, which includes Shakespearean, modern and children's plays. There also is a Summer Theatre Institute and Summer Video Institute.

Opportunities exist for individual volunteer efforts, including such programs as a two-day Urban Plunge among homeless people in Washington, D.C. There is an Office of Social Outreach designed for volunteer work in the Lehigh Valley. The university also has sponsored a Catholic Volunteer Service Fair for students interested in post-graduate community service.

Among other extracurricular opportunities are intramural leagues in six sports. For the more competitive, the DeSales Bulldogs compete in eight women's and eight men's sports at the NCAA Division III (non-scholarship) level. The baseball and women's and men's basketball teams have been quite successful in recent years.

Residential Life

Seventy percent of undergraduates live on campus, and they are housed in eight residence halls or townhouse complexes. Two of these are female only; one is reserved for men; and the others are coed. Residence halls that are coed are segregated by gender in separate wings.

The university handbook, which is replete with quotes from St. Francis de Sales, lists the hours of opposite-sex visitation for residence halls and floors. It also notes: "Because the full expression of love through sexual union requires the commitment to a total living and sharing together of two persons in marriage, the university believes that sexual union should only occur in marriage."

Drinking problems, which sadly seem to be present on many campuses, exist but the residential staffers are reported to be more vigilant on the issue. There also is a disciplinary board. The handbook points out in detail laws violated by underage drinking and substance abuse and identifies health problems associated with such use.

The Community

The Lehigh Valley is a vibrant small metropolitan area. The city of Allentown, with a population of about 106,000, offers a number of economic, shopping and cultural opportunities. An example of the latter is the Allentown Art Museum, which contains the works of a number of masters.

The area, with a strong industrial heritage associated with Mack Trucks and Bethlehem Steel, now has a more diversified economy. It also has a more diverse population, straying far from its one-time Pennsylvania German influence. Crime is at or above the national average in various categories, with a notable problem with drugs and gangs.

The DeSales campus, located in a quiet suburban area, is relatively safe. Still, the campus police have been diligent, recently initiating a student escort program. Campus crime violations seem to be for non-violent offenses.

Allentown is located about one hour north of Philadelphia along Route 309. New York City is one and one-half-hours away. The local road systems provide easy access to these major cities as well as to Harrisburg, the state capital, about 75 miles west of Allentown. There is no train service, but the Lehigh Valley International Airport accommodates eight regional commuter carriers. Major airports are located at Philadelphia and Newark.

The Bottom Line

One long-time staff member at the university told us, "The difference between DeSales today and 18 years ago is like night and day. In the 1980s, there was not much going on here in terms of Catholic identity." That's different now, and the Salesian identity is pervasive.

Today, there are a number of areas worthy of praise, including a strong, orthodox department of philosophy and theology. What is missing, surprisingly, is an engaged campus ministry that could address student spiritual apathy.

The university has created some very impressive and marketable majors for those students whose primary focus is not the strict liberal arts. These disciplines, including sports management, have benefited from DeSales's Catholic values. Students here can be exposed to a quality core curriculum and receive a good education.

Mount St. Mary's University

Emmitsburg, Maryland

www.msmary.edu

Overview

Within cannon shot of the legendary Gettysburg battlefield is an historic Catholic college that has been educating religious leaders and laypeople since 1808. Poised to celebrate its bicentennial, Mount St .Mary's University remains faithful to its original mission.

The history of the Emmitsburg, Maryland, institution includes some legendary figures in American Catholicism. Saint Elizabeth Ann Bayley Seton, the first American-born saint, founded the Sisters of Charity in Emmitsburg. She also established Saint Joseph's Academy and Free School, which became part of St. Mary's College when it was founded in 1808. At the time, the only other Catholic institution of higher education in the United States was Georgetown College.

She worked closely with the college's founding president, the French-born Father John DuBois. Father DuBois led the college for 18 years and then was appointed Bishop of New York, where he served until 1839.

Today, the university has three corporate parts, each of which has had an important impact on the Archdiocese of Baltimore and the nation. The seminary, the second oldest in the United States, is called the "Cradle of Bishops" because it has produced 48 bishops, including one 19th-century cardinal. The National Shrine Grotto of Our Lady of Lourdes, a replica of the shrine located in France, has been receiving thousands of pilgrims since 1875.

The lay institution that was long part of Mount St. Mary's College and Seminary acquired its current name in 2004 to reflect the growth that had taken place, including expansion into graduate programs in education, business, divinity and theology.

But despite changes that have taken place, the Mount has remained faithfully Catholic. Perhaps symbolic of this is the 120-foot tower and golden statute of the Blessed Mother at the Grotto, which looms large over the campus.

Dr. Thomas Powell, who has been university president for the past four years, has worked to enhance its Catholic identity. This is reflected in its strong new mission statement, which consists of four "pillars" and begins with "faith." In June 2007, the board of trustees issued a declaration of Catholic identity.

The university also emphasizes its Catholic identity in its core curriculum, which includes a year-long Freshman Seminar, required courses and choices among several required liberal arts disciplines. The first goal of the undergraduate program, according to the university, is: "An understanding of the Western humanist tradition, including its American expression, particularly as that tradition has been interpreted in Catholic thought and practice (primarily a goal of the core curriculum)."

This mix, along with an opportunity to study on a beautiful 1,400-acre campus in the Catoctin Mountains, attracted students from 28 states and 10 foreign countries to study at the university in the 2006–07 academic year. It is a particularly appealing option for those in Maryland, a state that accounts for about 60 percent of the student body; overall, 91 percent of students are from the Mid-Atlantic region.

Students can pursue more than 40 undergraduate majors, concentrations and minors. These include the traditional liberal arts disciplines as well as more modern ones such as computer science and environmental science. Among the university's academic partnerships is a six-year, undergraduate-graduate program offered in occupational therapy with Sacred Heart University.

Mount St. Mary's offers an M.B.A. and two master's degrees in education at a small campus in Frederick, 20 miles south of Emmitsburg. It also offers its M.B.A. in Hagerstown, a Master of Arts in Liberal Studies at Frederick and part-time programs in Frederick and Westminster, Maryland. The university is fully accredited by the Middle States Association of Colleges and Schools.

The university, recognizing the need to boost its current $35 million endowment, is aiming to increase it another $25 million by 2009.

A target for this fundraising is the 14,000-member alumni association, which is organized into 13 local chapters. One of the non-financial ways that alumni aid the university is through the Mount Alumni-Student Mentor Program, where graduates are paired up with freshmen.

Governance

A predominantly lay, 35-member board of trustees governs the university. Many of the members are prominent business leaders from Maryland and beyond. Ten of the board are clerics, including Archbishop William Cardinal Keeler and Auxiliary Bishop Francis Malooly, both of the Archdiocese of Baltimore, and Bishop Kevin Rhoades of the Diocese of Harrisburg, Pennsylvania.

Bishop Rhoades, who attended Mount St. Mary's College, was rector of the seminary for seven years before he was appointed to his current position in 2004.

Dr. Powell, the 23rd president of the university, was appointed in 2003. Four of the last five presidents have been lay academics. Dr. Powell, whose academic discipline is special education, had previously served as president of Glenville State College, a small central West Virginia institution, which has long specialized in teacher preparation.

Public Identity

President Powell has been working on strengthening the university's Catholic identity. The university's 2006–12 plan, "A Community Growing Together: A Vision for Future Generations," lists "continue to enhance our strong Catholic identity" as the first priority. Among the seven goals that have been identified to promote that objective is to infuse the university's Governing Documents with a commitment to *Ex corde Ecclesiae*.

That was partially done when the board of trustees adopted a vigorous statement on Catholic identity in June 2007. Noting "[a] strong Catholic identity is central to the mission of Mount St. Mary's University," the board stress four tenets which emphasize the primacy of the Gospel and the Church teachings, "full compliance with both the letter and spirit of *Ex corde Ecclesiae*," and the deference to the Holy See and the Archbishop of Baltimore.

The university also has initiated a hiring-for-mission program. The president personally meets with faculty and staff upon hiring and seeking tenure. He expects respect for and no public opposition to Catholic teaching.

The university's Catholic identity is an integral part of the current bicentennial celebration. Bishop Rhoades celebrated the opening event, the Founders Mass, on August 24, 2007. Later that day, a three-ton statue of Father DuBois was dedicated in the center of the campus. Among other events during the 2007–08 academic year will be a Bishops' Mass on November 11 and a pilgrimage to Rome and elsewhere in Italy in April 2008. The seminary has planned a number of separate events, including retreats.

One professor said, "The presence of the seminary on campus has helped out in many indirect ways." There are, of course, the Masses and various spiritual activities at the seminary's St. Bernard Chapel. Seminarians also are seen around campus and initiated a series of annual retreats for teenagers, the last one being Mount 2007 in February 2007.

Another initiative launched by Dr. Powell has been to assign seminarians to be chaplains to each of the university's 19 intercollegiate sports teams. They normally come to all the home games, lead the teams in prayer before games and attend the sports banquets.

The interim athletic director, Lynne Robinson, told us, "The chaplains may stay with their team for several years, up through their ordination to the priesthood. We have had cases where a seminarian has been chaplain to a team for four years. Recently, one who had been chaplain to the soccer team was ordained, and the soccer coaches and a number of team players attended his ordination."

The seminary currently has students from 32 U.S. dioceses as well as the Archdiocese of Grenada in Spain and the Diocese of Cajamarca in Peru. Men from three religious orders also are there. Its fall 2007 figure of 165 seminarians is larger than its number a decade ago. The seminary has trained 2,000 priests since 1808; about 1,200 are currently serving in 45 dioceses.

The third part of the university's corporation, the National Shrine Grotto of Our Lady of Lourdes, is a beautiful haven of spiritual tranquility. It includes the Chapel of St. Mary on the Hill, the small Corpus Christi Chapel, an outdoor Stations of the Cross complex and several statues.

The impressive Pangborn Memorial Campanile bell tower, which is 95 feet tall, has the gold-leafed 25-foot statue of the Blessed Mother at the top. A printed guide to the grotto says the 14 pealing bells have been a call to reflection: "Tradition has it that when John DuBois built his church on this lofty site he did so in order that the people in the valley at their daily tasks would look up, see the Cross and their Blessed Mother and would keep the faith."

Beyond the Grotto, there are other physical manifestations of Catholicism on campus such as Catholic artwork, crucifixes and statues. There also is a lounge identified as the John Paul II Plaza and a building named for a former archbishop of Baltimore, Archbishop William Borders. A recent addition to the seminary is named John R. Keating Hall, honoring the late Bishop of Arlington, Virginia, who was a strong supporter of vocations.

One unique religious observance at Mount St. Mary's is the annual Mass at which college rings are blessed. The Class of 2009 Ring Mass is scheduled for November 11, 2007.

The university is fairly vigilant in ensuring that speakers who might contradict Church teachings do not speak on issues of disagreement. The commencement speakers have been strong. The last three commencement speakers were the Most Reverend Gordon Bennett, Bishop of the Diocese of Mandeville, Jamaica, in 2005; then-Lt.Gov. Michael Steele of Maryland, an active pro-life Catholic and former seminarian, in 2006; and Archbishop Pietro Sambi, Apostolic Nuncio to the United States, in 2007. The 2007 commencement was the university's 199th.

Spiritual Life

The Chapel of the Immaculate Conception, opened in 1910, is the site of what the university calls the "principal university Mass" on Sunday at 7:30 p.m. It is also the location of a Saturday vigil Mass.

Daily Masses, Monday through Friday, are offered at the St. Bernard's Chapel at the seminary, and at noon and 10 p.m. (except Friday) at Mary Queen of Peace Chapel in Pangborn Hall, a residence facility. Masses are reported to be orthodox. Confessions are available three times a week and by appointment. Nearly 70 percent of the undergraduates are Catholic.

The Campus Ministry Organization presents opportunities for students to serve as lectors, ushers, Eucharistic ministers and in other capacities. There also are retreat weekends, Bible study, prayer groups and women's and men's vocation discernment groups. A peer ministry program in which older students work with younger ones in the residence halls and interact with the chaplain was begun in 2006.

The Mount's Callings Program, funded by a Lilly Endowment grant, sponsors numerous ways "to explore faith and life choices." This is done through campus ministry activities as well as an annual conference on campus. More than 1,000 students, faculty and others attended the March 2007 conference. The 2008 conference will examine the future of ministry in the American Church.

Other spiritual opportunities, including Masses, confessions, benediction, novenas and Eucharistic adoration, are available at the adjacent Grotto. This outdoor complex provides a setting for quiet, peaceful meditation.

There are three Catholic parish churches in the immediate vicinity. Saint Anthony Shrine Parish is about one-quarter mile south of the campus and its related church, Our Lady of Mount Carmel, is five miles away; each offers two Masses each Sunday. Less than three miles away in the town of Emmitsburg is Saint Joseph's Church, a Vincentian-run parish; it offers three Masses on Sunday.

Catholicism in the Classroom

The university is proud of its sequenced core curriculum of 19 courses. All first-year students take the Freshman Seminar in the fall and spring semesters. They are taught study skills and are intellectually oriented to college work.

Students focus on cultural studies the first year, two courses of philosophy are taken in the second year and two courses of theology are taken in the third year. Among other requirements are foreign language, non-Western studies and information technology.

The theology department is reported to be strong. All theology professors hold the *mandatum*, but the university does not make it a requirement for employment. There is a theology major—with the opportunity for an emphasis in religious education, pastoral ministry or youth ministry—and a theology minor.

We were told that theology professors see their role as teachers to include a pastoral component, and they strive to help their students integrate their academic work into their personal development.

Among recommended faculty members in the theology department are Father James Donohue, C.R., whose interests are in liturgy, sacraments, pastoral theology and systematic theology; Dr. David McCarthy, systematic and moral theology; and Dr. William Collinge, who pursues Catholic social teaching and the history and philosophy of religion.

The philosophy department also is strong. No philosophy courses or professors promote teachings in opposition to the Catholic faith. The department recognizes, according to one professor there, "a Catholic intellectual tradition and that you don't understand the history of philosophy without understanding the Catholic tradition."

The mission statement of the department is in line with *Fides et Ratio*, Pope John Paul II's 1998 papal encyclical on Faith and Reason. As further evidence of the university's support for this area, a new master's degree in philosophy is near approval.

We understand that two particularly impressive philosophy professors are the department chair, Dr. John Donvan, whose area is modern philosophy, and Dr. Michael Miller, a specialist in medieval philosophy and the philosophy of religion.

There is collegiality between the two departments. For example, in spring 2006 they joined in a faculty development seminar group to enhance their effectiveness and share teaching strategies for the capstone senior ethics course, which can be taken in either theology or philosophy.

They also have collaborated on a new student journal, *Tolle Lege*, which is being launched in the fall 2007 semester. This publication will feature student essays on theology and philosophy, and it expected to have its first issue released in December 2007. The title of the publication is a reference to St. Augustine's conversion.

Our interviewees indicated that Catholic identity varies by department. For example, one professor told us that it was less strong in the education, English, history and psychology departments. But Dr. Powell continues to work on strengthening the overall identity. We are encouraged by his personal involvement and strong endorsement of *Ex corde Ecclesiae*.

As part of its priority to strengthen its academics (priority two of five in its 2006–12 strategic plan), the university is seeking to establish a Center for Catholic Social Justice. It hopes that this initiative will include an endowed professorship and internships.

In the 2006–07 academic year, 43 percent of freshmen were majoring in liberal arts disciplines, 24 percent in the business and accounting programs, 14 percent in science and 12 percent in education.

An honors program is available to students. Included in the program are seminar-type classes and an opportunity to present research to the school at large. Honors students are able to attend special lectures, social and cultural events and periodic dinners at the university president's home.

There is a modest study-abroad program that is arranged by the American Institute for Foreign Studies. During the period 2006–09, semester-long programs have been or will be offered in Austria, Costa Rica, the Czech Republic, France, Ireland, Italy, Spain and the United Kingdom. Faculty members join students and sometimes teach courses.

The Mount has an active Service Learning Program, which encompasses what is known as the 4th Credit Option and Integrated Service Learning. The former allows students to add an additional credit to a course, without financial charge, by doing 30 hours of pertinent outside service and writing about it. Integrated Service Learning is service work integrated into the syllabus of a course.

Student Activities

Students can choose from about 70 clubs to join. These run the gamut of typical groups such as a chess club, chorale and career-related clubs. There also is the Committee to End the Death Penalty, a Knights of Columbus council and the Legion of Mary. There is a Student Government Association as well.

The Mount Students for Life participates in the annual March for Life in Washington, D.C., and other activities. In April 2007, they launched a campus-wide Pro-Life T-Shirt Day as part of a national program sponsored by the American Life League.

There is a homosexual group known as Allies, but it is not an official student club and is housed within campus ministry. According to the university, its "primary purpose is to support one another and to educate others about gays, lesbians, and bisexual issues. This organization recognizes, respects, and supports the Church's teaching on human sexuality, particularly that all single people are called to a life of chastity."

Outdoors activities are available through a group called Challenging Recreation, Unleashing Experience (CRUX). Among its spring 2007 activities were backpacking, canoeing, caving, hiking, rock climbing, snowshoeing and whitewater rafting.

The university has a student-run newspaper, *The Mountain Echo*, which dates back to 1879; it is available in print and online. There also is a campus radio station, WMTB 89.9 FM, which broadcasts 17 hours a day.

Students get involved in service projects which include food drives, help for the homeless, working with individuals with disabilities, soup kitchens, Habit for Humanity and tutoring. Among some specific activities are visiting Villa Saint Michael, a Daughters of Charity retirement home, and St. Catherine's Nursing Center; both are in Emmitsburg. Students also have participated in overseas service trips to Mexico and Peru.

For those interested in sports, there are club sports in dance, equestrian, hockey and rugby. Intramural opportunities are available in nearly two dozen sports, from bocce to volleyball. One respondent said that about one-quarter of all students are engaged in sports.

The Mount fields 19 intercollegiate teams in NCAA Division I, making it the fourth smallest university in that top division. Since 1989 they have competed in the Northeast Conference, which is composed of 11 universities in five states. The 1,000-seat Waldron Family Stadium Complex, which accommodates lacrosse and soccer, was dedicated in August 2007. A new baseball stadium is planned.

The legendary men's basketball coach Jim Phelan amassed 830 wins for the university during his 49-year career that ended in 2003. He won a national championship for the Mount in 1962. The basketball court has been renamed the "Jim Phelan Court" for the quiet leader who was famous for his bowties.

Students also participate in the university's Annual Crab Feast, the Christmas Dance and concerts performed at the Knott Athletic Recreation Convention Complex (ARCC), which seats 3,500 people.

Residential Life

About 90 percent of Mount St. Mary's students live on campus. Housing arrangements separate men and women by floor, and each floor has a resident advisor. Students live either in a Terrace complex of five residence halls, apartments with three towers or in Sheridan Hall. Bicentennial Hall is under construction and is scheduled to open in early 2008.

Some students elect to participate in the Lifestyles of Fellowship, Opportunity and Temperance (LOFT) initiative. These students have an interest in outdoor activities, service projects, healthy living and abstinence from alcohol. They live either in Pangborn Hall or in the Bradley Annex Suites. There also is a floor at Pangborn reserved for Women in Science. Off-campus rental opportunities are identified on the university's website.

Our interviewees noted that student drinking does take place, but it seems not to be a serious problem. All indications are that residential hall life is fairly typical of peer Catholic institutions. One university official said, "For any student who wants to live a good spiritual life and live uprightly, they won't have trouble here."

In an effort to keep parents and families informed about activities at the Mount, the university sponsors a Mount Family Association, coordinated by Dr. Powell's wife, Irene Quinn Powell. Its activities include a newsletter, a Mount Family Prayer Memo online, orientation and a fall Family Fest.

The university operates a wellness center. The nearest hospital, Gettysburg Hospital, is about 15 minutes away. Major research hospitals are located in the Baltimore and Washington, D.C., metropolitan areas.

The Community

Mount St. Mary's is located outside the town of Emmitsburg, which was founded on the frontier in 1785 and today has a population of 2,400 people. One of the landmarks of the town is the National Fire Academy, run by the U.S. Fire Administration and which trains firefighters.

Both serious crime and property crime in Emmitsburg is low, below the national average. But the town did see a doubling of crime between 2005 and 2006, reflected in breaking and entering and larceny crimes.

The campus is only a few miles from the Maryland-Pennsylvania border, which is the Mason-Dixon Line, historically separating the North from the South. Gettysburg, Pennsylvania, the historic Civil War town, is about 10 miles to the north while Frederick, Maryland, is about 20 miles to the south.

All three localities are off U.S. Route 15, which also provides easy access to the Catoctin Mountain Park, part of the U.S. National Park Service, and Cunningham Falls State Park, which offers hiking and water sports. The nearest national highway is Interstate 70, which can be accessed at either Frederick or Hagerstown. The highway runs from Baltimore in the east to Utah in the west.

Emmitsburg is one hour to the west of Baltimore, Maryland's largest city, and one hour north of Washington, D.C., and all the attractions of the nation's capital. Both major cities offer a large number of cultural, social and sports opportunities, including two Major League Baseball and two National Football League teams.

Three major international airports are located about one hour away: Baltimore/Washington International Thurgood Marshall Airport, Ronald Reagan Washington National Airport and Dulles International Airport. Virtually every major domestic and international carrier flies into one or more of these airports.

The Bottom Line

Mount St. Mary's University is proud to be linked to the rich Catholic heritage of the United States, both through its college and seminary. As the university celebrates its bicentennial with a rich array of events, its Catholic identity is prominently featured.

The university has recently strengthened its Catholic mission, and President Thomas Powell has been at the heart of this effort. His leadership in a number of ways comes at the right time as many long-established Catholic colleges are presented with issues of growth, academic freedom and economic constraints.

The Mount appeals most strongly to students in Maryland and the Mid-Atlantic region. But because of its Catholicism, solid curriculum, vibrant student life and impressive location, it will continue to appeal to students from other regions. It is a university that offers much as it enters its third century.

St. Gregory's University

Shawnee, Oklahoma

www.stgregorys.edu

Overview

Benedictine monks reached central Oklahoma in 1875 and immediately laid the framework for a Catholic college. By the early 20th century, their college was moved to Shawnee and became known as the Catholic University of Oklahoma. It grew modestly and was renamed St. Gregory's College and then, in 1997, St. Gregory's University.

The university is the only Catholic college in a state that has a Catholic population of about four percent of its nearly four million residents. It also is the oldest higher education institution in Oklahoma.

St. Gregory's has grown with the city of Shawnee, which has a population today of 29,000 and is located a half-hour east of Oklahoma City. The university has an undergraduate enrollment of 740 students, a majority of them at the Shawnee campus next to St. Gregory's Abbey. There is also a College for Working Adults at Shawnee and at a center in Tulsa about 100 miles away.

The university emphasizes its dedication to the Catholic, Benedictine tradition; its flexibility in academic programs; and its focus on a sense of community. This latter is reflected in what they call "A Community for Life," an appreciation for the sacredness of life and the importance of human relationships.

Students can major in several broad fields in humanities, theology, business, social science, natural science and health and sports science. There also is a teacher education pro-

QUICK FACTS

Founded: 1875
Type of institution: Small liberal arts college
Setting: Suburban
Undergraduate enrollment: 740 (2006–07 academic year)
Total undergraduate cost: $19,980 (tuition, room and board for 2007–08)
Undergraduate majors: Five (and numerous concentrations)

FIVE KEY POINTS

1. Catholic environment reflecting Benedictine Abbey influence.

2. Has programs for student evangelization and interaction with monks.

3. Offers flexible course programs.

4. Appeals to non-traditional students through the College for Working Adults.

5. A regional college that recruits primarily from Oklahoma and nearby states.

gram. A unique aspect of the curriculum is a Design-A-Degree option, through which undergraduates can focus their studies on a particular concentration. In effect, this allows for nearly 50 concentrations.

The university is committed to helping non-traditional students gain associate degrees in a number of fields, including medical technician, liberal arts programs and sacred music. The adult campus in Tulsa offers primarily business degrees at the associate, bachelor and master levels. There are 40 graduate students at the university.

About 58 percent of the students are from Oklahoma, but they also come from 14 other states as well as more than 20 other countries.

Governance

The university is separately incorporated but is a corporate ministry of St. Gregory's Abbey. The primarily lay board of 31 members includes five Benedictines as well as Archbishop Eusebius Beltran of the Archdiocese of Oklahoma City.

St. Gregory's third lay president, Dr. Dave Wagie, took office in April 2007. Dr. Wagie has had an impressive career. In addition to being an active Catholic, he was a career army officer, retiring with the rank of brigadier general; he holds a Ph.D. in engineering; was provost at the U.S. Air Force Academy; and has worked full-time on establishing schools in the United Arab Emirates.

Dr. Wagie succeeded Abbot Lawrence Stasyszen, O.S.B., who had been university president for seven years and who promoted *Ex corde Ecclesiae*. Today he is head of St. Gregory's Abbey and is chancellor of the university, focusing on the relationship between the two institutions as well as on the university's Catholic identity.

Public Identity

St. Gregory's strongly promotes its identity as a Catholic and Benedictine university. Certainly, the presence of the abbey as well as the involvement of the Benedictine monks has helped. The university motto is *Fides Lumen Praebeat* or "May Faith Grant Light." The community frequently refers to eight Benedictine traits: hospitality, community, reverence, attentiveness, service, balance, integrity and excellence.

There is an opening Mass at the beginning of the academic year. One former student told us, "A question arose whether non-Catholic students must attend this Mass, and the faculty insisted that the school must maintain its Catholic identity regardless of the varying faiths of the student body. They pointed out that non-Catholic students were choosing to attend a Catholic university."

We have found no evidence that inappropriate speakers or questionable extracurricular activities have taken place on campus.

Spiritual Life

Campus spiritual life revolves around the Abbey Church, where there are daily Masses. There also are Masses Wednesday and Sunday evenings in St. Benedict's Chapel in one of the three residence facilities, Duperou Hall. Eucharistic adoration is held once a month. Confessions are weekly.

In addition to the Opening Mass of the Holy Spirit, there are Praise and Worship services, Founder's Day prayer services and other special religious activities. During the times of these events, classes are canceled and all offices on campus are closed to allow students and faculty to attend.

Interviewees repeatedly discussed with us the importance of the Buckley Outreach Team, which consists of approximately 10 students who volunteer to organize and perform retreats for Catholic junior high and high school students in Oklahoma, Texas and Arkansas. In the fall of 2006, for example, retreats were sponsored as far away as one in North Little Rock, Arkansas, 300 miles from the university.

Established in 1990 from a bequest by the parents of Academic Vice President Father Charles Buckley, O.S.B., the Buckley Team promotes evangelization in about 20 retreats in 50 parishes and reaches 1,000 students each year. One faculty member told us, "The Buckley Team is *the* main attraction and program at SGU."

Campus ministry is active. There is, for example, a special Lenten and Advent program known as "Food for Thought." This program invites students, staff and faculty to enjoy a homemade bowl of soup while listening to meditations.

The campus ministry recently began a four-cycle of courses on Catholic teachings, an example of a catechetical program that is completely separate from the theology or other academic units. This program focuses only upon Church teachings, and is open to anyone of any faith. The topics for the courses in the rotation include the Sacraments, the Eucharist, God, moral theology and works of mercy.

There also are such outreach activities as pro-life efforts, including participating in the annual March for Life in Washington, D.C., each January, the Angel Tree program that provides Christmas presents to children of incarcerated parents and spring break mis-

sion trips. A Career Vocations and Volunteer Fair allows students to explore religious orders, vocations and lay mission and volunteer services.

There is a student and monk community dinner that gives students further interaction with the monks and priests. Another related, unique program is the Observation Program for University Students (OPUS), where young men of the campus are able to observe monks in their daily lives. Although not many avail themselves of the opportunity, young men are able here to live in the monastery and experience monastic life first hand for a semester.

Catholicism in the Classroom

Theology courses are reported to be orthodox. A former student says that the faithfulness of the theology department exemplifies the Catholic identity of the university. One theology professor frequently recommended in our interviews is Sister Marcianne Kappes, C.S.T.

The area with the largest enrollment is business, followed by natural sciences, education, social science, humanities and arts. Nothing was uncovered by our research that indicates problems with any of the disciplines.

The Common Core is 56 credits earned through courses required of all students. It includes "Tradition and Conversation," a four-semester sequence of seminars based upon the heritage of Western civilization. Four courses are required under the heading of "Faith and Reason," encompassing introductions to theology, philosophy, scripture and ethics. Other traditional subjects in the liberal arts, such as mathematics, history, fine arts and writing, are included in the Common Core.

Everyone also takes six to eight credits of professional development work dealing with computers and orientation to the work world. The university prides itself on its commitment to technology, calling itself "Wireless Laptop University" because of its Local Area Wireless Network.

Student Activities

There are 25 campus student organizations. These include four honor societies; two local fraternities and two local sororities with service components; the student newspaper, *The Chant*; and such diverse groups as Students in Free Enterprise, American Indian Student Association and Habitat for Humanity. There is a Knights of Columbus council and a Fellowship for Christian Athletes group.

There are no organizations that are at variance with the Church. One university official told us that prohibiting them is a "quiet way" of enforcing Catholic teaching.

The St. Gregory Cavaliers participate as one of the 12 members of the Sooner Athletic Conference under the auspices of the National Association of Intercollegiate Athletics.

Residential Life

All full-time students unless exempt by virtue of age, marriage or being a local resident are required to live in an on-campus residential facility. There are three residence halls, two of which are designated solely for women and one that has both men and women but in separate sections.

A strict visitation schedule exists, and there is no visitation anytime after midnight. The university is a "dry" campus as well as drug-free one, and there are few disciplinary problems regarding either issue. One staff member said, "The dry campus allows students to enjoy their college experience without being surrounded by drunkenness."

The campus is safe, and crimes that do occur are usually petty violations. We could find no evidence of violent crime over the last several years. Shawnee's crime rate is generally at or above the U.S. average in most categories. Overall, the city's crime index is more than 25 percent above the national figure.

The Community

Shawnee is a small city that is somewhat of a suburb of Oklahoma City, about 40 miles away. Oklahoma City has a population of 530,000 and has such major attractions as the Oklahoma City Museum of Arts, a zoo, a science center, a cowboy museum and various minor league sports teams.

Will Rogers World Airport, a half-hour from Shawnee, is the gateway for students arriving at St. Gregory's from some distance. Interstate 40 is a major highway that many others would use.

The Bottom Line

St. Gregory's University is not well known nationally. However, what we have seen impresses us. The university benefits from its relationship with St. Gregory's Abbey and its commitment to the Benedictine tradition.

There are a number of attractive points to the university, including its flexible curriculum that allows students to effectively design their major and degree. Similarly, they have a commendable focus on working and adult students, clearly an important emphasis for the future. We also are impressed by the Buckley Outreach Team that evangelizes and supports young adults in three states. For all these reasons, students—especially those from the Great Plains—will want to consider St. Gregory's.

Epilogue

What About Notre Dame?

In compiling this guide, we researched all Catholic colleges and universities that provide undergraduate degrees. Clearly, a number of them have fallen victim to secularization and have chosen to minimize their Catholic identity. There also are those struggling to determine their direction. *The Newman Guide to Choosing a Catholic College* focuses on those 21 institutions that have been exemplary in living their Catholic mission, and we are proud to recommend them.

The greatest challenge came in evaluating the University of Notre Dame. For many people, Catholics and non-Catholics alike, Notre Dame symbolizes Catholic higher education. As we interviewed faculty, students and alumni, and as we researched the record of the university over the past 10 years, we alternated between excitement and discouragement.

Clearly, the academic reputation of many of its colleges and departments as well its overall renown is a source of pride for its alumni and supporters. We also are impressed by the vibrant spiritual life that comes at a time when most large Catholic universities have become increasingly more secularized.

But there are issues, many of which have concerned us for some time, that prevent us from recommending Notre Dame. Overall, these involve matters of "academic freedom" and speaker policies. Among specific examples are a history of performances of *The Vagina Monologues*, homosexual programs and faculty members who are critical of Church teachings.

Fortunately, there are signs of improvement. Thanks to the concerns raised by Father John Jenkins, C.S.C., Notre Dame's president since 2005, *The Vagina Monologues* finally moved off campus in 2007. He also has launched an initiative to strengthen Catholic hiring, which is sorely in need of strengthening.

Ultimately, we decided that no guide to Catholic universities would be complete without discussing Notre Dame. For that reason, we are providing the same analysis that we presented for the preceding institutions, highlighting the strengths and the significant challenges, but without recommendation.

Notre Dame is not an anomaly among large Catholic universities. Most of them share a desire to move from their traditional Catholic liberal arts moorings to a financially driven research university model that characterizes secular institutions. Among its peers, however, Notre Dame emerges at the top of this group in terms of its Catholic identity.

For many Catholic students, attending Notre Dame is a dream come true. But we alert them and their parents that to thrive at Notre Dame requires a good Catholic formation and the exercise of caution in their course selections and social life. And so, we are providing a cautionary note.

Overview

The University of Notre Dame is the most well-known Catholic university in the United States. Its impressive 128-year-old Golden Dome (with the Blessed Virgin Mary on top) has become a symbol of Catholic higher education.

Founded in 1842 by the Congregation of Holy Cross, Notre Dame achieved prominence in the 1920s as a result of its exceptional football teams coached by Knute Rockne. Millions of Catholics became "subway alumni" who aspired to have their children attend the college and be part of the "Fighting Irish" tradition.

Today, Notre Dame consistently ranks in the top tier of U.S. universities, certainly helped by a hefty $4.4 billion endowment, the largest—by far—of any Catholic university. In May 2007, the university began an unprecedented $1.5 billion "Spirit of Notre Dame" capital campaign.

By all accounts, Notre Dame provides a broad-based, quality education. There are 59 bachelor's degree programs, and students have the opportunity to prepare for various professions. The university has eight colleges or schools.

The graduate school dates back to 1918 and was significantly strengthened by the late John Cardinal O'Hara when he was president in the 1930s. The law school, established in 1869, was the first at a Catholic university in the United States. There are a number of other respected programs, including those in architecture and at the Mendoza College of Business. The list goes on. As one respected faculty member said to us, "Notre Dame is a special place."

Governance

Father Edward Sorin, C.S.C., founded the university, and it remained under the control of the Congregation of the Holy Cross until 1967, when governance shifted. Today there is a 12-member Fellows committee, evenly divided between lay and religious members, which controls the university.

The Fellows name the board of trustees, a group that is headed by former Qwest executive Richard Notebaert. There are currently 56 members on the board.

This two-tiered structure, with the higher tier largely in the hands of the religious of the Congregation of the Holy Cross, is unusual among larger Catholic universities and presents an opportunity to protect the Catholic interests of the institution.

The president must be a member of both the Congregation of the Holy Cross and the Fellows. Upon his election, the new president is not required to take an Oath of Fidelity to the Catholic Magisterium, although the president does have to make a commitment to the university's mission statement and its policies.

The mission statement includes the following: "The University of Notre Dame is a Catholic academic community of higher learning, animated from its origins by the Congregation of the Holy Cross. The University is dedicated to the pursuit and sharing of truth for its own sake. As a Catholic university one of its distinctive goals is to provide a forum where through free inquiry and open discussion the various lines of Catholic thought may intersect with all the forms of knowledge found in the arts, sciences, professions, and every other area of human scholarship creativity."

Public Identity

Concerns

There is no question about the academic reputation of this university. But for those concerned about faithfulness to Catholic teaching, the story at Notre Dame is sometimes mixed.

Father Edward Malloy, C.S.C., who resigned in 2005 after 18 years as Notre Dame president, said in 1994 that certain provisions of *Ex corde Ecclesiae* were "offensive to the Catholic theological community." Fortunately, his successor, Father Jenkins, endorses the principles of *Ex corde Ecclesiae,* and he has presented to the faculty reasons why a misguided definition of academic freedom needs to be addressed at Catholic institutions.

Accordingly, many at Notre Dame and others, including alumni and bishops, hoped that Father Jenkins would forthrightly resolve embarrassing contradictions to the university's Catholic identity, such as the annual "queer film festival" and performances of the lewd and morally offensive *Vagina Monologues.* Improvements are being made, but many alumni told us that they are frustrated by the slow pace.

For five years, Father Malloy took no steps to restrict campus performances of the *Monologues* play despite the criticism that it generated among the alumni and Fort Wayne-South Bend Bishop John D'Arcy, who called the play "antithetical to Catholic teaching on human sexuality." By contrast, in 2006 Father Jenkins publicly expressed concern about the content of the play and its variance with Catholic teaching, even while accepting the flawed argument that lewd entertainment is protected by academic freedom.

Father Jenkins prevented ticket sales and moved the play to a classroom, and by 2007 no academic department was willing to sponsor *The Vagina Monologues*, which was moved off campus. Future campus performances are less likely than in previous years, but they are not forbidden by any clear standards of student or faculty conduct.

It is also hoped that Father Jenkins will curb invitations to campus speakers and honorees who clearly are in opposition to Church teaching. The *Monologues'* author, Eve Ensler, spoke in 2005. The following year, President Mary McAleese of Ireland, a critic of the Church, delivered a commencement address and received an honorary degree.

And in May 2007, University of Michigan president and biochemist Dr. Mary Sue Coleman delivered the commencement address to the graduate school. She is a strong public supporter of embryonic stem-cell research.

In another conflict with Church teaching, Notre Dame has embraced events promoted by homosexuals even while withholding official recognition of a student homosexual club. One example is the annual "queer film festival," which has featured dissident speakers and films that celebrate a homosexual lifestyle.

Father Jenkins has taken steps to reduce the profile of the "queer film festival" by changing its name and requesting a more academic approach to discussing the films, but the event still has an apparent goal of celebrating a homosexual "culture" that is hostile to Catholic teaching.

While concerned about such moral contradictions on a prominent Catholic campus, we acknowledge the many challenges that face Father Jenkins as he seeks to strengthen Notre Dame's Catholic identity. We are impressed by his pronouncements on Catholic identity and are hopeful that as he solidifies his influence, questionable activities will be curbed.

Progress

In fact, we see a number of positive signs of Notre Dame's public support for Church teaching. Some of this is student initiated, such as the Edith Stein Project, an annual conference that has promoted a paradigm for a new feminism as an alternative to the approach of *The Vagina Monologues*. This effort has been aided by Notre Dame's Center for Ethics and Culture, a wonderful institute that taps into Catholicism's rich intellectual heritage. The Edith Stein Project was also funded in part by the Cardinal Newman Society in 2007. Father Jenkins has endorsed this project.

There have been speakers who represent traditional Catholic viewpoints. Father John Harvey, O.S.F.S., the founder of Courage, has spoken on the need for homosexuals to live a chaste life. Among notable Church leaders to appear on campus was the formidable Francis Cardinal Arinze of Nigeria, regarded as *papabile*. Among other good speakers have been papal biographer George Weigel and Francis Cardinal George, O.M.I., of nearby Chicago.

Fortunately, there is a dedicated group of alumni, banding together as Project Sycamore, who are working to promote Catholic identity at Notre Dame. This group, which includes former Reagan National Security Advisor Richard Allen, has raised concerns about the *Monologues*, the "queer film festival" and other issues.

Spiritual Life

At the heart of a Catholic university is its spiritual life, and here Notre Dame shines; this helps set "Our Lady's University" apart from many peers. The university offers about 131 Masses on campus every week, the largest number of any university in the nation. There are chapels in every dorm, and Masses are offered every Sunday night in each of them.

One student told us that the most memorable experience for him at Notre Dame was the presence of the Eucharist. In addition to Masses, there is a strong adoration movement that is promoted by students and is available around the clock in the campus ministry building. Such offerings are consistent with a large university where the percentage of students who are Catholic is 85 percent.

Much of this spiritual life of the campus revolves around the magnificent 19th-century Basilica of the Sacred Heart. It has seven chapels; a carillon, dating back to 1852, is the oldest on the continent; and the grotto is a Lourdes replica. The basilica hosts six choirs and holds Sunday vespers.

A cadre of young Holy Cross priests draws high praise for moving spiritual life in the right direction. They have helped promote a Eucharistic procession on Divine Mercy Sunday the past several years, and benediction is offered at four sites, marking the return of a tradition that had been dormant for half a century. Confessions are offered 15 times a week during the academic year.

The Campus Ministry, which has more than 40 staff members, sponsors a broad range of targeted retreats. It also has outreach programs to African American, Latino and Asian American students. Examples include Chinese and Korean Bible study and multilingual Rosaries for Asian Americans. There is an active RCIA program.

Catholicism in the Classroom

Catholic Fidelity

All freshmen are part of the First Year of Studies College. Created in 1962, this program helps ease students into college life on several levels. They are supported here so well that the attrition rate from the freshman to sophomore year is only one percent, a remarkable feat accomplished by only a select few American colleges. Overall, 88 percent of students graduate in four years and about 95 percent within six years.

As part of graduation requirements, students need to take 13 courses selected from a number of disciplines. These include a university seminar that provides an academic orientation, a first-year composition course and a course in fine arts or literature. Other requirements include one course in history and social science and two courses each in mathematics, natural science, philosophy and theology.

Catholic identity in these areas varies. A decentralized approach to faculty hiring over the years has permitted a somewhat haphazard mixture of good and disappointing departments. The flexibility given to students to select from a broad range of courses to meet the broad 13-course requirement creates an environment which one senior professor called a "Disneyland" to pick and choose whatever courses they want. Some can be very good and some can be very bad.

Consider, for example, the theology requirement. One of two courses needed is Catholic oriented, but the other can be selected from more than two dozen offerings. Among these is a course entitled "Catholicism," taught by Father Richard McBrien, a controversial critic of Church teachings.

And we learn from Project Sycamore that of the six credits needed in philosophy, "none [are] in courses necessarily taught from a Catholic perspective."

Fortunately, the theology department, clearly disappointing in the 1980s, has been improving largely through the efforts of department chair John Cavadini. A 2000 graduate of the university said of Cavadini: "He is working in a place that is deeply entrenched, and he is trying to make the changes that are needed."

Foremost among those entrenched professors is Father McBrien. Another is Dominican priest Gustavo Gutierrez Merino, a 79-year-old Peruvian who holds an endowed chair. Considered the father of liberation theology, Gutierrez's work has been criticized by the Vatican.

Faculty members are not required to hold a *mandatum* proclaiming their fidelity to Church teachings—as mandated by Canon law and *Ex corde Ecclesiae*—but about 40 professors have asked for and received it. This issue becomes especially important when looking at replacements for elderly professors (including Father McBrien, who is approaching retirement age).

The philosophy department had been generally very good, bolstered by several outstanding teachers such as Alasdair McIntyre, a major contributor to virtue ethics; Thomists Alfred Freddoso and John O'Callaghan; and David Solomon. Ralph McInerny, a distinguished philosopher and a founder of *Crisis* magazine, has been teaching at Notre Dame since 1955.

Both McIntyre and McInerny are 78 years old, and they will be missed when they retire. Some Notre Dame professors said that with the loss of the best professors, the department is turning toward non-Catholic faculty and, according to one, is "falling apart." We are guardedly optimistic that the new hiring program, described below, might address this issue.

There are other especially notable departments and colleges, including the law school. Among the respected Catholic faculty members there are Gerald Bradley and Father John Coughlin, O.F.M. One faculty member observed that a "significant number of the faculty are into the Catholic tradition. The law school puts legal studies in the context of faith. Most of the faculty will teach law the same as a secular university but with no hostility to belief."

Among other strong faculty is Kent Emery of the Medieval Institute and the Great Books Seminar, and diplomatic history professor Father Wilson Miscamble. *The Irish Rover*, a student newspaper, said of Father Miscamble, "He brings history alive, and perhaps no one does it better."

About 22 percent of undergraduate students major in business fields. The most popular single major is political science, followed by psychology, finance, biological sciences and English. In fall 2006, there were 111 theology majors, about one-quarter of the number of political science majors.

Catholic Hiring

A growing concern at Notre Dame is the number of Catholic professors, currently estimated at about 53 percent. This is a significant decline from about 85 percent in the 1970s.

An initiative launched by Father Jenkins to reverse this trend has been implemented by Dr. Mark Roche, dean of the College of Arts and Letters; his school has, by far, the most faculty and undergraduates. He is aiming to raise the Catholic faculty level within the col-

lege. Dr. Roche has taken a personal interest in the campaign by engaging the selection committees and using inducements to attract Catholic applicants.

Dr. Roche announced in May 2007 that he would be resigning the deanship, effective May 2008. It is unclear what his resignation will mean for the hiring initiative. He will remain as a professor of German language and literature.

For this venture to succeed, Father Jenkins will need to personally step in rather than allow decisions to be made at the department level. According to our investigation, that has not yet happened. In fact, according to Dean Roche, 65 percent of the faculty and researchers hired in 2005–06 were not Catholics.

But there have been some notable high-level hires. The university benefited from the largesse of Donald Keogh, former Coca-Cola president and one-time Notre Dame board chair. He has funded two chairs, known as the Keough-Hesburgh Professorships, for which Catholics are to be given priority.

One recent explicitly Catholic addition to the faculty was the noted microeconomist Dr. Williams Evans, who was selected as the first Keogh-Hesburgh Professor in May 2007. He was attracted from the University of Maryland.

And in August 2007 the university announced the appointment of Dr. Peter Kilpatrick as the dean of the College of Engineering. In announcing the hiring, Provost Thomas Burish said Kilpatrick "has unwavering commitment to advancing the distinctive Catholic character of Notre Dame." The new dean had been chair of North Carolina State University's department of chemical and biomolecular engineering.

Another initiative comes from additional money from Keogh to assist a recruitment effort headed by Father Robert Sullivan, C.S.C., who will look toward compiling a database of solid Catholic academicians. He is a member of the history faculty and head of the Erasmus Institute.

The challenge to achieve success in this area has been encapsulated by a former university official, Richard Conklin. He said of Father Jenkins and the hiring plan: "His point was clear: the DNA for Catholicism on campus is carried by the faculty, not the administration or the students. He promised to work with academic leaders to find ways to attract 'a faculty which includes a diversity of perspectives and commitments but which has a preponderance of Catholics.'"

Father Jenkins recognizes the challenge present in working to achieve an appropriate balance between diversity and orthodoxy. In the winter 2006–07 issue of *Notre Dame Magazine*, the alumni publication, he discusses the need for attracting Catholic faculty: "Consequently, we must remain vigilant about the percentage of new hires who are Catholic, devise strategies to attract superb Catholic scholars and explain why we do so."

"At the same time," he said, "I want to say something that is obvious but may perhaps need more emphasis: Faculty members who are not Catholic are indispensable to the life and success of Notre Dame—in promoting scholarship, in building community, in provoking debate, in pushing for excellence, in ensuring a diversity of perspectives."

Special Programs

The Catholic intellectual life of the university also benefits from several in-house think tanks, two of them particularly noteworthy. One is the Center for Ethics and Culture, headed by Dr. Solomon of the philosophy department. It sponsors scholars, research and conferences that support several of Pope John Paul II's most notable encyclicals. The center's advisory board is a virtual who's who of orthodox Catholic intellectuals.

Another intellectual center on campus is The Jacques Maritain Center, which has been promoting the views of that notable French thinker and Catholic convert since 1957. Maritain (1882–1973) had a close connection with Notre Dame. The Center was once led by Ralph McInerny and now is directed by Dr. O'Callaghan of the philosophy department.

The university has undertaken significant efforts to support Catholic education at the primary and secondary level. The highest profile program is this area is the Alliance for Catholic Education. Every year the university supports graduates who teach at Catholic elementary and secondary schools across the country. No other Catholic university in the country has made such a broad commitment.

Finally, the Office of International Studies offers semester-long and summer programs at many locations on six continents, including targeted programs in Rome, London, Cairo and China. While usually not religious in nature, these offerings enrich the curriculum by allowing students to delve into such areas as art and architecture, classical studies, languages, history, politics and many others.

Student Activities

Not surprisingly, following the Fighting Irish football team is a matter of great interest to students. The football program, perhaps the most storied collegiate athletic program in the nation, helps defines the student body's autumn activities.

But there are many other intercollegiate sports that attract student athletes and fans.

The men's and women's basketball teams play in the highly competitive Big East conference. Under coach Muffet McGraw, the women's team has been a perennial power and won the national title in 2001.

Also noteworthy is The Notre Dame Boxing Club, with a tradition going back to 1923 and Knute Rockne. This clean, amateur program—which emphasizes skill, training and sportsmanship—has long raised money for overseas missions. Charles Rice, now retired, of the law school has been a coach for the club.

There are nearly 300 student groups and organizations on campus. They run the gamut in every sense of the word. One notable intellectual one is The Orestes Brownson Council on American Catholicism and Politics, which regularly meets to help students discuss Catholicism in the public square.

Notre Dame Right to Life is very active and sponsors an annual bus trip to the March for Life in Washington in January that usually draws about 150 students. The club hosted the Pro-Life Collegiate Conference in spring of 2006 and a chastity and pro-life collegiate rally in March 2007.

There also is a Knights of Columbus council, Irish Fighting for St. Jude Kids and Special Friends Club of Notre Dame, in which students work with autistic or special needs children. There is an extensive number of cultural, political, sports and performing arts organizations. There is a strong ROTC program here, too.

We are concerned, however, about some groups such as the Progressive Student Alliance, which advocates for homosexual and workers rights. One area of activity for them concerns the failure of the administration to add "sexual orientation" to its non-discrimination clause.

Less aggressive but equally committed to a variety of activities of concern to orthodox Catholics is a co-op known as ND Watch. It provides guidance on a range of issues, including artificial contraception. While it is clear that ND Watch is hostile to many university policies, its website remains on the university's main web page. Also of note, though run by faculty and staff, is a feminist webspace known as Watch.

The university does not officially recognize homosexual groups, but there is an unofficial Gay-Straight Alliance. Homosexual-oriented events flourish on campus, including a week-long National Coming Out Day in the fall.

The university confuses students by generally forbidding support for such activities and *The Vagina Monologues* through student clubs, yet allowing them when sponsored by faculty or deemed appropriate to students' free discussion and dialogue.

Many of these issues are chronicled in student publications. The university's daily student newspaper, *The Observer,* is occasionally disappointing, giving space to offensive views. A good alternative to the university-funded *Observer* is *The Irish Rover,* an independent, 3,500-circulation biweekly founded in 2003. Both newspapers have online editions.

Residential Life

Eighty percent of Notre Dame's undergraduates live on campus in 27 single-sex residence halls. The university places a strong emphasis on creating the right academic, social and religious tone in the residence halls. Every residence hall has its own rector, who in almost all cases is a priest, nun or brother.

The rector is a full-time university employee who also provides direction to the resident assistants and is responsible for arranging Mass on Saturday or Sunday evening in the residence hall. The religious leader is also available to chat with the students and guide them in their studies and social relations.

"Parietals," hours when members of the opposite sex are permitted in individual dormitory rooms, run from 9 a.m. to midnight Sunday through Thursday and 9 a.m. to 2 a.m. Friday and Saturday; overnight violations are punished. The residence halls all have lounges where people can meet 24 hours a day. There also are various places around campus that are open 24 hours for studying, eating and meeting.

Alcohol has been a problem on the Notre Dame campus. As a result, beer kegs are not permitted in any residence halls or elsewhere on university property. Students are not permitted to provide alcohol to any underage person, including at tailgate events. Hosts of tailgating—tailgating is a staple of the football season—are held responsible for violation of university regulations or Indiana laws. Tailgating during the game is prohibited. There is not a significant drug problem.

The Community

The campus is safe, but the adjacent gritty town of South Bend is not. This one-time industrial city of about 108,000 has an overall crime rate that is consistently 50 percent or more above the national average.

South Bend is the hub of a 15-county Greater Michiana region that covers northern Indiana and a portion of Michigan. Studebaker cars were once manufactured in South Bend. Now education and other service sector businesses support the local economy.

Notre Dame students have been involved with the community. Among the programs are Saint Joseph's Chapin Street Health Center volunteers, a tutoring initiative known as Slice of Life and Neighborhood Study Help Program and a local Habitat for Humanity contingent.

South Bend is about 90 miles east of Chicago. The South Shore Lines commuter rail connects both cities in about 3.5 hours. Amtrak and a busy South Bend Regional Airport also serve the area. Interstate 80, stretching from the east to west coast, can be accessed a few miles from South Bend.

The winters are severe, with average snowfall that is about double the U.S. average. It is the upper Midwest, after all. But the autumn, particularly with the sun shining on the landmark Golden Dome, is a magnificent time to be on campus.

The Bottom Line

Notre Dame is a high-quality university with an international reputation and an extensive alumni network. In many ways, the university clearly takes its Catholic identity seriously. But administrators seem sometimes caught between a commitment to Catholic teachings and a desire to maintain and build its reputation as a research university committed to a secular view of academic freedom.

Catholic identity and academic reputation are not incompatible, but successfully pursuing both requires strong leadership. Despite our disappointment with some decisions, we are optimistic about Father Jenkins's character and ability to achieve reform. The Catholic hiring program is one notable example, although we are awaiting more evidence of its impact. We also are impressed by the existence of a strong spiritual environment, which is a partnership of both students and young priests.

The situation at Notre Dame, in our opinion, is complex. One eminent professor there told us "a kid who is struggling with his faith will sink like a stone." Clearly, that is a chilling comment. And for that reason, we encourage students to discern whether they are prepared for the Notre Dame experience and what it offers and fails to offer.

It is our hope that Notre Dame will "wake up the echoes" of its wonderful, faithful history and be a beacon for other large universities in returning to its original and much-needed mission.

Appendices

Ex corde Ecclesiae

Apostolic Constitution of the Supreme Pontiff John Paul II on Catholic Universities

Given in Rome, at Saint Peter's, on 15 August, the Solemnity of the Assumption of the Blessed Virgin Mary into Heaven, in the year 1990, the twelfth of the Pontificate.

Introduction

Born from the heart of the Church, a Catholic University is located in that course of tradition which may be traced back to the very origin of the University as an institution. It has always been recognized as an incomparable centre of creativity and dissemination of knowledge for the good of humanity. By vocation, the *Universitas magistrorum et scholarium* is dedicated to research, to teaching and to the education of students who freely associate with their teachers in a common love of knowledge.[1] With every other University it shares that *gaudium de veritate,* so precious to Saint Augustine, which is that joy of searching for, discovering and communicating truth[2] in every field of knowledge. A Catholic University's privileged task is "to unite existentially by intellectual effort two orders of reality that too frequently tend to be placed in opposition as though they were antithetical: the search for truth, and the certainty of already knowing the fount of truth."[3]

2. For many years I myself was deeply enriched by the beneficial experience of university life: the ardent search for truth and its unselfish transmission to youth and to all those learning to think rigorously, so as to act rightly and to serve humanity better.

Therefore, I desire to share with everyone my profound respect for Catholic Universities, and to express my great appreciation for the work that is being done in them in the various spheres of knowledge. In a particular way, I wish to manifest my joy at the numerous meetings which the Lord has permitted me to have in the course of my apostolic journeys with the Catholic University communities of various continents. They are for me a lively and promising sign of the fecundity of the Christian mind in the heart of every culture. They give me a well-founded hope for a new flowering of Christian culture in the rich and varied context of our changing times, which certainly face serious challenges but which also bear so much promise under the action of the Spirit of truth and of love.

1. Cf. The letter of Pope Alexander IV to the University of Paris, 14 April 1255, Introduction: *Bullarium Diplomatum...,* vol. III, Turin 1858, p. 602.

2. SAINT AUGUSTINE, *Confes.* X, xxiii, 33: "In fact, the blessed life consists in *the joy that comes from the truth,* since this joy comes from You who are Truth, God my light, salvation of my face, my God". PL 32, 793-794. Cf. SAINT THOMAS AQUINAS, *De Malo,* IX, 1: "It is actually natural to man to strive for knowledge of the truth".

3. JOHN PAUL II, Discourse to the "Institut Catholique de Paris", 1 June 1980: *Insegnamenti di Giovanni Paolo II,* Vol. III/1 (1980), p. 1581.

It is also my desire to express my pleasure and gratitude to the very many Catholic scholars engaged in teaching and research in non-Catholic Universities. Their task as academics and scientists, lived out in the light of the Christian faith, is to be considered precious for the good of the Universities in which they teach. Their presence, in fact, is a continuous stimulus to the selfless search for truth and for the wisdom that comes from above.

3. Since the beginning of this Pontificate, I have shared these ideas and sentiments with my closest collaborators, the Cardinals, with the Congregation for Catholic Education, and with men and women of culture throughout the world. In fact, the dialogue of the Church with the cultures of our times is that vital area where "the future of the Church and of the world is being played out as we conclude the twentieth century."[4] There is only one culture: that of man, by man and for man.[5] And thanks to her Catholic Universities and their humanistic and scientific inheritance, the Church, expert in humanity, as my predecessor, Paul VI, expressed it at the United Nations,[6] explores the mysteries of humanity and of the world, clarifying them in the light of Revelation.

4. It is the honour and responsibility of a Catholic University to consecrate itself without reserve to *the cause of truth.* This is its way of serving at one and the same time both the dignity of man and the good of the Church, which has "an intimate conviction that truth is (its) real ally . . . and that knowledge and reason are sure ministers to faith."[7] Without in any way neglecting the acquisition of useful knowledge, a Catholic University is distinguished by its free search for the whole truth about nature, man and God. The present age is in urgent need of this kind of disinterested service, namely of *proclaiming the meaning of truth,* that fundamental value without which freedom, justice and human dignity are extinguished. By means of a kind of universal humanism a Catholic University is completely dedicated to the research of all aspects of truth in their essential connection with the supreme Truth, who is God. It does this without fear but rather with enthusiasm, dedicating itself to every path of knowledge, aware of being preceded by him who is "the Way, the Truth, and the Life,"[8] the *Logos,* whose Spirit of intelligence and love enables the human person with his or her own intelligence to find the ultimate reality of which he is the source and end and who alone is capable of giving fully that Wisdom without which the future of the world would be in danger.

5. It is in the context of the impartial search for truth that the relationship between faith and reason is brought to light and meaning. The invitation of Saint Augustine, *"Intellege ut credas; crede ut intellegas,"*[9] is relevant to Catholic Universities that are called to explore courageously the riches of Revelation and of nature so that the united endeavour of intelligence and faith will enable people to come to the full measure of their humanity, created in the image and likeness of God, renewed even more marvellously, after sin, in Christ, and called to shine forth in the light of the Spirit.

---

4. JOHN PAUL II, Discourse to the Cardinals, 10 November 1979: *Insegnamenti di Giovanni Paolo II*, Vol. II/2 (1979), p. 1096; cf. Discourse to UNESCO, Paris, 2 June 1980: AAS 72 (1980), pp. 735-752.

5. Cf. JOHN PAUL II, Discourse to the University of Coimbra, 15 May 1982: *Insegnamenti di Giovanni Paolo II*, Vol. V/2 (1982), p. 1692.

6. PAUL VI, Allocution to Representatives of States, 4 October 1965: *Insegnamenti di Paolo VI*, Vol. III (1965), p. 508.

7. JOHN HENRY CARDINAL NEWMAN, *The Idea of a University,* London, Longmans, Green and Company, 1931, p. XI.

8. *Jn* 14:6.

9. Cf. SAINT AUGUSTINE, Serm. 43, 9: PL 38, 258. Cf. also SAINT ANSELM, *Proslogion,* chap. I: PL 158, 227.

6. Through the encounter which it establishes between the unfathomable richness of the salvific message of the Gospel and the variety and immensity of the fields of knowledge in which that richness is incarnated by it, a Catholic University enables the Church to institute an incomparably fertile dialogue with people of every culture. Man's life is given dignity by culture, and, while he finds his fullness in Christ, there can be no doubt that the Gospel which reaches and renews him in every dimension is also fruitful for the culture in which he lives.

7. In the world today, characterized by such rapid developments in science and technology, the tasks of a Catholic University assume an ever greater importance and urgency. Scientific and technological discoveries create an enormous economic and industrial growth, but they also inescapably require the correspondingly necessary *search for meaning* in order to guarantee that the new discoveries be used for the authentic good of individuals and of human society as a whole. If it is the responsibility of every University to search for such meaning, a Catholic University is called in a particular way to respond to this need: its Christian inspiration enables it to include the moral, spiritual and religious dimension in its research, and to evaluate the attainments of science and technology in the perspective of the totality of the human person.

In this context, Catholic Universities are called to a continuous renewal, both as "Universities" and as "Catholic". For, "What is at stake is the *very meaning of scientific and technological research, of social life and of culture*, but, on an even more profound level, what is at stake is *the very meaning of the human person.*"[10] Such renewal requires a clear awareness that, by its Catholic character, a University is made more capable of conducting an *impartial* search for truth, a search that is neither subordinated to nor conditioned by particular interests of any kind.

8. Having already dedicated the Apostolic Constitution *Sapientia Christiana* to Ecclesiastical Faculties and Universities,[11] I then felt obliged to propose an analogous Document for Catholic Universities as a sort of "magna carta", enriched by the long and fruitful experience of the Church in the realm of Universities and open to the promise of future achievements that will require courageous creativity and rigorous fidelity.

9. The present Document is addressed especially to those who conduct Catholic Universities, to the respective academic communities, to all those who have an interest in them, particularly the Bishops, Religious Congregations and ecclesial *Institutions,* and to the numerous laity who are committed to the great mission of higher education. Its purpose is that "the Christian mind may achieve, as it were, a public, persistent and universal presence in the whole enterprise of advancing higher culture and that the students of these institutions become people outstanding in learning, ready to shoulder society's heavier burdens and to witness the faith to the world."[12]

10. In addition to Catholic Universities, I also turn to the many Catholic Institutions of higher education. According to their nature and proper objectives, they share some or all of the characteristics of a University and they offer their own contribution to the Church and to society, whether

---

10. Cf. JOHN PAUL II, Allocution to the International Congress on Catholic Universities, 25 April 1989, n. 3: AAS 18 (1989), p. 1218.

11. JOHN PAUL II, Apostolic Constitution Sapientia Christiana concerning the Ecclesiastical Universities and Faculties, 15 April 1979: AAS 71 (1979), pp. 469-521.

12. VATICAN COUNCIL II, Declaration on Catholic Education *Gravissimum Educationis,* n. 10: AAS 58 (1966), p. 737.

through research, education or professional training. While this Document specifically concerns Catholic Universities, it is also meant to include all Catholic Institutions of higher education engaged in instilling the Gospel message of Christ in souls and cultures.

Therefore, it is with great trust and hope that I invite all Catholic Universities to pursue their irreplaceable task. Their mission appears increasingly necessary for the encounter of the Church with the development of the sciences and with the cultures of our age.

Together with all my brother Bishops who share pastoral responsibility with me, I would like to manifest my deep conviction that a Catholic University is without any doubt one of the best instruments that the Church offers to our age which is searching for certainty and wisdom. Having the mission of bringing the Good News to everyone, the Church should never fail to interest herself in this Institution. By research and teaching, Catholic Universities assist the Church in the manner most appropriate to modern times to find cultural treasures both old and new, *"nova et vetera"*, according to the words of Jesus.[13]

11. Finally, I turn to the whole Church, convinced that Catholic Universities are essential to her growth and to the development of Christian culture and human progress. For this reason, the entire ecclesial Community is invited to give its support to Catholic Institutions of higher education and to assist them in their process of development and renewal. It is invited in a special way to guard the rights and freedom of these Institutions in civil society, and to offer them economic aid, especially in those countries where they have more urgent need of it, and to furnish assistance in founding new Catholic Universities wherever this might be necessary.

My hope is that these prescriptions, based on the teaching of Vatican Council II and the directives of the Code of Canon Law, will enable Catholic Universities and other Institutes of higher studies to fulfill their indispensable mission in the new advent of grace that is opening up to the new Millennium.

Part I

Identity and Mission

A. THE IDENTITY OF A CATHOLIC UNIVERSITY

1. Nature and Objectives

12. Every Catholic University, *as a university*, is an academic community which, in a rigorous and critical fashion, assists in the protection and advancement of human dignity and of a cultural heritage through research, teaching and various services offered to the local, national and international

---

13. *Mt* 13:52.

communities.[14] It possesses that institutional autonomy necessary to perform its functions effectively and guarantees its members academic freedom, so long as the rights of the individual person and of the community are preserved within the confines of the truth and the common good.[15]

13. Since the objective of a Catholic University is to assure in an institutional manner a Christian presence in the university world confronting the great problems of society and culture,[16] every Catholic University, as *Catholic*, must have the following *essential characteristics:*

"1. a Christian inspiration not only of individuals but of the university community as such;

2. a continuing reflection in the light of the Catholic faith upon the growing treasury of human knowledge, to which it seeks to contribute by its own research;

3. fidelity to the Christian message as it comes to us through the Church;

4. an institutional commitment to the service of the people of God and of the human family in their pilgrimage to the transcendent goal which gives meaning to life."[17]

14. "In the light of these four characteristics, it is evident that besides the teaching, research and services common to all Universities, a Catholic University, by *institutional commitment*, brings to its task the inspiration and light of the *Christian message*. In a Catholic University, therefore, Catholic ideals, attitudes and principles penetrate and inform university activities in accordance with the proper nature and autonomy of these activities. In a word, being both a University and Catholic, it must be both a community of scholars representing various branches of human knowledge, and an academic institution in which Catholicism is vitally present and operative."[18]

15. A Catholic University, therefore, is a place of research, where scholars *scrutinize reality* with the methods proper to each academic discipline, and so contribute to the treasury of human knowl-

---

14. Cf. *The Magna Carta of the European Universities*, Bologna, Italy, 18 September 1988, "Fundamental Principles".

15. Cf. VATICAN COUNCIL II, Pastoral Constitution on the Church in the Modern World *Gaudium et Spes*, n. 59: AAS 58 (1966), p. 1080; Declaration on Catholic Education *Gravissimum Educationis*, n. 10: AAS 58 (1966), p. 737. "Institutional autonomy" means that the governance of an academic institution is and remains internal to the institution; "academic freedom" is the guarantee given to those involved in teaching and research that, within their specific specialized branch of knowledge, and according to the methods proper to that specific area, they may search for the truth wherever analysis and evidence leads them, and may teach and publish the results of this search, keeping in mind the cited criteria, that is, safeguarding the rights of the individual and of society within the confines of the truth and the common good.

16. There is a two-fold notion of *culture* used in this document: the *humanistic* and the *socio-historical*. "The word 'culture' in its general sense indicates all those factors by which man refines and unfolds his manifold spiritual and bodily qualities. It means his effort to bring the world itself under his control by his knowledge and his labor. It includes the fact that by improving customs and institutions he renders social life more human both within the family and in the civic community. Finally, it is a feature of culture that throughout the course of time man expresses, communicates, and conserves in his works great spiritual experiences and desires, so that these may be of advantage to the progress of many, even of the whole human family. Hence it follows that human culture necessarily has a historical and social aspect and that the word 'culture' often takes on a sociological and ethnological sense". VATICAN COUNCIL II, Pastoral Constitution on the Church in the Modern World *Gaudium et Spes*, n. 53: AAS 58 (1966), p. 1075.

17. *L'Université Catholique dans le monde moderne. Document final du* 2ème *Congrès des Délégués des Universités Catholiques*, Rome, 20-29 November 1972, § 1.

18. *Ibid.*

edge. Each individual discipline is studied in a systematic manner; moreover, the various disciplines are brought into dialogue for their mutual enhancement.

In addition to assisting men and women in their continuing quest for the truth, this research provides an effective witness, especially necessary today, to the Church's belief in the intrinsic value of knowledge and research.

In a Catholic University, research necessarily includes *(a)* the search for an *integration of knowledge, (b)* a *dialogue between faith and reason, (c)* an *ethical concern*, and *(d)* a *theological perspective*.

16. *Integration of knowledge* is a process, one which will always remain incomplete; moreover, the explosion of knowledge in recent decades, together with the rigid compartmentalization of knowledge within individual academic disciplines, makes the task increasingly difficult. But a University, and especially a Catholic University, *"has to be a 'living union' of individual organisms* dedicated to the search for truth ... It is necessary *to work towards a higher synthesis* of knowledge, in which alone lies the possibility of satisfying that thirst for truth which is profoundly inscribed on the heart of the human person."[19] Aided by the specific contributions of philosophy and theology, university scholars will be engaged in a constant effort to determine the relative place and meaning of each of the various disciplines within the context of a vision of the human person and the world that is enlightened by the Gospel, and therefore by a faith in Christ, the *Logos,* as the centre of creation and of human history.

17. In promoting this integration of knowledge, a specific part of a Catholic University's task is to promote *dialogue between faith and reason,* so that it can be seen more profoundly how faith and reason bear harmonious witness to the unity of all truth. While each academic discipline retains its own integrity and has its own methods, this dialogue demonstrates that "methodical research within every branch of learning, when carried out in a truly scientific manner and in accord with moral norms, can never truly conflict with faith. For the things of the earth and the concerns of faith derive from the same God."[20] A vital interaction of two distinct levels of coming to know the one truth leads to a greater love for truth itself, and contributes to a more comprehensive understanding of the meaning of human life and of the purpose of God's creation.

18. Because knowledge is meant to serve the human person, research in a Catholic University is always carried out with a concern for the *ethical* and *moral implications* both of its methods and of its discoveries. This concern, while it must be present in all research, is particularly important in the areas of science and technology. "It is essential that we be convinced of the priority of the ethical over the technical, of the primacy of the person over things, of the superiority of the spirit over matter. The cause of the human person will only be served if knowledge is joined to conscience. Men

---

19. JOHN PAUL II, Allocution to the International Congress on Catholic Universities, 25 Aprii 1989, n. 4: *AAS* 81 (1989), p. 1219. Cf. also VATICAN COUNCIL II, Pastoral Constitution on the Church in the Modern World*Gaudium et Spes,* n. 61: AAS 58 (1966), pp. 1081-1082. Cardinal Newman observes that a University "professes to assign to each study which it receives, its proper place and its just boundaries; to define the rights, to establish the mutual relations and to effect the intercommunion of one and all". (Op. cit., p. 457).

20. VATICAN COUNCIL II, Pastoral Constitution on the Church in the Modern World *Gaudium et Spes,* n. 36: AAS 58 (1966), p. 1054. To a group of scientists I pointed out that "while reason and faith surely represent two distinct orders of knowledge, each autonomous with regard to its own methods, the two must finally converge in the discovery of a single whole reality which has its origin in God". (JOHN PAUL II, *Address at the Meeting on Galileo, 9* May 1983, n. 3: AAS 75 [1983], p. 690).

and women of science will truly aid humanity only if they preserve 'the sense of the transcendence of the human person over the world and of God over the human person.'"[21]

19. *Theology* plays a particularly important role in the search for a synthesis of knowledge as well as in the dialogue between faith and reason. It serves all other disciplines in their search for meaning, not only by helping them to investigate how their discoveries will affect individuals and society but also by bringing a perspective and an orientation not contained within their own methodologies. In turn, interaction with these other disciplines and their discoveries enriches theology, offering it a better understanding of the world today, and making theological research more relevant to current needs. Because of its specific importance among the academic disciplines, every Catholic University should have a faculty, or at least a chair, of theology.[22]

20. Given the close connection between research and teaching, the research qualities indicated above will have their influence on all teaching. While each discipline is taught systematically and according to its own methods, *interdisciplinary studies,* assisted by a careful and thorough study of philosophy and theology, enable students to acquire an organic vision of reality and to develop a continuing desire for intellectual progress. In the communication of knowledge, emphasis is then placed on how *human reason in its reflection* opens to increasingly broader questions, and how the complete answer to them can only come from above through faith. Furthermore, the *moral implications* that are present in each discipline are examined as an integral part of the teaching of that discipline so that the entire educative process be directed towards the whole development of the person. Finally, Catholic theology, taught in a manner faithful to Scripture, Tradition, and the Church's Magisterium, provides an awareness of the Gospel principles which will enrich the meaning of human life and give it a new dignity.

Through research and teaching the students are educated in the various disciplines so as to become truly competent in the specific sectors in which they will devote themselves to the service of society and of the Church, but at the same time prepared to give the witness of their faith to the world.

2. *The University Community*

21. A Catholic University pursues its objectives through its formation of an authentic human community animated by the spirit of Christ. The source of its unity springs from a common dedication to the truth, a common vision of the dignity of the human person and, ultimately, the person and message of Christ which gives the Institution its distinctive character. As a result of this inspiration, the community is animated by a spirit of freedom and charity; it is characterized by mutual respect, sincere dialogue, and protection of the rights of individuals. It assists each of its members to achieve wholeness as human persons; in turn, everyone in the community helps in promoting unity, and each one, according to his or her role and capacity, contributes towards decisions which affect the community, and also towards maintaining and strengthening the distinctive Catholic character of the Institution.

21. JOHN PAUL II, Address at UNESCO, 2 June 1980, n. 22: AAS 72 (1980), p. 750. The last part of the quotation uses words directed to the Pontifical Academy of Sciences, 10 November 1979: *Insegnamenti di Giovanni Paolo II,* Vol. II/2 (1979), p. 1109.

22. Cf. VATICAN COUNCIL II, Declaration on Catholic Education *Gravissimum Educationis,* n. 10: *AAS* 58 (1966), p. 737.

22. *University teachers* should seek to improve their competence and endeavour to set the content, objectives, methods, and results of research in an individual discipline within the framework of a coherent world vision. Christians among the teachers are called to be witnesses and educators of authentic Christian life, which evidences attained integration between faith and life, and between professional competence and Christian wisdom. All teachers are to be inspired by academic ideals and by the principles of an authentically human life.

23. *Students* are challenged to pursue an education that combines excellence in humanistic and cultural development with specialized professional training. Most especially, they are challenged to continue the search for truth and for meaning throughout their lives, since "the human spirit must be cultivated in such a way that there results a growth in its ability to wonder, to understand, to contemplate, to make personal judgments, and to develop a religious, moral, and social sense."[23] This enables them to acquire or, if they have already done so, to deepen a Christian way of life that is authentic. They should realize the responsibility of their professional life, the enthusiasm of being the trained 'leaders' of tomorrow, of being witnesses to Christ in whatever place they may exercise their profession.

24. *Directors* and *administrators* in a Catholic University promote the constant growth of the University and its community through a leadership of service; the dedication and witness of the *non-academic staff* are vital for the identity and life of the University.

25. Many Catholic Universities were founded by Religious Congregations, and continue to depend on their support; those Religious Congregations dedicated to the apostolate of higher education are urged to assist these Institutions in the renewal of their commitment, and to continue to prepare religious men and women who can positively contribute to the mission of a Catholic University.

Lay people have found in university activities a means by which they too could exercise an important apostolic role in the Church and, in most Catholic Universities today, the academic community is largely composed of laity; in increasing numbers, lay men and women are assuming important functions and responsibilities for the direction of these Institutions. These lay Catholics are responding to the Church's call "to be present, as signs of courage and intellectual creativity, in the privileged places of culture, that is, the world of education-school and university."[24] The future of Catholic Universities depends to a great extent on the competent and dedicated service of lay Catholics. The Church sees their developing presence in these institutions both as a sign of hope and as a confirmation of the irreplaceable lay vocation in the Church and in the world, confident that lay people will, in the exercise of their own distinctive role, "illumine and organize these (temporal) affairs in such a way that they always start out, develop, and continue according to Christ's mind, to the praise of the Creator and the Redeemer."[25]

---

23. VATICAN COUNCIL II, Pastoral Constitution on the Church in the Modern World *Gaudium et Spes,* n. 59: AAS 58 (1966), p. 1080. Cardinal Newman describes the ideal to be sought in this way: "A habit of mind is formed which lasts through life, of which the attributes are freedom, equitableness, calmness, moderation and wisdom". (*Op. cit.,* pp. 101-102).

24. JOHN PAUL II, Post-Synodal Apostolic Exhortation *Christifideles Laici,* 30 December 1988, n. 44: AAS 81 (1989), p. 479.

25. VATICAN COUNCIL II, Dogmatic Constitution on the Church *Lumen Gentium,* n. 31: *AAS* 57 (1965), pp. 37-38. Cf. Decree on the Apostolate of the Laity *Apostolicam Actuositatem,* passim: AAS 58 (1966), pp. 837ff. Cf. also *Gaudium et Spes,* n. 43: *AAS* 58 (1966), pp. 1061-1064.

26. The university community of many Catholic institutions includes members of other Churches, ecclesial communities and religions, and also those who profess no religious belief. These men and women offer their training and experience in furthering the various academic disciplines or other university tasks.

3. *The Catholic University in the Church*

27. Every Catholic University, without ceasing to be a University, has a relationship to the Church that is essential to its institutional identity. As such, it participates most directly in the life of the local Church in which it is situated; at the same time, because it is an academic institution and therefore a part of the international community of scholarship and inquiry, each institution participates in and contributes to the life and the mission of the universal Church, assuming consequently a special bond with the Holy See by reason of the service to unity which it is called to render to the whole Church. One consequence of its essential relationship to the Church is that the institutional fidelity of the University to the Christian message includes a recognition of and adherence to the teaching authority of the Church in matters of faith and morals. Catholic members of the university community are also called to a personal fidelity to the Church with all that this implies. Non-Catholic members are required to respect the Catholic character of the University, while the University in turn respects their religious liberty.26

28. Bishops have a particular responsibility to promote Catholic Universities, and especially to promote and assist in the preservation and strengthening of their Catholic identity, including the protection of their Catholic identity in relation to civil authorities. This will be achieved more effectively if close personal and pastoral relationships exist between University and Church authorities, characterized by mutual trust, close and consistent cooperation and continuing dialogue. Even when they do not enter directly into the internal governance of the University, Bishops "should be seen not as external agents but as participants in the life of the Catholic University."[27]

29. The Church, accepting "the legitimate autonomy of human culture and especially of the sciences", recognizes the academic freedom of scholars in each discipline in accordance with its own principles and proper methods,[28] and within the confines of the truth and the common good.

Theology has its legitimate place in the University alongside other disciplines. It has proper principles and methods which define it as a branch of knowledge. Theologians enjoy this same freedom so long as they are faithful to these principles and methods.

Bishops should encourage the creative work of theologians. They serve the Church through research done in a way that respects theological method. They seek to understand better, further

---

26. Cf. VATICAN COUNCIL II, Declaration on Religious Liberty *Dignitatis Humanae*, n. 2: AAS 58 (1966), pp. 930-931.

27. JOHN PAUL II, Address to Leaders of Catholic Higher Education, Xavier University of Louisiana, U.S.A., 12 September 1987, n. 4: AAS 80 (1988), p. 764.

28. VATICAN COUNCIL II, Pastoral Constitution on the Church in the Modern World *Gaudium et Spes*, n. 59: *AAS* 58 (1966), p. 1080.

develop and more effectively communicate the meaning of Christian Revelation as transmitted in Scripture and Tradition and in the Church's Magisterium. They also investigate the ways in which theology can shed light on specific questions raised by contemporary culture. At the same time, since theology seeks an understanding of revealed truth whose authentic interpretation is entrusted to the Bishops of the Church,[29] it is intrinsic to the principles and methods of their research and teaching in their academic discipline that theologians respect the authority of the Bishops, and assent to Catholic doctrine according to the degree of authority with which it is taught.[30] Because of their interrelated roles, dialogue between Bishops and theologians is essential; this is especially true today, when the results of research are so quickly and so widely communicated through the media.[31]

B. THE MISSION OF SERVICE OF A CATHOLIC UNIVERSITY

30. The basic mission of a University is a continuous quest for truth through its research, and the preservation and communication of knowledge for the good of society. A Catholic University participates in this mission with its own specific characteristics and purposes.

1. Service to Church and Society

31. Through teaching and research, a Catholic University offers an indispensable contribution to the Church. In fact, it prepares men and women who, inspired by Christian principles and helped to live their Christian vocation in a mature and responsible manner, will be able to assume positions of responsibility in the Church. Moreover, by offering the results of its scientific research, a Catholic University will be able to help the Church respond to the problems and needs of this age.

32. A Catholic University, as any University, is immersed in human society; as an extension of its service to the Church, and always within its proper competence, it is called on to become an ever more effective instrument of cultural progress for individuals as well as for society. Included among its research activities, therefore, will be a study of *serious contemporary problems* in areas such as the dignity of human life, the promotion of justice for all, the quality of personal and family life, the protection of nature, the search for peace and political stability, a more just sharing in the world's resources, and a new economic and political order that will better serve the human community at a national and international level. University research will seek to discover the roots and causes of the serious problems of our time, paying special attention to their ethical and religious dimensions.

---

29. Cf. VATICAN COUNCIL II, Dogmatic Constitution on Divine Revelation *Dei Verbum*, nn. 8-10: *AAS* 58 (1966), pp. 820-822.

30. Cf. VATICAN COUNCIL II, Dogmatic Constitution on the Church *Lumen Gentium*, n. 25: *AAS* 57 (1965), pp. 29-31.

31. Cf. "Instruction on the Ecclesial Vocation of the Theologian" of the Congregation for the Doctrine of the Faith of 24 May 1990.

If need be, a Catholic University must have the courage to speak uncomfortable truths which do not please public opinion, but which are necessary to safeguard the authentic good of society.

33. A specific priority is the need to examine and evaluate the predominant values and norms of modern society and culture in a Christian perspective, and the responsibility to try to communicate to society those *ethical and religious principles which give full meaning to human life.* In this way a University can contribute further to the development of a true Christian anthropology, founded on the person of Christ, which will bring the dynamism of the creation and redemption to bear on reality and on the correct solution to the problems of life.

34. The Christian spirit of service to others for the *promotion of social justice* is of particular importance for each Catholic University, to be shared by its teachers and developed in its students. The Church is firmly committed to the integral growth of all men and women.[32] The Gospel, interpreted in the social teachings of the Church, is an urgent call to promote "the development of those peoples who are striving to escape from hunger, misery, endemic diseases and ignorance; of those who are looking for a wider share in the benefits of civilization and a more active improvement of their human qualities; of those who are aiming purposefully at their complete fulfilment."[33] Every Catholic University feels responsible to contribute concretely to the progress of the society within which it works: for example it will be capable of searching for ways to make university education accessible to all those who are able to benefit from it, especially the poor or members of minority groups who customarily have been deprived of it. A Catholic University also has the responsibility, to the degree that it is able, to help to promote the development of the emerging nations.

35. In its attempts to resolve these complex issues that touch on so many different dimensions of human life and of society, a Catholic University will insist on cooperation among the different academic disciplines, each offering its distinct contribution in the search for solutions; moreover, since the economic and personal resources of a single Institution are limited, cooperation in *common research projects* among Catholic Universities, as well as with other private and governmental institutions, is imperative. In this regard, and also in what pertains to the other fields of the specific activity of a Catholic University, the role played by various national and international associations of Catholic Universities is to be emphasized. Among these associations the mission of *The International Federation of Catholic Universities,* founded by the Holy See,[34] is particularly to be remembered. The Holy See anticipates further fruitful collaboration with this Federation.

36. Through programmes of *continuing education* offered to the wider community, by making its scholars available for consulting services, by taking advantage of modern means of communication, and in a variety of other ways, a Catholic University can assist in making the growing body of human knowledge and a developing understanding of the faith available to a wider public, thus expanding university services beyond its own academic community.

32. Cf. JOHN PAUL II, Encyclical Letter Sollicitudo Rei Socialis, nn. 27-34: *AAS* 80 (1988), pp. 547-560.

33. PAUL VI, Encyclical Letter *Populorum Progressio*, n. 1: AAS 59 (1967), p. 257.

34. "Therefore, in that there has been a pleasing multiplication of centres of higher learning, it has become apparent that it would be opportune for the faculty and the alumni to unite in common association which, working in reciprocal understanding and close collaboration, and based upon the authority of the Supreme Pontiff, as father and universal doctor, they might more efficaciously spread and extend the light of Christ". (Plus XII, Apostolic Letter *Catholicas Studiorum Universitates*, with which The International Federation of Catholic Universities was established: AAS 42 [1950], p. 386).

37. In its service to society, a Catholic University *will relate especially to the academic, cultural and scientific world* of the region in which it is located. Original forms of dialogue and collaboration are to be encouraged between the Catholic Universities and the other Universities of a nation on behalf of development, of understanding between cultures, and of the defence of nature in accordance with an awareness of the international ecological situation.

Catholic Universities join other private and public Institutions in serving the public interest through higher education and research; they are one among the variety of different types of institution that are necessary for the free expression of cultural diversity, and they are committed to the promotion of solidarity and its meaning in society and in the world. Therefore they have the full right to expect that civil society and public authorities will recognize and defend their institutional autonomy and academic freedom; moreover, they have the right to the financial support that is necessary for their continued existence and development.

2. Pastoral Ministry

38. Pastoral ministry is that activity of the University which offers the members of the university community an opportunity to integrate religious and moral principles with their academic study and non-academic activities, *thus integrating faith with life*. It is part of the mission of the Church within the University, and is also a constitutive element of a Catholic University itself, both in its structure and in its life. A university community concerned with promoting the Institution's Catholic character will be conscious of this pastoral dimension and sensitive to the ways in which it can have an influence on all university activities.

39. As a natural expression of the Catholic identity of the University, the university community *should give a practical demonstration of its faith in its daily activity*, with important moments of reflection and of prayer. Catholic members of this community will be offered opportunities to assimilate Catholic teaching and practice into their lives and will be encouraged to participate in the celebration of the sacraments, especially the Eucharist as the most perfect act of community worship. When the academic community includes members of other Churches, ecclesial communities or religions, their initiatives for reflection and prayer in accordance with their own beliefs are to be respected.

40. Those involved in pastoral ministry will encourage teachers and students to become more aware of their responsibility towards those who are suffering physically or spiritually. Following the example of Christ, they will be particularly attentive to the poorest and to those who suffer economic, social, cultural or religious injustice. This responsibility begins within the academic community, but it also finds application beyond it.

41. Pastoral ministry is an indispensable means by which Catholic students can, in fulfilment of their baptism, *be prepared for active participation in the life of the Church*; it can assist in developing and nurturing the value of marriage and family life, fostering vocations to the priesthood and religious life, stimulating the Christian commitment of the laity and imbuing every activity with the spirit of the Gospel. Close cooperation between pastoral ministry in a Catholic University and the other

activities within the local Church, under the guidance or with the approval of the diocesan Bishop, will contribute to their mutual growth.[35]

42. Various associations or movements of spiritual and apostolic life, especially those developed specifically for students, can be of great assistance in developing the pastoral aspects of university life.

3. Cultural Dialogue

43. By its very nature, a University develops culture through its research, helps to transmit the local culture to each succeeding generation through its teaching, and assists cultural activities through its educational services. It is open to all human experience and is ready to dialogue with and learn from any culture. A Catholic University shares in this, offering the rich experience of the Church's own culture. In addition, a Catholic University, aware that human culture is open to Revelation and transcendence, is also a primary and privileged place for a *fruitful dialogue between the Gospel and culture.*

44. Through this dialogue a Catholic University assists the Church, enabling it to come to a better knowledge of diverse cultures, discern their positive and negative aspects, to receive their authentically human contributions, and to develop means by which it can make the faith better understood by the men and women of a particular culture.[36] While it is true that the Gospel cannot be identified with any particular culture and transcends all cultures, it is also true that "the Kingdom which the Gospel proclaims is lived by men and women who are profoundly linked to a culture, and the building up of the Kingdom cannot avoid borrowing the elements of human culture or cultures.[37] "A faith that places itself on the margin of what is human, of what is therefore culture, would be a faith unfaithful to the fullness of what the Word of God manifests and reveals, a decapitated faith, worse still, a faith in the process of self-annihilation."[38]

45. A Catholic University must become *more attentive to the cultures of the world of today,* and to the *various cultural traditions existing within the Church* in a way that will promote a continuous and profitable dialogue between the Gospel and modern society. Among the criteria that characterize the values of a culture are above all, the *meaning of the human person,* his or her liberty, dignity, *sense of*

---

35. The Code of Canon Law indicates the general responsibility of the Bishop toward university students: "The diocesan bishop is to have serious pastoral concern for students by erecting a parish for them or by assigning priests for this purpose on a stable basis; he is also to provide for Catholic university centers at universities, even non-Catholic ones, to give assistance, especially spiritual to young people". (*CIC*, can. 813).

36. "Living in various circumstances during the course of time, the Church, too, has used in her preaching the discoveries of different cultures to spread and explain the message of Christ to all nations, to probe it and more deeply understand it, and to give it better expression in liturgical celebrations and in the life of the diversified community of the faithful". (VATICAN COUNCIL II, Pastoral Constitution on the Church in the Modern World *Gaudium et Spes*, n. 58: AAS 58 [1966], p. 1079).

37. PAUL VI, Apostolic Exhortation Evangelii Nuntiandi, n. 20: AAS 68 (1976), p. 18. Cf. VATICAN COUNCIL II, Pastotal Constitution on the Church in the Modern World *Gaudium et Spes*, n. 58: AAS 58 (1966), p. 1079.

38. JOHN PAUL II, Address to Intellectuals, to Students and to University Personnel at Medellín, Colombia, 5 July 1986, n. 3: AAS 79 (1987), p. 99. Cf. also VATICAN COUNCIL II, Pastoral Constitution on the Church in the Modern World *Gaudium et Spes*, n. 58: *AAS* 58 (1966), p. 1079.

responsibility, and openness to the transcendent. To a respect for persons is joined *the preeminent value of the family,* the primary unit of every human culture.

Catholic Universities will seek to discern and evaluate both the aspirations and the contradictions of modern culture, in order to make it more suited to the total development of individuals and peoples. In particular, it is recommended that by means of appropriate studies, the impact of modern technology and especially of the mass media on persons, the family, and the institutions and whole of modem culture be studied deeply. Traditional cultures are to be defended in their identity, helping them to receive modern values without sacrificing their own heritage, which is a wealth for the whole of the human family. Universities, situated within the ambience of these cultures, will seek to harmonize local cultures with the positive contributions of modern cultures.

46. An area that particularly interests a Catholic University is the *dialogue between Christian thought and the modern sciences.* This task requires persons particularly well versed in the individual disciplines and who are at the same time adequately prepared theologically, and who are capable of confronting epistemological questions at the level of the relationship between faith and reason. Such dialogue concerns the natural sciences as much as the human sciences which posit new and complex philosophical and ethical problems. The Christian researcher should demonstrate the way in which human intelligence is enriched by the higher truth that comes from the Gospel: "The intelligence is never diminished, rather, it is stimulated and reinforced by that interior fount of deep understanding that is the Word of God, and by the hierarchy of values that results from it... In its unique manner, the Catholic University helps to manifest the superiority of the spirit, that can never, without the risk of losing its very self, be placed at the service of something other than the search for truth."[39]

47. Besides cultural dialogue, a Catholic University, in accordance with its specific ends, and keeping in mind the various religious-cultural contexts, following the directives promulgated by competent ecclesiastical authority, can offer a contribution to ecumenical dialogue. It does so to further the search for unity among all Christians. In inter-religious dialogue it will assist in discerning the spiritual values that are present in the different religions.

4. Evangelization

48. The primary mission of the Church is to preach the Gospel in such a way that a relationship between faith and life is established in each individual and in the socio-cultural context in which individuals live and act and communicate with one another. Evangelization means "bringing the Good News into all the strata of humanity, and through its influence transforming humanity from within and making it new. . . . It is a question not only of preaching the Gospel in ever wider geographic areas or to ever greater numbers of people, but also of affecting and, as it were, upsetting, through the power of the Gospel, humanity's criteria of judgment, determining values, points of interest, lines of thought, sources of inspiration and models of life, which are in contrast with the Word of

---

39. PAUL VI, to the Delegates of The International Federation of Catholic Universities, 27 November 1972: *AAS* 64 (1972), p. 770.

God and the plan of salvation."[40]

49. By its very nature, each Catholic University makes an important contribution to the Church's work of evangelization. It is a living *institutional* witness to Christ and his message, so vitally important in cultures marked by secularism, or where Christ and his message are still virtually unknown. Moreover, all the basic academic activities of a Catholic University are connected with and in harmony with the evangelizing mission of the Church: research carried out in the light of the Christian message which puts new human discoveries at the service of individuals and society; education offered in a faith-context that forms men and women capable of rational and critical judgment and conscious of the transcendent dignity of the human person; professional training that incorporates ethical values and a sense of service to individuals and to society; the dialogue with culture that makes the faith better understood, and the theological research that translates the faith into contemporary language. "Precisely because it is more and more conscious of its salvific mission in this world, the Church wants to have these centres closely connected with it; it wants to have them present and operative in spreading the authentic message of Christ."[41]

Part II

General Norms

Article 1. *The Nature of these General Norms*

§ 1. These General Norms are based on, and are a further development of, the Code of Canon Law[42] and the complementary Church legislation, without prejudice to the right of the Holy See to intervene should this become necessary. They are valid for all Catholic Universities and other Catholic Institutes of Higher Studies throughout the world.

§ 2. The General Norms are to be applied concretely at the local and regional levels by Episcopal Conferences and other Assemblies of Catholic Hierarchy[43] in conformity with the Code of Canon Law and complementary Church legislation, taking into account the Statutes of each University or Institute and, as far as possible and appropriate, civil law. After review by the Holy See,[44] these local or regional "Ordinances" will be valid for all Catholic Universities and other Catholic Institutes of Higher Studies in the region, except for Ecclesiastical Universities and Faculties. These latter Institu-

---

40. PAUL VI, Apostolic Exhortation *Evangelii Nuntiandi,* nn. 18ff.: *AAS* 68 (1976), pp. 17-18.

41. PAUL VI, Address to Presidents and Rectors of the Universities of the Society of Jesus, 6 August 1975, n. 2: AAS 67 (1975), p. 533. Speaking to the participants of the International Congress on Catholic Universities, 25 April 1989, I added (n. 5): "Within a Catholic University the evangelical mission of the Church and the mission of research and teaching become *interrelated* and *coordinated*": Cf. *AAS* 81 (1989), p. 1220.

42. Cf. in particular the Chapter of the Code: "Catholic Universities and other Institutes of Higher Studies" *(CIC,* cann. 807-814).

43. Episcopal Conferences were established in the Latin Rite. Other Rites have other Assemblies of Catholic Hierarchy.

44. Cf. *CIC,* Can. 455, §2.

tions, including Ecclesiastical Faculties which are part of a Catholic University, are governed by the norms of the Apostolic Constitution *Sapientia Christiana.*[45]

§ 3. A University established or approved by the Holy See, by an Episcopal Conference or another Assembly of Catholic Hierarchy, or by a diocesan Bishop is to incorporate these General Norms and their local and regional applications into its governing documents, and conform its existing Statutes both to the General Norms and to their applications, and submit them for approval to the competent ecclesiastical Authority. It is contemplated that other Catholic Universities, that is, those not established or approved in any of the above ways, with the agreement of the local ecclesiastical Authority, will make their own the General Norms and their local and regional applications, internalizing them into their governing documents, and, as far as possible, will conform their existing Statutes both to these General Norms and to their applications.

Article 2. *The Nature of a Catholic University*

§ 1. A Catholic University, like every university, is a community of scholars representing various branches of human knowledge. It is dedicated to research, to teaching, and to various kinds of service in accordance with its cultural mission.

§ 2. A Catholic University, as Catholic, informs and carries out its research, teaching, and all other activities with Catholic ideals, principles and attitudes. It is linked with the Church either by a formal, constitutive and statutory bond or by reason of an institutional commitment made by those responsible for it.

§ 3. Every Catholic University is to make known its Catholic identity, either in a mission statement or in some other appropriate public document, unless authorized otherwise by the competent ecclesiastical Authority. The University, particularly through its structure and its regulations, is to provide means which will guarantee the expression and the preservation of this identity in a manner consistent with §2.

§ 4. Catholic teaching and discipline are to influence all university activities, while the freedom of conscience of each person is to be fully respected.[46] Any official action or commitment of the University is to be in accord with its Catholic identity.

§ 5. A Catholic University possesses the autonomy necessary to develop its distinctive identity and pursue its proper mission. Freedom in research and teaching is recognized and respected according to the principles and methods of each individual discipline, so long as the rights of the individual and of the community are preserved within the confines of the truth and the common good.[47]

---

45. Cf. *Sapientia Christiana: AAS* 71 (1979), pp. 469-521. Ecclesiastical Universities and Faculties are those that have the right to confer academic degress by the authority of the Holy See.

46. Cf. VATICAN COUNCIL II, Declaration on Religious Liberty *Dignitatis Humanae,* n. 2: *AAS* 58 (1966), pp. 930-931.

47. Cf. VATICAN COUNCIL II, Pastoral Constitution on the Church in the Modern World *Gaudium et Spes,* nn. 57 and 59: *AAS* 58 (1966), pp. 1077-1080; *Gravissimum Educationis,* n. 10: *AAS* 58 (1966), p. 737.

Article 3. *The Establishment of a Catholic University*

§ 1. A Catholic University may be established or approved by the Holy See, by an Episcopal Conference or another Assembly of Catholic Hierarchy, or by a diocesan Bishop.

§ 2. With the consent of the diocesan Bishop, a Catholic University may also be established by a Religious Institute or other public juridical person.

§ 3. A Catholic University may also be established by other ecclesiastical or lay persons; such a University may refer to itself as a Catholic University only with the consent of the competent ecclesiastical Authority, in accordance with the conditions upon which both parties shall agree.[48]

§ 4. In the cases of §§ 1 and 2, the Statutes must be approved by the competent ecclesiastical Authority.

Article 4. *The University Community*

§ 1. The responsibility for maintaining and strengthening the Catholic identity of the University rests primarily with the University itself. While this responsibility is entrusted principally to university authorities (including, when the positions exist, the Chancellor and/or a Board of Trustees or equivalent body), it is shared in varying degrees by all members of the university community, and therefore calls for the recruitment of adequate university personnel, especially teachers and administrators, who are both willing and able to promote that identity. The identity of a Catholic University is essentially linked to the quality of its teachers and to respect for Catholic doctrine. It is the responsibility of the competent Authority to watch over these two fundamental needs in accordance with what is indicated in Canon Law.[49]

§ 2. All teachers and all administrators, at the time of their appointment, are to be informed about the Catholic identity of the Institution and its implications, and about their responsibility to promote, or at least to respect, that identity.

§ 3. In ways appropriate to the different academic disciplines, all Catholic teachers are to be faithful to, and all other teachers are to respect, Catholic doctrine and morals in their research and teaching. In particular, Catholic theologians, aware that they fulfil a mandate received from the Church,

---

48. Both the establishment of such a university and the conditions by which it may refer to itself as a Catholic University are to be in accordance with the prescriptions issued by the Holy See, Episcopal Conference or other Assembly of Catholic Hierarchy.

49. Canon 810 of CIC, specifies the responsibility of the competent Authorities in this area: § 1 "It is the responsibility of the authority who is competent in accord with the statutes to provide for the appointment of teachers to Catholic universities who, besides their scientific and pedagogical suitability, are also outstanding in their integrity of doctrine and probity of life; when those requisite qualities are lacking they are to be removed from their positions in accord with the procedure set forth in the statutes. § 2 The conference of bishops and the diocesan bishops concerned have the duty and right of being vigilant that in these universities the principles of Catholic doctrine are faithfully observed". Cf. also Article 5, 2 ahead in these "Norms".

are to be faithful to the Magisterium of the Church as the authentic interpreter of Sacred Scripture and Sacred Tradition.[50]

§ 4. Those university teachers and administrators who belong to other Churches, ecclesial communities, or religions, as well as those who profess no religious belief, and also all students, are to recognize and respect the distinctive Catholic identity of the University. In order not to endanger the Catholic identity of the University or Institute of Higher Studies, the number of non-Catholic teachers should not be allowed to constitute a majority within the Institution, which is and must remain Catholic.

§ 5. The education of students is to combine academic and professional development with formation in moral and religious principles and the social teachings of the Church; the programme of studies for each of the various professions is to include an appropriate ethical formation in that profession. Courses in Catholic doctrine are to be made available to all students.[51]

Article 5. *The Catholic University within the Church*

§ 1. Every Catholic University is to maintain communion with the universal Church and the Holy See; it is to be in close communion with the local Church and in particular with the diocesan Bishops of the region or nation in which it is located. In ways consistent with its nature as a University, a Catholic University will contribute to the Church's work of evangelization.

§ 2. Each Bishop has a responsibility to promote the welfare of the Catholic Universities in his diocese and has the right and duty to watch over the preservation and strengthening of their Catholic character. If problems should arise concerning this Catholic character, the local Bishop is to take the initiatives necessary to resolve the matter, working with the competent university authorities in accordance with established procedures[52] and, if necessary, with the help of the Holy See.

§ 3. Periodically, each Catholic University, to which Artide 3, 1 and 2 refers, is to communicate relevant information about the University and its activities to the competent ecclesiastical Authority. Other Catholic Universities are to communicate this information to the Bishop of the diocese in which the principal seat of the Institution is located.

---

50. VATICAN COUNCIL II, Dogmatic Constitution on the Church *Lumen Gentium*, n. 25: *AAS* 57 (1965), p. 29; *Dei Verbum*, nn. 8-10: *AAS* 58 (1966), pp. 820-822; Cf. *CIC*, can. 812: "It is necessary that those who teach theological disciplines in any institute of higher studies have a mandate from the competent ecclesiastical authority".

51. Cf. *CIC*, can 811 § 2.

52. For Universities to which Article 3 §§ 1 and 2 refer, these procedures are to be established in the university statutes approved by the competent ecclesiastical Authority; for other Catholic Universities, they are to be determined by Episcopal Conferences or other Assemblies of Catholic Hierarchy.

Article 6. *Pastoral Ministry*

§ 1. A Catholic University is to promote the pastoral care of all members of the university community, and to be especially attentive to the spiritual development of those who are Catholics. Priority is to be given to those means which will facilitate the integration of human and professional education with religious values in the light of Catholic doctrine, in order to unite intellectual learning with the religious dimension of life.

§ 2. A sufficient number of qualified people-priests, religious, and lay persons-are to be appointed to provide pastoral ministry for the university community, carried on in harmony and cooperation with the pastoral activities of the local Church under the guidance or with the approval of the diocesan Bishop. All members of the university community are to be invited to assist the work of pastoral ministry, and to collaborate in its activities.

Article 7. *Cooperation*

§ 1. In order better to confront the complex problems facing modern society, and in order to strengthen the Catholic identity of the Institutions, regional, national and international cooperation is to be promoted in research, teaching, and other university activities among all Catholic Universities, including Ecclesiastical Universities and Faculties.[53] Such cooperation is also to be promoted between Catholic Universities and other Universities, and with other research and educational Institutions, both private and governmental.

§ 2. Catholic Universities will, when possible and in accord with Catholic principles and doctrine, cooperate with government programmes and the programmes of other national and international Organizations on behalf of justice, development and progress.

Transitional Norms

Art. 8. The present Constitution will come into effect on the first day to the academic year 1991.

Art. 9. The application of the Constitution is committed to the Congregation for Catholic Education, which has the duty to promulgate the necessary directives that will serve towards that end.

Art. 10. It will be the competence of the Congregation for Catholic Education, when with the passage of time circumstances require it, to propose changes to be made in the present Constitution in order that it may be adapted continuously to the needs of Catholic Universities.

Art. 11. Any particular laws or customs presently in effect that are contrary to this Constitution are abolished. Also, any privileges granted up to this day by the Holy See whether to physical or moral persons that are contrary to this present Constitution are abolished.

---

53. Cf. *CIC*, can. 820. Cf. also *Sapientia Christiana*, Norms of Application, Article 49: *AAS* 71 (1979), p. 512.

Conclusion

The mission that the Church, with great hope, entrusts to Catholic Universities holds a cultural and religious meaning of vital importance because it concerns the very future of humanity. The renewal requested of Catholic Universities will make them better able to respond to the task of bringing the message of Christ to man, to society, to the various cultures: "Every human reality, both individual and social has been liberated by Christ: persons, as well as the activities of men and women, of which culture is the highest and incarnate expression. The salvific action of the Church on cultures is achieved, first of all, by means of persons, families and educators. . . . Jesus Christ, our Saviour, offers his light and his hope to all those who promote the sciences, the arts, letters and the numerous fields developed by modem culture. Therefore, all the sons and daughters of the Church should become aware of their mission and discover how the strength of the Gospel can penetrate and regenerate the mentalities and dominant values that inspire individual cultures, as well as the opinions and mental attitudes that are derived from it."[54]

It is with fervent hope that I address this Document to all the men and women engaged in various ways in the significant mission of Catholic higher education.

Beloved Brothers and Sisters, my encouragement and my trust go with you in your weighty daily task that becomes ever more important, more urgent and necessary on behalf of Evangelization for the future of culture and of all cultures. The Church and the world have great need of your witness and of your capable, free, and responsible contribution.

---

54. JOHN PAUL II, to the Pontifical Council for Culture, 13 January 1989, n. 2: *AAS* 81 (1989), pp. 857-858.

Some Useful Comparative Information

The following section provides information that helps draw comparisons among colleges in *The Newman Guide* and identifies some unique characteristics. It is presented to complement the material in the profiles, and it is a selective snapshot of some key points.

General Information

❖ There are eight colleges or universities in this *Guide* that have full-time undergraduate enrollment of more than 1,000 students. They are, in descending order: The Catholic University of America, Franciscan University of Steubenville, University of St. Thomas, Mount St. Mary's University, DeSales University, University of Dallas, Benedictine College and Belmont Abbey College.

❖ There are seven colleges that have full-time undergraduate enrollment of fewer than 100 students. The smallest is Holy Apostles College & Seminary, followed by John Paul the Great Catholic University, Wyoming Catholic College, Our Lady Seat of Wisdom Academy, The College of Saint Thomas More, Magdalen College and The Thomas More College of Liberal Arts.

❖ Seven colleges offer more than two dozen majors. These are, in order of number of majors, The Catholic University of America, Benedictine College, DeSales University, University of Dallas, Franciscan University of Steubenville, University of St. Thomas and Mount St. Mary's University.

❖ On the other hand, four colleges have only one "major." These are Magdalen College, The College of Saint Thomas More, Thomas Aquinas College and Wyoming Catholic College.

❖ Mount St. Mary's University, which was founded in 1808 and is currently celebrating its bicentennial, is the second-oldest college Catholic in the U.S. The newest in this *Guide* is Wyoming Catholic College, which opened its doors in September 2007.

❖ Wyoming Catholic College became the first Catholic college in that state, just as Southern Catholic College became the first in Georgia in 2005. Both states are experiencing rising Catholic populations.

❖ The Catholic University of America is a pontifical university founded by U.S. Catholic bishops as a national graduate institution in Washington, D.C., in 1887.

❖ A Great Books focus is emphasized at Magdalen College, Thomas Aquinas College, The College of Saint Thomas More, The Thomas More College of Liberal Arts and Wyoming Catholic College. Christendom College and the University of Dallas also include elements of it.

❖ The Thomas More College of Liberal Arts has a unique humanities cycle curriculum that is taken by all students at the same time.

❖ Colleges that require Latin or Greek as part of their core curriculum are Ave Maria University, The Thomas More College of Liberal Arts, The College of Saint Thomas More, Magdalen College, Our Lady Seat of Wisdom Academy and Wyoming Catholic College.

❖ The Catholic University of America and the University of Dallas have Phi Beta Kappa chapters.

❖ Magdalen College awards every qualifying graduate an Apostolic Catechetical Diploma in addition to a bachelor of arts degree.

❖ Among popular Catholic publications that are based on a campus are *Envoy* magazine at Belmont Abbey College and *Second Spring: An International Journal of Faith and Culture* at The Thomas More College of Liberal Arts. Franciscan University of Steubenville announced in 2007 that it began co-publication of the 86-year-old European Catholic publication *The Sower*. Several other colleges sponsor scholarly publications.

❖ The University of Dallas, Christendom College and The Thomas More College of Liberal Arts sponsor one-semester study-abroad programs that all or most of their students attend, usually in the sophomore year.

❖ Magdalen College and The College of Saint Thomas More have short foreign study programs. Franciscan University of Steubenville has a program in Gaming, Austria. Several of the other colleges have some arrangements for students to study abroad.

❖ Belmont Abbey College and Ave Maria University have been especially creative in developing new scholarships to attract Catholic students.

❖ Tuition for two colleges, Our Lady Seat of Wisdom Academy and Holy Apostles College & Seminary, is below $8,000 per year.

❖ Colleges that are primarily commuter schools are Holy Apostles College & Seminary, Aquinas College and the University of St. Thomas.

❖ The College of Saint Thomas More appeals to non-traditional students. Only about 25 percent of incoming freshmen enter from high school. Most of the students are in their 20s while some are in their 30s or older.

❖ Nearly 80 percent of students at Aquinas College are women.

❖ The University of St. Thomas has the most ethnically diverse student body. Nearly one-half of undergraduates are non-white and about one-third are Hispanic.

❖ Christendom College, Thomas Aquinas College, Our Lady Seat of Wisdom Academy, Ave Maria University, Magdalen College and The Thomas More College of Liberal Arts have attracted significant numbers of homeschooled students.

❖ Franciscan University is a prime example of a one-time troubled Catholic college that turned itself around to become one of the gems of U.S. Catholic higher education.

❖ Magdalen College requires all students to participate in its vocal music program every year.

❖ The largest cities represented by colleges in the *Guide* are: Houston (fourth largest in the U.S.), with the University of St. Thomas; and San Diego (eighth largest in the U.S.) with John Paul the Great Catholic University.

❖ Mount St. Mary's University is the only *Guide*-recommended college that participates in NCAA Division I sports. It also has a unique program where seminarians serve as team chaplains for each of its 19 intercollegiate sports teams.

Specific Programs

❖ DeSales University offers a major in marriage and family studies. The major finds its inspiration in the teaching of Pope John Paul II's Theology of the Body.

❖ Ave Maria University and Franciscan University of Steubenville offer majors in sacred music.

❖ The Catholic University of America and DeSales University have extensive drama departments. Belmont Abbey College's Abbey Players dates back to 1883.

❖ John Paul the Great Catholic University has an unusual niche, focusing on business entrepreneurship and training leaders in New Media, including the entertainment industry.

❖ Mount St. Mary's University has two cooperative health-related programs with other universities. There is a five-year program in biology and nursing (two bachelor's degrees) with The Johns Hopkins University and a six-year undergraduate-graduate program in occupational therapy with Sacred Heart University.

❖ Undergraduate degrees in nursing also are available at Aquinas College, The Catholic University of America, DeSales University and Franciscan University of Steubenville.

❖ DeSales University also has a notable undergraduate and graduate Physician Assistant program. As part of its community outreach, students in the program launched the DeSales Free Clinic for homeless people in Allentown, Pennsylvania, in 2007. Faculty members and students operate it.

❖ The Catholic University of America offers an undergraduate degree in engineering. The University of St. Thomas has cooperative agreements for dual-degree programs in the fields of engineering and technology with Texas A & M University, University of Houston and the University of Notre Dame.

❖ Among The Catholic University's 12 schools is the School of Architecture and Planning, which offers a bachelor's degree in architecture as well as professional and post-professional master's degrees. It is the only recommended college with an architecture program.

❖ Belmont Abbey College, located near the capital of NASCAR racing in Charlotte, North Carolina, has a unique major in motor sports management, complete with an internship.

❖ Sports management programs are offered at Belmont Abbey College, DeSales University, Franciscan University of Steubenville and Mount St. Mary's University.

❖ Wyoming Catholic College has an equestrian program as part of its required curriculum.

❖ Reserve Officers Training Corps (ROTC) programs are available through various cooperative programs at Belmont Abbey College, Benedictine University, The Catholic University of America, The College of Saint Thomas More, DeSales University, Franciscan University of Steubenville,

Mount St. Mary's University, St. Gregory's University, University of Dallas and the University of St. Thomas.

Religious Matters

❖ Colleges with a percentage of Catholic students greater than 90 percent are Ave Maria University, Christendom College, Franciscan University of Steubenville, Holy Apostles College & Seminary, John Paul the Great Catholic University, Magdalen College, Our Lady Seat of Wisdom Academy and Thomas Aquinas College.

❖ Belmont Abbey College, Benedictine College and St. Gregory's University are Benedictine institutions with abbeys on the grounds.

❖ DeSales University is affiliated with the Oblates of St. Francis de Sales (Salesians), Franciscan University of Steubenville with the Third Order Regular of St. Francis (T.O.R.), University of St. Thomas with the Congregation of St. Basil (Basilians), and Holy Apostles College & Seminary with the Society of the Missionaries of the Holy Apostles.

❖ Aquinas College is the only institution in the *Guide* run by religious sisters, in this case the Dominican Sisters of the Congregation of Saint Cecilia ("Nashville Dominicans").

❖ The Dominican Sisters operate a coed elementary-middle school and a girls' high school on Aquinas College campus grounds.

❖ At The College of Saint Thomas More, there is a small preparatory school for students aged 12 to 18 on campus. About one-quarter of the graduates of Lady Margaret Roper School eventually enroll at the college.

❖ Ave Maria Grammar and Preparatory School opened at Ave Maria University with 140 students in August 2007. The K-12 school includes teachers from the Dominican Sisters of Mary, Mother of the Eucharist.

❖ Recommended colleges that have seminarians who are an integral part of the lay institution are Holy Apostles College & Seminary and Mount St. Mary's University.

❖ Mount St. Mary's University's seminary is known as the "Cradle of Bishops" because it has produced 48 bishops, including one 19th-century cardinal.

❖ Saint Elizabeth Ann Bayley Seton, the first American-born saint, was involved in the early history of Mount St. Mary's University, including its founding.

❖ The Catholic University of America has as its next-door neighbor the magnificent Basilica of the National Shrine of the Immaculate Conception, the nation's largest Catholic church.

❖ Thomas Aquinas College, Christendom College and Magdalen College have produced large numbers of vocations. About one-tenth of the students/graduates of each college has entered the priesthood or religious life.

❖ The Thomas More College of Liberal Arts announced in July 2007 that it was setting up two funds that should help remove one impediment to vocations. The Saint John Vianney Fund for Future Priests and The Saint Mother Katherine Drexel Fund for Future Nuns will absorb student loans accumulated by its graduates who are going into a seminary or convent.

❖ Franciscan University of Steubenville and Ave Maria University have a pre-theologate program.

❖ Southern Catholic College, which opened in 2005, has a five-member board of fellows, whose only role is to evaluate and uphold the Catholic identity of the college.

❖ The University of Dallas School of Ministry provides religious outreach through its graduate, deaconate and online courses. Thirty-seven Texas parishes were represented at its Catholic Bible School graduation ceremony in May 2007.

❖ Franciscan University of Steubenville pioneered an extensive household residential program, which provides living quarters in an atmosphere that encourages various forms of spiritual activity. Ave Maria University has developed a similar program.

❖ Among the less common Catholic student organizations are Aquinas College's Frassati Society, named for Blessed Pier Giorgio Frassati, an early 20th-century Dominican tertiary who exemplified the Beatitudes; and Ave Maria University's Communion and Liberation group, dedicated to studying the works of the late Monsignor Luigi Giovanni Giussani, an Italian who founded the *Comunione e Liberazione* movement.

❖ Benedictine College and Franciscan University of Steubenville have large campus ministry organizations, and many others have active programs.

❖ St. Gregory's University has a unique and highly regarded Buckley Outreach Team, which sponsors retreats for Catholic junior high and high school students in Oklahoma, Texas and Arkansas.

❖ The Fellowship of Catholic University Students (FOCUS), an outreach and evangelization program primarily located on secular college campuses, has chapters at Benedictine College and the University of St. Thomas.

❖ Evening Rosary walks are very popular at Ava Maria University. They include Father Joseph Fessio, S.J., the university's Theologian in Residence. He received his doctorate in theology from the University of Regensburg (Germany), where he studied under then-Professor Joseph Ratzinger (now Pope Benedict XVI).

❖ One of the founders and advisory board members of Our Lady Seat of Wisdom Academy is Canadian Catholic novelist and painter Michael O'Brien. He is the author of *Father Elijah: An Apocalypse, Strangers and Sojourners* and *Sophia House.*

About the Cardinal Newman Society

Founded in 1993, the Cardinal Newman Society is dedicated to renewing and strengthening Catholic identity at the 224 Catholic colleges and universities in the United States.

The Society focuses its work on assisting students, school officials and alumni; urging fidelity to the Magisterium of the Catholic Church; and researching activities both on campus and in the classroom. The Society is a 501(c)(3) tax-exempt, nonprofit organization supported by more than 20,000 private individuals, corporations and foundations.

In addition to publishing *The Newman Guide*, the Society promotes Catholic values on life and sexual ethics on campuses and in dorm rooms through its Love & Responsibility Program. It also operates a Campus Speaker Monitoring Project to support the guidelines the U.S. Bishops have established to prohibit Catholic institutions from giving opponents of Catholic teachings honors or platforms for their views, and maintains a speakers bureau of leading Catholic figures as a resource for student groups. Additionally, the Society promotes Eucharistic adoration and is the national coordinator for the display of the Vatican's International Exposition *The Eucharistic Miracles of the World* on campuses.

For more information on the Cardinal Newman Society and its programs, or to become a member, visit CardinalNewmanSociety.org or write to Cardinal Newman Society, 9167 Key Commons Court, Manassas, Virginia 20110–5330. The telephone number is (703) 367-0333.